D1191727

BASEBALL GOES WEST

BASEBALL GOES WEST

*The Dodgers, the Giants, and the
Shaping of the Major Leagues*

LINCOLN A. MITCHELL

The Kent State University Press

KENT, OHIO

© 2018 by The Kent State University Press, Kent, Ohio 44242
All rights reserved
Library of Congress Catalog Number 2018008750
ISBN 978-1-60635-359-2
Manufactured in the United States of America

Library of Congress Cataloging-in-Publication Data
Names: Mitchell, Lincoln Abraham, author.
Title: Baseball goes west : the Dodgers, the Giants, and the shaping of the major
    leagues / Lincoln A. Mitchell.
Description: Kent, Ohio : The Kent State University Press, [2018] | Includes
    bibliographical references and index.
Identifiers: LCCN 2018008750 | ISBN 9781606353592 (hardcover : alk. paper)
Subjects: LCSH: Baseball--United States--History. | Brooklyn Dodgers (Baseball
    team)--History. | New York Giants (Baseball team)--History. | Los Angeles Dodgers
    (Baseball team)--History. | San Francisco Giants (Baseball team)--History.
Classification: LCC GV863.A1 M55 2018 | DDC 796.357/640979409045--dc23
LC record available at https://lccn.loc.gov/2018008750

22 21 20 19 18   5 4 3 2 1

CONTENTS

ACKNOWLEDGMENTS

I am grateful for the many people who contributed to *Baseball Goes West: The Dodgers, the Giants, and the Shaping of the Major Leagues*. Susan Wadsworth-Booth, Will Underwood, and their team at Kent State University Press were patient and helpful to me as I wrote it. John Horne at the National Baseball Hall of Fame assisted in finding the photos used in the book. Joseph D'Anna, Christian Ettinger, Charles A. Fracchia Jr., Charles Karren, John Maschino, and Tova Wang have been my baseball sounding boards most of my life. It was with my late brother Jonathan Mitchell that I first experienced the rivalry between the Giants and Dodgers. The Baseball Freaks Facebook group continues to be a source of support, humor, and insight into the game for me. My wife, Marta Sanders, has encouraged my writing for more than 20 years. My sons, Asher and Reuben, have indulged their father's stories about baseball players of long ago for years, although they remain more interested in improving their own skills on the diamond. My writing companion, Isis the dog, has slept quietly by my side while I wrote and revised this book, and was always ready for a walk when I needed a break.

This book arose in part out of a lifetime of being a baseball fan in San Francisco and New York. Over the years, there were two conversations that I overheard periodically—at ballgames, all over the borough of Brooklyn, occasionally even from older Manhattanites, in the cafes and ballfields of San Francisco, on the New York City subway, and on the old ballpark express in San Francisco. One conversation was that of older New Yorkers still bemoaning the loss of the Giants and, more frequently, the Dodgers. The other was from San Franciscans of the same generation who had grown up rooting for the Seals and felt compelled to remind younger fans that, in their view, there had been big league baseball in San Francisco long before the Giants ever got there. The Brooklyn Dodgers, New York Giants, Hollywood Stars, and San Francisco Seals are not coming back, but this book is dedicated to the fans of those long-gone teams, particularly those who decided to give the San Francisco Giants, Los Angeles Dodgers, and New York Mets a chance.

INTRODUCTION

All baseball fans with a sense of the game's history are familiar with the events of October 3, 1951. That was the day when the New York Giants completed a comeback from what had at one time been a 13-game deficit, and clinched the National League pennant on the final pitch of the final game of an exciting three-game playoff against their archrivals, the Brooklyn Dodgers. That game ended with perhaps the most dramatic and famous single play in baseball history. The Giants went into the bottom of the ninth inning trailing 4–1, but managed to get one run in and two runners on with one out and Bobby Thomson, one of their best players, at bat. Thomson hit a clutch three-run home run to give the Giants a 5–4 victory and the National League pennant. In the almost 70 years since, millions of baseball fans have seen the video of that home run and heard Giants radio announcer Russ Hodges, famously repeating the phrase "The Giants win the pennant."

It is an eerie coincidence, and one about which most fans are entirely un-aware, that the two teams met again in the final game of a three-game playoff to decide the National League pennant 11 years later. That game also occurred on October 3. The Dodgers led the third game of the 1962 playoff against the Giants in the ninth inning as well, but this time by two runs, and, like they had done 11 years earlier to the day, found a way to lose that game—and the pennant—to the Giants. In 1962, no single play was as famous or important as Thomson's home run. Instead, the Giants sent ten players to the plate in the top of the ninth inning, and managed to stitch together four runs on two singles, four walks, and one Dodgers error.

There are other similarities between these two series. In both years the Giants won the first game, the Dodgers won the second, and the Giants the third. The Giants in both 1951 and 1962 went on to lose in the World Series to the New York Yankees. Alvin Dark, who was part of the winning rally in

1951, managed the Giants in 1962. Willie Mays was a rookie and on deck when Thomson hit the home run in 1951; he got a big single in the 1962 winning rally. Duke Snider, the Dodgers' star center fielder in 1951, was still on the club in 1962, but only as a useful backup outfielder.

A glaring difference between the events of October 3, 1951, and October 3, 1962, is that while the earlier game is something that almost every more-than-casual baseball fan knows, the later game is something that few people know—unless they are big Giants or Dodgers fans and over 60 years old. This is partially due to the unparalleled drama of Bobby Thomson's home run, but also because the first series occurred in New York City and the second series in California, after the Dodgers and Giants had moved west. The disparity between how the 1951 and 1962 Dodgers–Giants playoffs are remembered reflects how the history of those two teams, and of baseball in general during these two decades, is usually understood. This is particularly true in New York and the Northeast, but it is also the case in the United States as a whole.

The year 1951 may have been the high point of baseball's long history in New York City. The Dodgers and Giants ended the 154-game season with identical records of 96–58, fully 15 games ahead of the third-place Cardinals. In the American League, the Yankees went 98–56 and won the pennant, their third of what would be five consecutive pennants, by five games. Thus, the New York teams had the three best records in baseball.

The 1951 season was also significant because both the Yankees and the Giants had rookie outfielders, Mickey Mantle and Willie Mays, respectively, who not only helped their team win the pennant, but went on to become the biggest stars of their generation. Mantle played 86 games in the outfield that year, but only appeared in center field three times. The primary center fielder on that Yankees team was Joe DiMaggio, who in 1951 was in the last year of his storied career. DiMaggio started 113 games for the Yankees that year, all in center field. The Dodgers center fielder that year was Duke Snider, who was just entering the prime of his Hall of Fame career. Thus, 1951 was both the beginning of the era of Willie, Mickey, and the Duke and the end of the Joe DiMaggio era in New York.[1]

By 1962, as any baseball fan knows, that golden era of New York City baseball was over. The Dodgers and Giants had been ripped out of the bosom of central Brooklyn and northern Manhattan and moved across the continent to Chavez Ravine and Candlestick Point. Admittedly, 1962 was also the year National League baseball returned to New York—but the hapless Mets, winners of 40 games that season, were, at the time, hardly a replacement for the Giants and the Dodgers.

The story of what happened between October 3, 1951, and October 3, 1962, is too frequently framed as one of loss for New York, often one that takes on a symbolic import beyond simply baseball. Much of this expresses a sense that New Yorkers were exploited by greedy team owners Walter O'Malley of the Dodgers and Horace Stoneham of the Giants, and that baseball suffered a big blow when the Dodgers and Giants moved west. The implicit opinion in many accounts—whether in journalism, fiction, or even music—is that baseball and America would have been better off if the Giants and particularly the Dodgers had never moved.[2]

Sam Anderson summarized this received view of the Dodgers' departure in a 2007 essay in *New York Magazine*:

The baseball gods murdered the Dodgers with a poisonous cocktail of post-war affluence, the automobile, television, suburban Long Island, stubborn city-planning mastermind Robert Moses, and—the greatest villain of all—a greedy owner named Walter O'Malley. (Old Brooklynites still joke that, if you were to find yourself in a room with Hitler, Stalin, and O'Malley, armed with only two bullets, you'd have to shoot O'Malley twice.) It was a brutal hit, since the team didn't just leave, they went on to an eternal and victorious afterlife in Los Angeles, the sprawling, public-transportationless anti-Brooklyn of the New World. Brooklyn's slow decline into irrelevance—begun in 1898, when the proud independent city was swallowed by the bureaucracy of Greater New York—turned into a nosedive. The borough fell off the map, devoting itself entirely to gang violence, heroin, race riots, arson, homelessness, crack, and becoming a suitable background for late-seventies Travolta projects (*Welcome Back, Kotter; Saturday Night Fever*). New York officially ceded its baseball centrality to California, which today has five teams to our two. This is the origin myth of modern Brooklyn, a story hammered as deep into the borough's collective psyche as the Odyssey to the ancient Greeks': The Dodgers united a multicultural Eden, but O'Money ate Southern California's forbidden fruit, and the borough fell into darkness.[3]

There is no doubt that hundreds of thousands of Dodgers fans in Brooklyn and somewhat fewer Giants fans in and around Manhattan were heartbroken and angry to see their team leave. Those sentiments and the corresponding anger toward Stoneham and O'Malley were genuine, and they are still maintained by some today. However, the sadness felt by erstwhile fans of the Brooklyn Dodgers and New York Giants often obscures the larger impact the move had on baseball. This book will show that the decision by O'Malley and Stoneham to move west was absolutely central to the making of modern Major League Baseball (MLB), and that those moves helped baseball continue to grow domestically, maintain a singularly important niche and role in American culture, and become the increasingly global institution that it is today.

The departure of the Giants and Dodgers from New York is generally understood as the end of an era—the era of New York City's dominance in baseball; of Willie, Mickey, and the Duke patrolling center field in three different boroughs; and of baseball at its best and most pure. Sometimes the metaphor is extended to suggest that the Giants' and Dodgers' leaving Brooklyn brought about, or at least symbolized, the decline of New York City, of postwar American dominance, and even of some abstract national innocence that is only peripherally related to baseball. This myopic, New York–centered view, however, obscures the reality that when the Dodgers and Giants moved west, they almost immediately modernized baseball, opened it up to a much larger audience, and made it a bigger and better sport.

Moreover, while the traditional view of the departure of the Dodgers and Giants from New York City as a calamity also implicitly suggests that the once great Dodgers–Giants rivalry was one of the casualties of this move, the Dodgers–Giants rivalry has continued and perhaps gotten even stronger in the six decades since both teams came west. From their first season on the West Coast, the rivalry between the two teams was strong. John Rosengren notes that "the move to the West Coast changed the complexion but not the intensity of the rivalry, which accentuated the animosity intrinsic between the capitals of Northern and Southern California."[4] Andrew Goldblatt also recognizes that the rivalry remained at least as strong after the move west.[5] The 1962 playoff series is one example of this, but the two teams fought in several close pennant races in the 1960s. Even when the Giants were not competitive—for example, in the mid-1970s—games between the teams have drawn large crowds and have had special meaning to fans. In some recent years the Dodgers–Giants rivalry has been the most electrifying in baseball, sometimes outpacing even the Yankees–Red Sox rivalry. In recent years, a Dodgers–Giants game late in the season, particularly if the starting pitchers are Clayton Kershaw and Madison Bumgarner, two of the top left-handed pitchers in the game, is both as exciting as any current matchup in baseball and also steeped in more than a century of intense rivalry between the teams and their fans.

The Dodgers–Giants rivalry has now been on the West Coast for about as long as it was in New York. For most of this time it has been, on the surface, somewhat lopsided, as the Dodgers won five pennants, and the Giants none between 1974 and 1988, and the Giants five and the Dodgers only one since 1989. There have, however, been numerous big games, close divisional races, and exciting moments that have kept this rivalry strong. In recent years the rivalry has occurred with equal intensity in Spanish and English, as anybody who has attended a Dodgers–Giants game, in either ballpark, knows.

BASEBALL BEGINS TO CHANGE

By the late 1950s, when the Giants and Dodgers moved west, baseball was changing. At the beginning of that decade, the 16 major league teams had all been in their current cities since essentially the turn of the century. No teams had been added or dropped during that period either. In 1950, St. Louis, home of the Browns and the Cardinals, represented the southern and western frontier of big league baseball. In the early and mid-1950s, there were some rumblings of change in baseball's alignment and geography. Following the 1952 season, the Braves moved from Boston to Milwaukee. A year later, the Browns moved from St. Louis to Baltimore and became the Orioles. A year after that, the Athletics moved from Philadelphia to Kansas City. The importance of these moves can be overstated. While these were the first changes of their kind in more than half a century, Baltimore and Milwaukee, and to a lesser degree Kansas City, hardly opened up new geographic or other frontiers for big league baseball. Only the Orioles found a permanent home in their new city. Within another 15 years or so, both the Braves and Athletics would move again.

None of these three teams were important or winning franchises at the time of their initial move. The Athletics, Browns, and Braves were in bad shape both on and off the field before the move. The Athletics did not win a pennant in their last 22 years in Philadelphia, finishing in last place in ten of those seasons. The Browns had won the pennant, their only one in St. Louis, as recently as 1944, but had not had a winning record since 1945.[6] The Braves had won the pennant in 1948 and before that in 1914; however, despite having two future Hall of Famers on their roster, Eddie Mathews and Warren Spahn, when they moved to Milwaukee, they were not comparable to the Giants and Dodgers. Nobody writing a history of baseball from 1900 to 1955 would have put a lot of attention on the Braves and Browns. The Athletics had been one of the most famous and successful franchises from 1900 to 1931, but had fallen on a couple of decades of losing seasons by the time they left Philadelphia.

Baltimore, Kansas City, and Milwaukee represented incremental movement to the west and south, but moving lesser franchises to second-tier Midwestern or mid-Atlantic cities was not a groundbreaking development that could forever alter baseball. Moving two teams to California would be a categorically different development for big league baseball. The fact that the Giants and Dodgers were high-profile teams that, at the time of the move, had appeared in six of the last seven (and seven of the last nine) World Series only made the moves more dramatic.

Hindsight tells us that it was imperative that big league baseball establish itself on the West Coast during this period, when the geographical and cultural centers of the country were shifting west from the Northeast. It is also now clear that moving two high-profile teams was a brilliant decision that brought these two hugely important West Coast cities not just big league baseball, but star-laden, championship-contending big league baseball teams. None of this, however, was obvious or uncontroversial at the time.

The move to California occurred in a complex economic, demographic, geographic, media, and infrastructural context that will be explored in greater detail throughout this book. Part of this environment was the long tradition of high-level professional baseball on the West Coast, largely in the form of the Pacific Coast League. By 1957, the Pacific Coast League was no longer an independent league, as all but one of its eight teams were affiliated with big league teams, but fans on the West Coast, not least in Los Angeles and San Francisco, viewed the Pacific Coast League as comparable to the big leagues. Accordingly, Los Angeles and San Francisco, while necessary cities for MLB if it was ever going to be truly national in scale, were not cities where a losing expansion team would have necessarily won the attention and affection of fans.[7]

The Dodgers and Giants, thus, not only brought MLB to these two major West Coast cities, but they brought popular and well-known players, making it much easier for these two teams to be embraced in their new homes. In 1958, the first year they were in San Francisco, the Giants went 80–74, finished in third place and were led by two future Hall of Famers, the rookie Orlando Cepeda and the incomparable Willie Mays. The Dodgers had a dismal record of 71–83, but they bounced all the way back and won the World Series in 1959. However, even that seventh-place Dodgers team in 1958 featured four future Hall of Famers: Pee Wee Reese, Duke Snider, Don Drysdale, and Sandy Koufax. At that time, Reese and Snider were established stars, Drysdale was beginning to break through as a major talent, and Koufax was still trying to establish himself. In addition to Reese and Snider, other well-known members of the

"Boys of Summer" Dodgers from the 1947–57 era who made the journey west with the team included Gil Hodges, Don Zimmer, Jim Gilliam, Carl Furillo, Johnny Podres, Carl Erskine, Clem Labine, Don Newcombe, and Ed Roebuck. That 1958 Dodgers team may not have been very good, but the team had many players who were recognizable to even moderate baseball fans.

The two teams changed baseball when they moved west. The details and impacts of those changes will be the primary subject of the book. The teams themselves also changed when they moved west. The narratives that defined their long tenure in New York no longer held up after moving to California. This has contributed to the gap between how the move west is perceived and what it really meant.

DID BASEBALL NEED SAVING?

The 1950s are generally thought of as a time when baseball was in pretty good shape; however, below the surface, problems of low attendance, changing demographics, and the inability of the team owners to figure out how to monetize the growing popularity of television suggested a more complex situation.

Hand-wringing about the decline of baseball has been around almost as long as the sport itself. As Brett Smiley wrote: "The sportswriting obsession with forecasting the demise of baseball spawned a *sub*-pastime: fact and theory-based defenses concerning baseball's health. Cynics and critics have persistently forecasted the end of baseball for at least 100 years—literally—and for just as long, other sportswriters have refuted the claims."[8] In a 2014 article, Bryan Curtis traces the evolution of the baseball-is-dying narrative over the decades. Referring to a 1955 article, he writes that "*even Golden Agers* thought baseball was fatally anachronistic. . . . It suggested that baseball would be usurped by the drive-in theater, the swimming pool, and the airplane." Curtis then describes the thinking behind this narrative in the following two decades:

> "The fact that baseball was your father's game, your father's Oldsmobile, I think we started to see this in the 1960s," [official MLB historian John] Thorn said, "as baseball on the field seemed to be in a declining stage as measured by offensive stats."
>
> In the '60s, baseball was going to die because of over-expansion. The winnowing of the minors. Outfield fences pushed back in bigger stadiums. "If baseball dies," the columnist Jim Murray wrote, "the murder weapon will be real estate."

Table 1. Attendance for MLB, 1953–57

Season	Annual Attendance per Team	Teams with Attendance over 947,000	Teams with Attendance below 473,000	Team with Highest Attendance	Team with Lowest Attendance
1953	925,042	6	0	New York Yankees (1,623,245)	Cincinnati Reds (578,535)
1954	1,031,226	9	0	New York Yankees (1,557,125)	Pittsburgh Pirates (501,910)
1955	1,096,285	8	2	New York Yankees (1,572,923)	Washington Senators (448,862)
1956	1,091,395	10	1	Milwaukee Braves (2,160,015)	Washington Senators (455,627)
1957	1,122,567	10	1	Milwaukee Braves (2,338,482)	Washington Senators (482,472)

Note: During 1953–57, there were 16 teams and 154 games per season. On both counts, this is less than in 1964–68. To account for this difference, 1950s data is projected over a 162-game schedule, with an estimated five home doubleheaders per team in each decade. The attendance thresholds of 947,000 and 473,000 in the 1950s are adjusted from 1,000,000 and 500,000 in the 1960s, while the annual attendance, highest attendance, and lowest attendance values are adjusted by dividing by 72 and multiplying by 76.
Source: "MLB Ballpark Attendance," Ballparks of Baseball (2017), http://www.ballparksofbaseball.com/baseball-ballpark-attendance/.

In the '70s, it was the winnowing of the minors (again). Bigger stadiums (again). And that elusive American character—now warped by Oswald, Vietnam, and Kent State. "While baseball hasn't passed," a *Toledo Blade* writer noted in 1972, "its current decline tells a lot about the changed American character. It's the collapse of small-town America, the rush to violence in sport, film, and other entertainment, the diminished competitive urge, and the lessened credibility of the American dream."[9]

These examples show that the baseball-is-dying story line is very adaptable. Any developments in American life can be mobilized to be shown as forces working against baseball. The real story, in many respects, has been the game's extraordinary resilience.

One of the reasons the baseball-is-dying motif has been so enduring is that for much of its history, big league baseball has faced economic and other

Table 2. Attendance for MLB, 1964–68

Season	Annual Attendance per Team	Teams with Attendance over 1,000,000	Teams with Attendance below 500,000	Highest Attendance	Lowest Attendance
1964	1,102,053	9	0	Los Angeles Dodgers (2,228,751)	Washington Senators (600,106)
1965	1,150,431	10	0	Los Angeles Dodgers (2,553,577)	Kansas City Athletics (528,344)
1966	1,259,110	10	0	Los Angeles Dodgers (2,617,029)	Washington Senators (576,260)
1967	1,215,422	11	0	St. Louis Cardinals (2,090,145)	Cleveland Indians (662,980)
1968	1,155,137	11	0	Detroit Tigers (2,031,847)	Washington Senators (546,661)

Note: For most of the 1960s, including 1964–68, there were 20 teams and 162 games per season.
Source: "MLB Ballpark Attendance," Ballparks of Baseball (2017), http://www.ballparksofbaseball
.com/baseball-ballpark-attendance/.

problems. The last two decades have been something of an exception to this, but there were many periods before that when the sense of crisis was real. In the late 1960s, the ascendancy of football—of the National Football League in particular—threatened MLB. In the early and mid-1970s, many franchises, including the San Francisco Giants, explored the idea of moving because they had such a difficult time drawing fans. As late as the 1990s, the possibility of MLB contracting by one or two teams was frequently discussed. The 1950s were an interesting time in this regard. The problems facing MLB were serious; however, because the game was doing so well in New York, at a time when that city's dominance of the media environment was so strong, those problems were often overlooked and are not always remembered.

Nonetheless, there is ample evidence that the problems facing baseball in the years leading up to the Dodgers and Giants moving west were very real. Some of this can be seen by comparing game attendance for the late 1950s with the late 1960s, specifically the five years before the move (1953–57) with the five years before MLB expanded and switched to a divisional format (1964–68). Tables 1 and 2 provide some of this data.

The two tables show that, once adjustments are made for schedules, attendance figures were consistently, but only slightly, higher in the 1964–68 period. Some of this is due to population growth, as there were 50 million more Americans in 1970 than in 1950. However, MLB was able to exploit that population growth only because of moves like the Dodgers and Giants to Los Angeles and San Francisco. Bill James, the baseball writer who pioneered advanced statistical analysis of the game, concluded that in the 1950s "the average American . . . attended a big league baseball game about once every ten years." According to James, the number dropped to one in nine years during the 1960s.[10]

The peripheral data here is valuable, too. In the years before the move west, several teams struggled to remain viable; however, by the 1964–68 period, every team drew at least 500,000 fans every year. The strong attendance for the Dodgers indicates that much of the strength of baseball in the mid-1960s, to the extent that it was indeed strong, was due to that franchise. Additionally, the stronger attendance numbers in the late 1950s were due to the short-lived romance between Milwaukee and the Braves. That romance was dying by 1962, when the Braves became one of the weaker draws in baseball, and ended after 1965 as the Braves moved to Atlanta for the 1966 season.

Attendance figures only reveal part of the relative health of baseball in these two eras. Baseball in the years before the move had little competitive balance. In the 11 years between 1947 and 1957, only six teams, representing five cities, appeared in the World Series.[11] In the 11 years following the move, 12 teams from 12 different cities played in the World Series.[12]

Beginning in the 1950s, as television became more widespread, MLB sought to figure out how best to make a profit through televising ballgames. This was not always easy as some in the game thought that televising games would keep people away from the ballpark, so blackouts or only televising road games were relatively common practices. However, in general during these years, baseball on television became more widespread.

As the people running big league baseball began to get a better understanding of the new medium, television profits began to increase. According to James Walker and Robert Bellamy, "By 1957, broadcasting was pumping $9.3 million in rights fees into Major League Baseball."[13] This only includes national contracts, not the local ones struck by each individual team. By October 1965, the nature of television revenue had changed. That year, "NBC won the rights [to the national MLB contract] for $30.6 million. . . . Major League Baseball's new network topped the previous high for television rights: the NFL's 28.2-million two year deal with CBS . . . [and] total revenues for MLB increased 60 percent over earlier national baseball contracts."[14]

Overall, the data indicate that baseball was in better shape in the late 1960s than in the mid- to late 1950s—but that is not the general perception. For several reasons, baseball in the 1950s is still viewed as a time when the game was in good shape, while the late 1960s is generally seen as a period when the game was in crisis. There are several reasons for this: First, in the 1950s, baseball was in better shape in the country's media capital, whereas by the mid-1960s the Yankees dynasty had ended and the Mets, while popular, were not winning anything (although the Mets' fortunes would change dramatically in 1969). Additionally, baseball in the mid- to late 1960s was so low scoring and dominated by pitchers that many found the game more slow and boring than ever. It is difficult to assess the extent to which cultural changes in this period affected an institution like baseball, which had always been conservative and tradition-based, but it is likely that these changes had an impact on the game's perceived popularity as well.

The biggest development in the late 1960s that had a direct effect on baseball was the rise of the NFL. The first Super Bowl, between the Packers and Chiefs, was played in January 1967. Its combined Nielsen rating of 41.1—it was broadcast on both NBC and CBS—significantly eclipsed that of the Cardinals–Tigers World Series played in October 1968. That was the first World Series for which Nielsen data is available. The 1968 Super Bowl, between the Packers and Raiders, had a 36.8 Nielsen rating, much better than the 22.8 for the 1968 World Series. The World Series goes at least four games, while the Super Bowl is only one game. Nonetheless, by the late 1960s, the Super Bowl had become the premier American television sports event, a position previously held by the World Series.[15]

During these years, books like Ralph Andreano's *No Joy in Mudville* (1965) probed the problems facing baseball. Andreano defined the "modern dilemma of baseball" as "a relative decline in the game's commercial popularity during an era of unprecedented prosperity. . . . It may be impossible to stop the trend, and spectator sports—baseball in particular—may be headed for a period of stagnation and decline."[16] During the 1960s, there were also early rumblings of the labor disputes that would have an enormous impact on the game in the 1970s and 1980s—and ultimately contribute to making MLB more profitable for players and owners. Similarly, the coverage of the game began to change as a new cadre of journalists moved away from the hagiography that had characterized most baseball writing through the early 1960s. Racial tensions were also never far from the surface as African American stars became more prominent and gradually more outspoken. This all occurred against the backdrop of the political, cultural, and social changes of the 1960s. Although most of these changes had roots in the 1950s, they were much less visible in that decade. It is not, therefore, surprising that the perception of baseball being in crisis was so strong in the 1960s.

DIFFERENT COASTS, DIFFERENT PERSONAS

During their decades in Brooklyn, the Dodgers had two different, but overlapping personas. They were the "Bums," or, as more frequently rendered in the local dialect, "Dem Bums." "Dem Bums" were a sad-sack team of lovable, but incompetent losers. This was the team that between 1901 and 1940 finished below .500 26 times and won only two pennants and no World Championships. Their manager for 18 of those years was a short, stocky former catcher named Wilbert Robinson, known as "Uncle Robbie."

One of the best players of that period was Babe Herman, who from 1926 to 1931 hit .340/.397/.559.[17] During these years, Herman was overshadowed by another Babe, who played in the Bronx and was setting records with the Yankees. Herman, however, is not remembered primarily for his hitting prowess, but for his ineptitude on the bases. Most memorably, he once hit a line drive, put his head down, and ran hard to third base, inadvertently passing two of his teammates on the basepaths. Thus, Herman famously doubled into a double play. This gave rise to the apocryphal story that captures the feeling of those pre-1941 Dodgers. A truck driver in Brooklyn arrives at a stoplight and asks a boy listening to a radio what the score of the game is. The boy responds, "The Bums are down by two, but they have three men on base," to which the trucker counters, "Which base?"

The Dodgers of that era were also defined by their home. In the early part of the twentieth century, Brooklyn was not the hip and pricey place it is today, but a grittier working-class borough that could seem light-years away from the glamor and excitement of Manhattan, despite the proximity of the two boroughs. Accordingly, the Dodgers' home also occasionally made them a target of jokes, not least because of the famous Brooklyn accent. Dixie Walker was a star outfielder with the Dodgers from 1939 to 1947. He was very popular in Brooklyn, his fourth major league team, despite hailing from Georgia. As such, he was known as "The People's Cherce."

Waite Hoyt was a Hall of Fame pitcher who had his best years with the Yankees in the 1920s, where he was a star hurler on a team whose offense was led by Babe Ruth and Lou Gehrig. Hoyt joined the Dodgers for two seasons in 1937–38, when he was in his late 30s and no longer a star, although in 1937 he was still a decent big league pitcher. While finishing his career with the Dodgers, Hoyt stumbled on the dugout steps one day and injured his knee. This led a concerned Dodgers fan to yell out, "Hurt's hoyt."

After World War II, two things happened to change the Dodgers' image. The first thing is that they continued to be a good team with an enduring core of players, including Pee Wee Reese, Gil Hodges, Duke Snider, Carl Furillo, Carl Erskine, and Clem Labine, thus building on their success in the early part of the 1940s. A team that loaded with talent could no longer be dismissed as lovable losers. Beginning in 1947, for a decade the Dodgers were the best team in the National League and, on paper at least, probably the best team in baseball. These players were not only good, but they were colorful and likable.

The second and related development was that the Dodgers, led by their famous general manager Branch Rickey, were the first big league team to flout the informally agreed upon segregation that had been a moral blemish on baseball throughout the twentieth century. The Brooklyn Dodgers of the 1947–56 era had many great players, but none were as important to the history of the game, and the country, as Jackie Robinson. Robinson played his first game with the Dodgers in 1947, but within a few years he was joined by two other great African American players, catcher Roy Campanella and pitcher Don Newcombe. By adding these three African American stars to their strong core of white players, the Dodgers ensured that they would be the best team in the National League for years.

Jackie Robinson's Dodgers are one of those teams that, from a historical perspective, are very hard not to like. Like earlier Dodgers teams, they were lovable, with colorful, charismatic, and heroic stars, but they were no longer lovable losers—they were also very good. Roger Kahn's *Boys of Summer* captured the feel of that team and assured its place in the collective baseball memory:

> During the early 1950s, the Jackie Robinson Brooklyn Dodgers were outspoken, opinionated, bigoted, tolerant, black, white, open, passionate; in short a fascinating mix of vigorous men. . . . Ebbets Field was a narrow cockpit, built of brick and iron and concrete, alongside a steep cobblestone slope of Bedford Avenue. Two tiers of grandstand pressed the playing area from three sides, and in thousands of seats fans could hear a ballplayer's chatter, notice a ballplayer's

gait and, at a time when television had not yet assaulted illusion with the Zoomar lens, you could actually see, the actual expression on the actual face of an actual major leaguer as he played. *You could know what he was like!*[18]

The moment that best captured the gestalt of that team occurred early in the 1947 season. The Dodgers were playing the Reds in Cincinnati. The fans were barraging Jackie Robinson with even more racial insults than usual. Robinson, a man of great dignity and courage, nonetheless seemed very alone standing at his position at first base, the only African American on the field. As the noise was getting worse, Reese walked across the infield from his shortstop position and put his arm around his teammate. The symbolism of the Kentucky-born white shortstop embracing his African American teammate was lost on nobody and is probably the best display of sportsmanship and teamwork in baseball history.

That, at least, is how the story goes. No photograph of the event exists. Newspaper reports of the game, which is said to have occurred on May 13, 1947, do not mention Reese's embrace of Robinson either.[19] Regardless of whether the embrace actually happened, it has become part of the lore and legacy of the Brooklyn Dodgers and is even celebrated by a statue depicting the two Dodgers greats at the home of the minor league Brooklyn Cyclones.

Those Dodgers were a great team, but they had one Achilles' heel, which made them more broadly appealing and only added to the charm of their story. Despite being a National League powerhouse, they could not get over the final barrier and win the World Series. That barrier took the form of another New York team, the Yankees. The Yankees beat the Dodgers in the World Series in 1941, 1947, 1949, 1952, and 1953. When the Dodgers finally beat the Yankees in 1955, few could have imagined that less than two years later they would play their last game in Brooklyn. In 1956, the Dodgers again lost to the Yankees in the World Series for the fifth time in ten years.

In Los Angeles, the Dodgers cast aside their Brooklyn persona and quickly transformed into a very different sort of team. Despite a bad first year in California, they were almost immediately a winning team. They won the World Series in 1959, only their second year in Los Angeles, and went on to win it again in 1963 and 1965. Moreover, although the team continued to have high-profile stars, the Los Angeles Dodgers always had a much more wholesome and all American feel than the scrappier and more colorful Brooklyn teams.

The two most famous Dodgers of the 1960s reflect that transition. Sandy Koufax was the best pitcher on those early Los Angeles Dodgers teams and indeed, from 1962 to 1966, in all of baseball. At 6'2", Koufax was a tall and handsome man who fit well into the film capital of the United States; he was also an old Brooklyn Dodger, who had actually grown up in that borough. More significantly, Koufax was Jewish. He was never an impact player in Brooklyn, where there was a huge Jewish population; however, by the 1960s, Los Angeles also had a large Jewish population, who happily embraced the best Jewish ballplayer of the era and (with the possible exception of Hank Greenberg) of all time.

The other great player on the early Los Angeles Dodgers teams was Don Drysdale. Drysdale, who grew up in the San Fernando Valley, was 6'5" and looked like a caricature of an all-American athlete. Throughout his career, he was comfortable in film culture and was frequently seen in Hollywood with people from the film industry. "Drysdale was perfect for a city that thrived on glamour and celebrity . . . and his cool sleek style seemed to mirror that of his city."[20] Drysdale was the prototype for the clean-cut Dodgers of the 1970s and 1980s, personified by people like Don Sutton, Tommy John, Ron Cey, and, more than anybody else, Steve Garvey.

Drysdale and Koufax were linked together in the minds of baseball fans because they were the top two starters on one of the best teams, but also because, despite their different backgrounds, they got along well. This relationship is probably best remembered for their joint holdout in the spring of 1966, when they demanded more money from the Dodgers.

Don Drysdale, incidentally, had a supporting role in one of the most famous moments in Jewish American sports history. In 1965, Koufax famously declined to pitch Game One of the World Series because it fell on Yom Kippur, the holiest day of the year in the Jewish calendar. Dodgers manager Walter Alston was fortunate to have Drysdale, who had gone 23–12 with a 2.77 ERA in the regular season, ready to pitch. Game One, however, did not go well for Drysdale. By the time Alston came to take him out of the game, with two outs in the third, the righty had given up seven hits, seven runs (only three earned), and walked one. Drysdale's greeting to his frustrated manager was "I bet you wish I was Jewish too." The Dodgers went on to beat the Twins in that World Series, not least because, once the High Holy Days were over, Koufax pitched 24 innings, giving up only two runs while throwing complete game shutouts in Game Five and Game Seven.

The Los Angeles Dodgers, particularly in their first 30 years, were largely a team of winners who—at least in the eyes of Southern Californians—were also lovable. The team that had integrated baseball with its first African American star continued to produce African American stars in this period. In the 1960s these players included Maury Wills, Tommy Davis, Willie Davis, and John

Roseboro; in the 1970s, star African American players included Dusty Baker and Reggie Smith. However, they were never the best-known stars on the team, even in the late 1970s when Baker and Smith contributed as least as much as better-known players like Cey and Garvey.

Pete Hamill captured this difference between how the Dodgers in Brooklyn and in Los Angeles were viewed, particularly by the New York media, in a 1987 essay in which he described Mets catcher Gary Carter: "Carter is Mister Good Guy America, right out of the wholesome Steve Garvey mold. You can imagine him as a Los Angeles Dodger—but not a Brooklyn Dodger."[21]

The Giants played a very different role in the early years of baseball. They were the most successful team in the National League through the beginning of World War II and, through at least the early 1920s, were the best-known team in the United States. The most famous Giant of the early twentieth century was not a lovable loser or seen as a clown. Christy Mathewson, one of the greatest pitchers in baseball history, was regarded as a gentleman and a role model; he was one of the first big baseball stars to have gone to college. Mathewson attended Bucknell, where he was more accomplished as a football player than as a baseball player. It is not clear whether he ever graduated from Bucknell, but even a few years of college was more than most players in the early twentieth century had.[22]

The biggest contrast between the public images of the two teams in the early twentieth century was reflected in their managers. John McGraw, who managed the Giants from the last part of the 1902 season through the first part of the 1932 season, winning ten pennants, was known as a strict and serious man, who demanded much from his players. In contrast to "Uncle Robbie," McGraw was known as "The Little Napoleon."[23]

By the 1950s, the Giants had shed much of this image, but still retained their status as one of the top teams in the National League and had remained competitive, winning two pennants during their last seven years in New York. The New York Giants were a consistently good and occasionally excellent organization. From 1903 to 1939, they finished under .500 only three times. By the time they left New York, that number had risen to 12, but was still an impressive figure over a 54-year span. In recent years, of course, the Giants have once again become one of baseball's premier franchises, winning the World Series in 2010, 2012, and 2014, while earning a reputation as one of the smartest organizations, with a very savvy approach to player development, marketing, fan relations, and the new media environment that is so important in the Bay Area.

For many years, however, the San Francisco Giants were a hard luck team, frequently either on the verge of leaving San Francisco or the victims of acute mismanagement. During the 1970s and 1980s, when the Dodgers were setting attendance records, the Giants were struggling to draw fans to their cold and inadequate ballpark. In the 1980s, the Giants resorted to gimmicks, including awarding a pin called the "Croix de Candlestick" to fans who stayed to the end of extra inning night games and having a mascot called the Crazy Crab, whom fans were encouraged to boo. This is a long way from the tight ship John McGraw used to run.

Josh Wilker's 2010 memoir *Cardboard Gods* includes an extended riff on a journeyman Giants pitcher of that era named John D'Acquisto that reflects how those post–Willie Mays Giants of the late 1970s and early 1980s were viewed outside the Bay Area:

> I had never seen the San Francisco Giants on television. They never surfaced in *Sports Illustrated* or anywhere near the top of the most distant of all divisions [Wilker lived in New England at the time], the National League West. In the All Star Game their yearly lone representative was no more noticeable than the half-second blip in the corner of the screen made by a white-shirted extra fleeing ruin in a disaster film. They seemed to me in those years, which were just after their iconic superstar Willie Mays had departed, to be not so much a team as a state of being, or somehow a lack of a state of being. A mystery. A mist.
>
> Gary Lucas was Gary Lavelle. Gary Maddox was Gary Mathews. . . . Gary Thomasson and Gary Alexander drifted into the ever expanding Gary-laced void.[24]

While the Dodgers won a championship in their second year on the West Coast, the Giants had to wait slightly longer, finally winning the World Series in their 53rd year in San Francisco. For much of the period between the 1972 season, during which Willie Mays was traded, and the 2010 championship season, the Giants rarely contended, winning only two pennants and were generally not a successful, wealthy, or prominent franchise.

During these years, whenever the Giants did appear in the national baseball media spotlight, it was often for odd reasons. In 1989, when they finally won their first pennant in 27 years, Game Three of the World Series—the first played in San Francisco since Willie McCovey lined out to Bobby Richardson with the tying and winning runs on base in the bottom of the ninth inning of the final game of the 1962 World Series—was postponed because, a few minutes before the first pitch, the Bay Area was hit by the biggest earthquake in the region since 1906. Game Three was supposed to be played on October 17, but the earthquake, and subsequent repairs and recovery, meant that the game was played on the October 27.

Fifteen years or so later, the Giants found themselves in the center of baseball's steroid controversy. Their best player, Barry Bonds, was one of many in the period from roughly 1993 to 2007 to have been associated with performance-enhancing drugs. Although Bonds's use of performance-enhancing drugs was never proven, few baseball fans outside of San Francisco doubted it. Bonds, who had been the best player in the game in the 1990s, allegedly began using steroids sometime after 1998, when his career should have been in its decline phase. Instead, Bonds transitioned from a powerful, but lithe athlete, capable of hitting 40 home runs in a season while stealing 30 bases—and winning a Gold Glove for his graceful play and great range in the outfield—to being a slow-moving, muscular power hitter. During the later years of his career, he set the single-season and career home run records, but not without the blemish of alleged use of performance-enhancing drugs. For many baseball fans, Bonds's cartoonish physique defined the Giants, and all that was wrong with baseball, from roughly 2001 to 2007.

The changing stories of the Giants and Dodgers after moving west help place their New York years, particularly the last decade or so, in perspective; they are also a reminder that baseball is a constantly changing institution. This book will tell the story not just of the Giants and Dodgers after moving west, but will look at how that move helped make the baseball we know today possible. It will also examine how these two teams, particularly in their first years in California, were instrumental in forging so many of the changes that define today's game.

Under the layers of nostalgia, poor understanding of baseball, demography, and culture in New York in the 1950s, and vilification of Walter O'Malley and Horace Stoneham—who ultimately made courageous and smart, but unpopular, business decisions—is an angle on the evolution of baseball history that, while perhaps glaringly obvious once said, almost always goes unsaid. O'Malley and Stoneham, regardless of what many fans of the Brooklyn Dodgers and New York Giants thought of them, did not destroy baseball or bring an end to its golden era. More accurately, they saved the game at the big league level, forced it out of a period of declining attendance, moribund franchises, plodding style of play, and limited national interest. They ensured that it would become genuinely national in scope and laid the groundwork for the increasingly global success of MLB today.

BASEBALL THEN AND NOW

The changes in big league baseball since 1957, when the New York Giants and Brooklyn Dodgers played their last games, have been enormous. On-the-field rule changes, primarily the introduction of the designated hitter in 1973, have had a major impact on how the game is played. Other developments in the style and strategy of the game, including the evolution of modern bullpens, the five-man pitching rotation, as well as rules and conventions limiting the ability of pitchers to throw inside, have also changed the game dramatically. Similarly, the sabrmetric revolution—which began with the innovative research of an underemployed security guard in Lawrence, Kansas, in the late 1970s named Bill James—has transformed the way baseball players are evaluated and how teams seek to win championships; it has in general contributed to making the modern game very different from the one the Dodgers and Giants played while they were still in Brooklyn and northern Manhattan.

Pitching, for example, looks very different today than it did in the 1950s. In 1957 the Dodgers and Giants combined for 79 complete games and 50 saves. In 2017, playing a season with eight more games, these two teams combined for only five complete games, but 83 saves. In those days nobody thought about pitch counts, and teams rarely carried more than ten pitchers on their 25-man rosters. Today most teams carry 12 pitchers, while many have 13 at least some of the time. The game the Dodgers and Giants played in their last decades in New York was one where home runs were central to offensive strategies, but hitting for average, moving runners along, and putting the bat on the ball, even if without much power, were still viewed as central to producing runs. In the late 1950s, baseball was still a game where striking out, even by power hitters, was considered a weakness. In 1957, Dodgers and Giants hitters combined to strike out 997 times. By 2017, that number had more than doubled to 2,584.

Although the on-the-field changes are interesting, particularly to older baseball fans who can remember if not the 1950s, then at least the 1970s, the game has changed in ways that may be more significant than simply how it is played, the introduction of a few new rules, or some new strategies. Off the field, the entire economic structure today is different than it was during the 1950s. Big league baseball, despite annual media paroxysms that baseball is dying, consistently draws higher attendance than it did 60 to 70 years ago. Baseball is much more international, as MLB includes players from all over the world, while the sport is becoming more popular in places ranging from Australia to the Netherlands that are not traditional baseball countries. Additionally, baseball has embraced modern technology, enabling today's fans to consume baseball in various forms across the internet and providing them with access to exponentially more data and video than their counterparts in the 1950s.

In this respect, baseball is not much different from many other institutions. Almost all American institutions, including those in finance, media, government, education, and other areas of society, have either undergone enormous change in the last 60 years, or they have disappeared. Americans get news, shop, and watch television differently than they did a half or even a quarter century ago. Nonetheless, an overview of those changes specific to baseball is helpful in understanding the role that the Dodgers and Giants moving west may have had on the developments in baseball during this period.

WHO PLAYED

One of the most striking differences between big league baseball in the late 1950s and the second decade of the twenty-first century is that the game is now played by a very different group of men. It remains the case that baseball is still played entirely by men, but that too may be changing as the movement to bring girls and women into baseball appears to be gaining some momentum. For example, in late 2015 the Oakland A's appointed Justine Siegal as the first woman to be a coach on a big league team. Organizations like Baseball for All and the popularity and impressive pitching of Mo'ne Davis in the 2014 Little League World Series have drawn more attention to the widespread exclusion of women and girls from all levels of baseball. The day when women play in the big leagues or when an enduring women's baseball league is created may still be far off, but it no longer seems an impossibility.

Although Jackie Robinson became the first African American player in the modern era of big league baseball in 1947, integration was still moving slowly in 1957. That year the Philadelphia Phillies became the last National League team to put an African American player on their roster, when shortstop John Kennedy played his first game for Philadelphia early in the season. Two American League teams, the Detroit Tigers and Boston Red Sox, still had no African American players. The Tigers did not have any nonwhite players until 1958. The Red Sox became, famously, the last team to integrate when they added infielder Pumpsie Green to the roster in July 1959. In the late 1950s, the informal agreement that no team would have more than three African American players had begun to be phased out; however, it remained true that most relief pitchers and backup infielders in the big leagues were white, as African American players still had to be stars, or at least impact players, to win and keep a big league job.

Toward the end of 1956, the Giants used a rookie third baseman for three games. Ozzie Virgil hit well enough in those three games, going five for 12 with a double and a triple, that he earned a spot on the team the following season as a backup infielder and outfielder. He hit a very respectable .278/.305/.583 as a 25-year-old rookie in 1957 on the way to a journeyman career that took him to the Tigers, Athletics, Orioles, and Pirates, before finishing his playing days with the San Francisco Giants in 1966 and 1969.

Virgil never was a great player, retiring with a .263 batting average and only 14 home runs over parts of nine seasons, but he is a significant figure in baseball history. Virgil was the first Dominican-born player in the major leagues. Virgil went to high school in the Bronx, after moving to New York as a young boy, but has retained strong ties to the Dominican Republic throughout his life.

When he stepped on the field for the Giants, Virgil became the first of many Dominican-born players (707 through the end of 2017) to play in the big leagues, but it was not until the 1960s that Dominicans began to make an impact. Only one other Dominican, another Giant, Felipe Alou, appeared in a big league game in the 1950s. In 2017, by contrast, 152 Dominican-born players were in the major leagues.

While Dominicans may be the most significant example of foreign-born players becoming more numerous and visible in the big leagues, the game in general has become much more international in the 60 years since the Giants and Dodgers moved west. In 1957, 94 percent of the players in the big leagues had been born in the United States, not including an additional 1.1 percent who had been born in Puerto Rico. Big league players that year hailed from only ten countries other than the United States and Puerto Rico. Most of those who had not been born in the United States had immigrated to the United States at a young age. By 2017, the proportion of American-born players had fallen to 70.5 percent, as well as 2.1 percent from Puerto Rico and two players from the U.S. Virgin Islands. The remaining players had been born in a total of 19 different countries.

The majority of foreign-born players still come from Latin America, with the Dominican Republic (11.2 percent) and Venezuela (8.1 percent) having the most players in the big leagues in 2017. However, the increasing internationalization of big league baseball has drawn from other regions as well. For the entire time the Giants and Dodgers were in New York, no Asian, or even Asian American, player appeared in the big leagues. Baseball has been popular in Japan, Korea, and Taiwan for almost the entire twentieth century, so there was no shortage of people playing baseball in Asia during those years. The Asian leagues, and therefore Asian ballplayers, were widely assumed to be inferior to their counterparts in the United States. This assumption was reinforced by barnstorming trips to Japan by big league players in Japan during the 1920s and 1930s, and then again after World War II was over. Those teams of barnstorming big leaguers almost never lost to their Japanese counterparts, often winning by lopsided scores. However, by the postwar era, great Japanese players like Sadaharu Oh were good enough to have played in the big leagues. Today Japanese players like Ichiro Suzuki, Masahiro Tanaka, Yu Darvish, Hideki Matsui, and many others have demonstrated they can more than hold their own in the big leagues. Players from Korea, like Shin-soo Choo and Jung-ho Kang, as well as from Taiwan, like Chien Ming Wang and Hong-Chih Kuo, have similarly shone for several teams.

In addition to drawing more heavily from baseball-playing regions, big league baseball, particularly in recent years, has begun to realize the fruit of MLB's efforts to increase its international reach. Players from countries where baseball is considerably newer, such as Australia, New Zealand, Brazil, and even a few European countries, have also been signed by big league teams and, in a few cases, played in the big leagues. In 2017 Pirates infielder Gift Ngoepe became the first South African player to appear in a big league game. It is not hard to imagine that in the next decade or two, there will be players from countries where baseball is now relatively new, such as China, playing in the big leagues.

The internationalization of big league baseball has meant that over the last 60 years the biggest change that the game has seen on the field is that it is now played by a very different, demographically speaking, group of players. This has made baseball a more interesting and diverse game and forced players, managers, and fans to navigate occasionally complex cultural questions. This was not always easy. In the 1960s, for example, Giants manager Alvin Dark struggled to manage a diverse team with several high-profile Latino stars like Juan Marichal, Orlando Cepeda, and the Alou brothers.[1]

This diversity has also improved the quality of play. Today, the best players in the world, much more than at any time in the past and almost no matter where they play—with the glaring exception of Cuba—have a path to big league baseball.

HOW AND WHERE THE GAME WAS PLAYED

It is relatively common to point out how much more international baseball is today compared to 60 years ago; it is less frequently noted that MLB today is more truly national than it was in the late 1950s. Even after the Browns, Athletics, and Braves moved cities—and in the case of the Browns, changed names—in the early and mid-1950s, big league baseball was still played in a relatively small swath of the United States, one that was unmistakably skewed toward the Northeast and Midwest, at a time when the population was shifting to the South and West. As late as 1957, the farthest distance between big league cities was 1,244 miles, from Boston to Kansas City. Today, in contrast, the farthest distance between big league cities is 3,297 miles—from Seattle to Miami.

Census data from 1960, a reasonably accurate reflection of the population in 1957, shows that people in eight of the country's 20 largest cities—Los Angeles, Houston, San Francisco, Dallas, New Orleans, San Antonio, San Diego, and Seattle—not only had no team, but did not live within 500 miles, and in most cases 1,000 miles, of one. Television and radio, by the late 1950s, were making big league baseball, at least in some form, available to many fans, but that was an inadequate substitute for attending, even occasionally, a big league game.

Because in the 1950s MLB did not reach into as much of the United States or as many of its population centers as it does today, baseball in other forms continued to thrive. Therefore, the national baseball landscape was very different. That changed relatively quickly after the Dodgers and Giants moved west and expansion and more franchise movement brought big league baseball to places like Houston, Atlanta, Dallas, and San Diego in the following years.

Thus, one of the biggest changes in baseball over the last 60 years is that MLB projects much more hegemony over baseball now. For much of the pre–World War II era, the big leagues existed alongside of semipro baseball, the Negro Leagues, independent minor leagues, and offseason barnstorming. During those years, racial barriers to playing in the big leagues not only kept some of the best players out of the big leagues, but ensured that the Negro Leagues could exist alongside the American and National Leagues. For many African American baseball fans, despite the uneven quality of play and frequent lack of continuity in the Negro Leagues, the Negro Leagues were considered as important as the white big leagues. Additionally, African Americans who attended Negro League games contributed to the economic success of those ventures rather than to the American or National League teams.

In the prewar years, independent minor league also thrived in parts of the country that were not served by the geographically confined American and National Leagues. The best known of these—and the most relevant for the story of the Giants and the Dodgers—was the Pacific Coast League (PCL). The PCL offered high-quality baseball to fans in western cities like San Francisco, Oakland, Seattle, Los Angeles, Portland, and San Diego. Hall of Famers like Ted Williams, Paul Waner, and Joe DiMaggio, as well as many other future big leaguers, passed through the PCL on their way to, and sometimes from, National and American League teams. Additionally, many players who were probably good enough to play for teams in the East, although not as stars, chose to remain closer to home and spent their entire careers in the PCL.

During these years, semipro and barnstorming were also critical parts of the professional baseball landscape. Semipro baseball existed in a grey area between professional and amateur. Semipro teams rarely belonged to any organized leagues, and, if they did, these leagues usually did not last very long. Rosters, management, schedules, and compensation were not formalized either. Players did not play for free so they were not true amateurs. Some were paid by companies where they worked part-time and focused on baseball; some were paid through informal methods such as weekly or even daily rates; others were paid by passing the hat and dividing the take after games, as well as in myriad other ways.

Barnstorming was, like semipro baseball, informal, but played a different role in the baseball economy of the prewar years. Barnstorming was a way for big league players to increase their income during an era when players' salaries were nowhere near what they are today, and when all but the very best players needed to work winter jobs to make an adequate income. Barnstorming also played a key role in bringing big league caliber play, or at least big league caliber players, to fans in parts of the country that did not have the opportunity to see these players during the regular season. In the years before television, this was particularly important. Big league players barnstormed throughout the United States during off seasons, focusing on parts of the country where the weather permitted winter baseball. Additionally, big league players participated in barnstorming trips abroad, most notably to Japan in the 1920s and early 1930s as well as to the Caribbean and other foreign destinations.

Barnstorming during these years was significant for two additional reasons. First, while barnstorming was not fully integrated, it provided opportunities for white and nonwhite players to compete with, and more frequently, against each other. Thus while, for example, Satchel Paige and Bob Feller, the best African American and white pitchers of the late 1930s and early 1940s, could not pitch against each other during the regular season due the segregation of big league baseball, fans could, and did, see that and other extraordinary matchups from barnstorming teams. Those two pitchers were later teammates on the pennant-winning Cleveland Indians team in 1948, when Paige finally was allowed to play in the big leagues. Second, for most of the prewar period, even the very best players barnstormed. This meant that fans in Texas, Nevada, Japan, and elsewhere had a chance to see Babe Ruth, Lou Gehrig, Josh Gibson, Jimmie Foxx, Lefty Grove, Feller, Paige, and the other great players of those years. Players who participated in barnstorming trips, traveled abroad, or who played on high-profile winter teams with stars like Ruth, Gehrig, or Grove were able to meaningfully bolster their otherwise relatively modest baseball salaries.

During the years before World War II, big league baseball was just one variety of baseball that fans could see. It was, on balance, clearly the best baseball in the United States, and the world, but it was not nearly as dominant as it has become in the years since then. Additionally, before Jackie Robinson, baseball's own version of apartheid kept some of the best players out of the big leagues. Geographical limits and small salaries also created a disincentive for many top players to move from the PCL or other minor leagues to the big leagues.

Much of this began to change in earnest after Jackie Robinson joined the Dodgers in 1947. Within a few years of Robinson becoming a member of the Brooklyn team, a number of other great African American players left the Negro Leagues to star in the big leagues, including Roy Campanella, Larry Doby, Monte Irvin, and Satchel Paige. Additionally, African American players just a few years younger than Robinson, who was born in 1919, were able to start their big league careers at a much younger age. Three of the biggest African American stars of the 1950s and 1960s, Willie Mays, Henry Aaron, and Ernie Banks, played their first big league game when they were 20, 20, and 22 years old, respectively. These three players all went on to stellar careers and rank among the greatest players ever, in part because they were able to give their best years to the big leagues.

It may, therefore, be a bit surprising that all three of these men also played in the post–Jackie Robinson Negro Leagues. Banks spent parts of the 1950 and 1953 seasons with the Kansas City Monarchs. In 1951 and 1952 he served in the military. Mays played for the Birmingham Black Barons in 1949 and 1950. Aaron was an infielder with the Indianapolis Clowns in 1951 and part of 1952 before the Braves purchased his contract. Aaron had a very long and superb career in the major leagues, playing until 1976, and was the last big leaguer to have played in the Negro Leagues.

By the middle of the 1950s, however, the Negro Leagues were no longer an incubator for top African American baseball talent. Two future first-ballot Hall of Famers, Willie McCovey and Frank Robinson began their respective careers with the Giants and Reds in 1959 and 1956—just a few years after Aaron, Banks, and Mays—but they never played in the Negro Leagues. Neither would any of the African American stars who came after them.

Even by the early 1950s, when great players like Banks and Aaron played for the Monarchs and Clowns on their way to the big leagues, the Negro Leagues were not in strong shape. The integration of the big leagues had destroyed the fan base, and economic niche, that Negro League teams had enjoyed through-out much of urban America. Thus, the quality and consistency of Negro League play steadily declined through the 1950s. Additionally, there was less stability during these years, with teams forming and collapsing between and during seasons. By the 1960s, the Negro Leagues, or, more accurately, the barnstorm-ing teams that were entirely African American, still existed, but they were on the fringes of organized baseball. They either barnstormed or played in small towns and rural areas, often in a hybrid form of baseball and entertainment.

The eventual collapse of the Negro Leagues began before the Dodgers and Giants moved west, and the two events were not very related. However, during the 1960s, barnstorming became much less common; independent and semipro minor leagues came to an end, more or less, as well. This was largely a result of the Giants and Dodgers opening up the western and southern parts of the United States, thus reducing the appeal of both barnstorming and semipro baseball. By Opening Day 1967, not even ten years after the move west, the national reach of big league baseball had substantially increased, with teams in San Francisco, Atlanta, Houston, and Minneapolis, as well as two teams in Los Angeles.

Big league baseball's expanding hegemony during the years immediately following World War II was attributable to non-baseball developments as well. The changing technological environment, specifically the rise of television, was a key part of this. For example, in 1950 only 9 percent of American households had televisions. That number had increased to 64.5 percent by 1955 and to 87.1 percent by 1960. It reached 92.6 percent in 1965. This means that, while in 1950 people who wanted to see baseball had to go to a ballpark of some kind, by 1960 the huge majority of Americans could watch big league baseball, at the very least once a week, on television in their homes. This obviously reduced the market for, and appeal of, barnstorming, semipro, and other forms of independent baseball.[2]

These trends, which began in the late 1950s and early 1960, have continued and perhaps even accelerated into the present. Major League Baseball is a more dominant force in American baseball than it ever has been and has expanded to 30 teams that play in 26 cities in the United States and one in Canada. Every AA and AAA minor league team is affiliated with a big league team, as are almost all teams in the lower minors. The handful of independent-league teams are generally in small cities or regions with limited fan bases. The route to the big leagues, particularly for American players, runs through the formal structures of college and affiliated minor leagues. Almost no American player gets to the big leagues any other way.

Today, MLB has greater hegemony over organized baseball than either the NFL or the NBA have over their respective sports. This is, in part, due to the absence of extensive minor league structures in football and basketball. This has grown to mean that collegiate athletics is the primary setting for the development of future NFL and NBA players. The NCAA, while working as essentially a feeder to professional football and basketball, or even as a de facto minor league system, does not answer to the NFL or NBA. It has independent governing structures and revenue streams as well as its own incentive structures. This is also true of college baseball, which is also organized largely by the NCAA, but college baseball is not a de facto minor league in the same way. Many American-born baseball players, and almost all players from Venezuela, the Dominican Republic, and elsewhere in Latin America, go straight from high school to the affiliated minor leagues, never attending college. Similarly, many baseball players who are drafted out of college still spend time in the minors. This gives MLB more power over player development and related revenue than either the NFL or the NBA.

A related point is that as late as the mid-1970s, the American Basketball Association (ABA) existed independently of the NBA. Some of basketball's greatest stars of that era including Artis Gilmore, Spencer Haywood, Moses Malone, and, most famously Dr. J—Julius Erving—played in the ABA before it merged with the NBA. A similar situation existed in professional football, as the United States Football League (USFL) existed for several years in the early 1980s, before shutting down in 1985. Several of the greatest football players of that era, including Herschel Walker, Reggie White, and Steve Young, spent some time in the USFL before moving to the NFL after the USFL folded. The USFL was shorter lived and did not leave as big a mark on the broader culture as the ABA.

Unlike what has happened in football and basketball, no formal league has emerged to challenge MLB in over a century. Additionally, no independent minor league has emerged to compete with the affiliated minor leagues; while college baseball is more popular than ever now, it is not nearly as popular as either college football or basketball, or even minor league baseball.

The last effort to form a third big league to compete with the National and American Leagues, an idea that had been pursued by the Federal League in 1914–45 and that had been a subject of discussion periodically regarding the PCL in the 1940s and 1950s, occurred in 1960, almost immediately after the Dodgers and Giants moved west. The departure of the Giants and Dodgers left the country's biggest media market, New York, with only one team, after having three for more than 60 years. Relatively quickly after the Dodgers and Giants left for the West Coast, it became clear there was a paucity of big league baseball in New York, a city that was not only the biggest in the country, but also one where passion for baseball had always been strong. This was an opportunity for somebody to make some money and have an impact on baseball. The negotiations around solving that problem were an important period for big league baseball.

The absence of National League baseball in New York ultimately led to the creation of the New York Mets. The Mets played their first two seasons in the Polo Grounds, the northern Manhattan ballpark that had previously been home to the New York Giants, before moving to Shea Stadium in Queens in 1964. By moving to Queens, the Mets assured themselves a base of fan support in Brooklyn, Queens, and the suburban Long Island counties of Nassau and Suffolk. These areas have remained strongholds of Mets support to this day.

The Mets also deliberately tried, and continue to try, to link themselves to the legacy of the Dodgers and Giants, their National League predecessors in New York. Their colors, orange and blue, are taken from the Giants and Dodgers. The interlocking orange "NY," borrowed from the Giants against a blue background, borrowed from the Dodgers, on the original Mets caps was an elegant hybrid of the New York Giants and Brooklyn Dodgers caps. Their new ballpark, Citi Field, where they began playing in 2009, features a Jackie Robinson rotunda and a façade modeled after that of Ebbets Field. This is a reflection of how the nostalgia in New York has long been mostly about the Dodgers with much less focus on the Giants. Robinson, for his part, never played a single game for the Mets.

When the Mets were created in 1962, the National League needed to add another team so that there would still be an even number of teams. That team was placed in Houston, thus finally giving a big league team to a southern city. The Houston team was originally the Colt .45s, but became the Astros in 1965, and moved over to the American League in 2013. The expansion to Houston, preceded in 1961 by the American League placing an expansion team in Los Angeles, was part of the second step of baseball's migration west and south. It was understood that the Dodgers and Giants moving west would only be the beginning of this process, but the details of what the process would look like did not become clear until the Colt .45s were added to the National League.

One of the factors that accelerated the creation of the Mets and the corresponding decision to award a National League franchise to New York was that in 1959–60 there was a movement, the last of its kind, to create a third big league. That league would have been known as the Continental League. The Continental League never amounted to anything, but at the time it was seen as a threat with which the big leagues needed to reckon. Had the Continental League established a team in New York before the National League did, it would have had an anchor franchise around which to build out the league.

Much of the credibility of the Continental League, and the threat it represented to the American and National Leagues, was due to the man who provided most of the strategy and energy for the proposed new league. Branch Rickey, the legendary general manager who was credited with the creation of the affiliated minor league system while he was running the Cardinals and with integrating the big leagues by bringing Jackie Robinson to the Dodgers, was the Continental League's strongest advocate. The failure of the Continental League in 1960, although barely a footnote in most histories of big league baseball, marked the moment when the possibility of a third major league or even a high-level independent minor league disappeared from the baseball environment.

Lurking around the fringes of the threat raised by the Continental League was the possibility that baseball could lose its antitrust exemption. This exemption had guaranteed, and continues to guarantee, that the American and National Leagues can essentially exercise a monopoly over high-level baseball and top baseball players. The key to that exemption is the reserve clause, which was still in effect in the late 1950s. The reserve clause stripped players of the right to negotiate or bargain with any team other than the one for which they had last played, unless they were released by that team.

On the other hand, the discussion around the possibility of the Continental League was not something that either occurred on the fringes of MLB or was perceived as anything but serious. It spurred the National League into moving more quickly and decisively than it otherwise might have, thus demonstrating that as late as 1960 or thereabouts big league baseball, specifically the owners of big league teams, saw the emergence of another league as a real possibility. Within even 20 years, that idea would get no support. Today it would be considered a joke.

BASEBALL AND THE CULTURE

The role baseball plays in American culture is complex, multifaceted, profound, and difficult to accurately describe, but it has undoubtedly changed a great deal since the Dodgers and Giants left New York. The general narrative about the position of baseball suggests that as the entertainment, media, and sports environment has changed, baseball has become less popular. According to this argument, the rise of everything from professional football and basketball, to the internet and video games has left baseball with a smaller share of the attention and disposable income of many Americans. Moreover, according to this narrative, as American culture has become less unified, more violent, impatient, and prurient, baseball, like America, has lost its special place or even its way. This might be called the "Mrs. Robinson" position, based on Simon and Garfunkel's 1967 song of that name in which they ask the question "Where have you gone, Joe DiMaggio? A nation turns its lonely eyes to you."

This view is hokey, impossible to prove, and comes across as the lamentation of a generation looking back at its youth; nonetheless, there is something to it. For many years, baseball was a deep part of the everyday life of America. Children, and adults, played it in various forms during a large share of their free time. On-the-field events like Joe DiMaggio's 56-game hitting streak in 1941 or the annual ritual of the World Series were widely discussed by Americans of all kinds. Baseball on the radio was the background sound of much of American life for decades. The French-born American philosopher and historian Jacques Barzun's famous line, "Whoever wants to know the heart and mind of America had better learn baseball," is still frequently quoted and used as part of efforts by MLB to promote the game. This line is used not by observers of the game or of American society, but usually by MLB itself as an effort to demonstrate the link, real or imagined, between baseball and American culture. Baseball fans, particularly those with a poetic or philosophical inclination may believe that those words, written in 1954, still reveal a fundamental truth about America.

A few paragraphs later, Barzun fleshes out this assertion while offering a view of America that was plausible, albeit barely, in 1954, but has not been a reflection of the American role in the world for decades: "We find also our American innocence in calling 'World Series' the annual games between the winners in each big league. The world doesn't know or care and couldn't compete if it wanted to, but since it's us children having fun, why, the world is our stage."[3]

It is very difficult to imagine an American or thoughtful foreign observer of the United States in the twenty-first century making similar observations. The word "arrogance" would fit better than "innocence" in the second quotation. Nobody at home or abroad views the United States as a young country playing funny games on the world stage anymore. Additionally, the globalization of baseball, which has led to it being played in more countries, not to mention the significant number of big leaguers from foreign countries, gives it a much less uniquely American feel than was the case in the middle of the last century.

Baseball has, by most measures, a smaller cultural impact and is on the minds of Americans less today than in 1954. Other sports like soccer and basketball have grown in popularity, so that fewer children play baseball, particularly in informal settings, than ever before. Annual events like the World Series and Opening Day are no longer the national touchpoints that they were for most of the twentieth century. Very few players have the cultural impact that Babe Ruth, Lou Gehrig, Joe DiMaggio, Jackie Robinson, Willie Mays, or a few others once did. Baseball is no longer the constant background of many American childhoods that it once was. Harder to pin down is the reduced centrality of baseball to the vibe or gestalt of America, but that decline is real.

Today there are still some people who are likely to agree with Barzun's assessment or with Roger Angell's observation, which is also frequently used by MLB to promote itself and its special role in the American character, that, "since baseball time is measured only in outs, all you have to do is succeed utterly; keep hitting, keep the rally alive, and you have defeated time. You remain forever young. Sitting in the stands, we sense this, if only dimly. The players below us—Mays, DiMaggio, Ruth, Snodgrass—swim and blur in memory, the ball floats over to Terry Turner, and the end of this game may never come."[4] These people, however, are probably older and whiter than the America that is taking shape in the twenty-first century. Baseball is still a great game, but as metaphor for America it has not fully survived into the twenty-first century.

Paradoxically, while baseball's position in the American culture has diminished in the last 60 years or so, it has only grown more popular and wealthy during those years. Big league baseball is seen by more people, both live and on television, even relative to the total population, than during the years before the Dodgers and Giants moved west. Table 3 shows the annual attendance for all of big league baseball for the last ten years the Dodgers and Giants were in New York. During the ten years in question, the average attendance for any given team in a year was 1,048,771. Given that in those years teams only played 154 games a year, the average big league baseball game from 1948 to 1957 had only 14,566 spectators.[5] The population in the United States in 1950 was 161,325,798. Using that number as a base, the overall attendance for the ten years from 1948 to 1957 was 104 percent that of the U.S. population in 1950.

Looking at similar data from 2008 to 2017, as shown in Table 4, reveals a sport that consistently drew much greater attendance than it did during the supposed golden era of the late 1940s and early 1950s. From 1951 to 1954, the average big league team did not draw even 1,000,000. Over the last decade, the average team drew 2.4 million fans or more every year. Even when adjusting for population, using the 2010 population of 308,745,538 as base, the numbers are striking, as the total attendance at big league games over the last ten years is 240 percent of the U.S. population. This number is a bit misleading because during this period only 29 of the 30 teams played in the United States. The thirtieth, the Toronto Blue Jays, made their home in Canada; however, leaving Toronto out of the data makes negligible impact, only reducing total attendance to about 234 percent of the U.S. population. Additionally, the average big league game played in 2008–17 was seen by just over 30,000 spectators, almost twice as many as during the earlier period.[6]

The overall increases in attendance from 1948 to 2016, however, did not occur linearly or immediately. As late as 1970, the average big league team drew fewer than 1.2 million fans per season. This number did not reach two million until 1987.[7]

The substantial increase in attendance figures overall, as well as on a per team or per capita basis, reflects the changing role of big league baseball within the broader baseball context, but it also indicates an increase in the popularity of the game. The former point is reasonably straightforward: As big league baseball moved to the West Coast and Texas and later to Arizona, Florida, and elsewhere, it became more accessible for more Americans than ever before. Additionally, as the Negro Leagues collapsed, and baseball became increasingly

Table 3. Attendance for MLB, 1948–57

Season	Overall Attendance	Average Attendance per Team
1948	20,938,388	1,308,649
1949	20,215,365	1,263,460
1950	17,153,172	1,072,273
1951	15,661,207	978,825
1952	14,005,944	875,372
1953	14,021,684	876,355
1954	15,631,217	976,951
1955	16,617,383	1,038,586
1956	16,543,250	1,033,953
1957	17,015,819	1,063,489
Total	167,803,429	1,048,771

Source: Ballparks of Baseball (2017), http://www.ballparksofbaseball.com.

Table 4. Attendance for MLB, 2008–17

Season	Overall Attendance	Average Attendance Per Team
2008	78,584,286	2,619,476
2009	73,401,938	2,446,731
2010	73,171,239	2,439,041
2011	73,451,522	2,448,384
2012	73,951,759	2,465,059
2013	74,026,895	2,467,563
2014	73,739,622	2,457,987
2015	75,959,167	2,531,972
2016	73,159,054	2,438,635
2017	72,670,423	2,422,347
Total	742,115,905	2,473,710

Sources: Ballparks of Baseball (2017), http://www.ballparksofbaseball.com; Maury Brown, "MLB Sees Nearly 73.8 Million in Attendance for 2015, Seventh-Highest All-Time," *Forbes,* Oct. 6, 2015.

racially integrated. Major League Baseball began to get revenue from African American baseball fans that a generation earlier would have gone to Negro League teams. Barnstorming also fell by the wayside as expansion made big league baseball accessible in all but the most sparsely populated areas of the continental United States.

Attendance is only one measure of baseball's growth over the last 60 years. Television and more recently the internet have also helped big league baseball reach more people than in the past. The evidence here is decidedly more mixed. For example, ratings for the World Series, baseball's most famous and important event, have declined precipitously in recent decades. As late as 1986–91, most World Series games were seen by 30 million television viewers, but for the most part the event has not reached an average of even 20 million viewers since 2004.[8] Only in 2016, when Game Seven between the Cubs and the Indians—one of the most highly anticipated games in baseball history—drew more than 40 million viewers, did the average for a World Series exceed 20 million viewers. The 2017 World Series between the Dodgers and the Astros also went seven games, but averaged only 18.9 million viewers per game.[9]

Despite the generally shrinking number of World Series viewers, baseball is more available on television than ever before, with all teams broadcasting all games, even many spring-training games. Until the 1980s, the number of games teams televised varied substantially. In most years this ranged from 30 to 130 depending on the team. Additionally, before the rise of cable television, there were fewer opportunities to watch games that did not involve local teams. The All-Star Game and World Series were televised in the 1950s, but other than that there was only the matchup broadcast on *Game of the Week,* available nationally on network television. This did not change much until the advent of cable made more games available to more viewers, beginning in the late 1970s and early 1980s.

More baseball on television, even with declining World Series ratings, has meant more revenue both for individual teams through local television contracts and deals and for MLB itself through national television contracts. Major League Baseball currently gets about $1.5 billion a year, or $50 million per team, from its national baseball contracts. This has contributed to making the sport bigger and richer than it has ever been.

For most fans this is most evident in the steadily rising salaries paid to baseball players. The enormous salaries earned by ballplayers today and the rapid acceleration of those salaries since the advent of free agency in the mid-1970s are other indicators of how baseball has become a bigger and more lucrative business over the last 60 years. In 1957, the last year the Dodgers and Giants played in New York, the highest paid player in the big leagues was Yankees catcher Yogi Berra, who made $65,000 that year. Adjusted for inflation, that would be about $550,000 in 2016 dollars, according to the Bureau of Labor Statistics. That is a lot of money, but it is about $1/50$ of the highest salaries today, and only $15,000 more than the minimum big league salary for 2017.[10]

The growth of baseball in recent decades is beginning to confront challenges, but it has had an enormous impact on how the game is experienced and its role in the culture.[11] At first, it may seem incongruous that baseball, while growing steadily, particularly in recent years, almost certainly no longer occupies the central and special role it once did in the broader American culture. One reason for this is simply that baseball now must compete with other sports, and other entertainment sources, ranging from cable television and the internet to movies, restaurants, and the like, all of which are more common in American life than they were in the early part of the twentieth century.

There is, however, more to it than that. As baseball has become bigger, it has begun to look more like other forms of entertainment, such as Hollywood movies and popular music. Baseball players, because of their extraordinarily high salaries, are not accessible the way they once were. No star player would continue to work selling cars in the winters in the same place as where he played in the summers as Gil Hodges did while playing for the Dodgers in the 1950s. It is unimaginable that a highly touted prospect during his first season with the big league team would live in a boardinghouse within two miles of the ballpark and occasionally join the neighborhood kids to play stickball on the streets as Willie Mays did in 1951.

Astronomically higher salaries have made baseball more oriented toward money at almost every level. For children today, baseball is not a beloved activity on which they can spend hours of free time away from adults. It has become structured from young ages all the way through the college level in a way that is radically different from how young people played baseball even 30 years ago. Folk tales of the great slugger who built his muscles pulling a plow, or the pitcher who was found in a cornfield in the Midwest somewhere, helped build the mythology of baseball, but today those players would have been identified, placed on elite travel teams, and been going to college showcases around the country by the time they were 16 (and probably even 12) years old.

WHAT DOES THIS HAVE TO DO WITH THE GIANTS AND DODGERS?

There is nothing profound about noting that baseball has changed a lot in the last 60 years, although there is more value in examining some of the ways in which it has changed. The question of what impact the Dodgers and Giants had on these changes, and thus on the making of modern big league baseball, is more significant, particularly given the more common narrative that their move west was a negative for baseball and even for America.

It is reasonably evident that the offseason of 1957–58 represented a very big turning point for big league baseball. The next few years would see the game become more national in reach due to increasing franchise moves and expansion. The game would also grow to include more African American and Latino ballplayers. However, this was only the beginning of that process. Baseball attendance did not proceed upward on a clear or immediate trajectory once the Dodgers and Giants moved west. Attendance, in fact, remained a problem through the 1970s when, ironically, one of the teams that struggled most to fill its ballpark was the San Francisco Giants.

The changes baseball has experienced since 1957 have been gradual and cumulative, but the move by the Dodgers and Giants was a key event in this process. It is a moment that neatly cleaves the game's history. There are a small handful of other moments like this in baseball history. Jackie Robinson's debut with the Dodgers in 1947 is one of them. Another might be the sale of Babe Ruth from the Red Sox to the Yankees in 1920, which allowed baseball's most famous star to spend the bulk of his career playing in the media capital of the United States.

Even if this 1957–58 turning point is recognized, that is not the same as suggesting that the Dodgers and Giants move to California led directly to these changes in baseball. Nevertheless, there is ample reason to think that this notion should be given substantial credence, no matter how hard it is to prove actual causality. The most immediate impact of the move west was that it greatly expanded the sense of what was possible for big league baseball. If the Dodgers and Giants, two of the game's most storied franchises, could leave New York, then big-picture change was possible. Uprooting two of the game's most famous franchises from their longtime homes in the biggest city in the country allowed ownership and players to see that the on-the-field rules of the game, structures governing relations between players and management, and the schedule and tempo of the season were all also subject to change.

Fans in other cities could think about winning expansion teams for their communities or about luring existing franchises there. Similarly, after the Giants and Dodgers moved, it was apparent that any franchise could move and that cities needed to actively court both potential new teams and the teams they already had if they wanted to keep them. That new variable changed the relationship between cities and their home teams. In the short run this contributed to additional franchise moves: In 1960–61, the Senators moved from Washington, D.C., to Minnesota and became the Twins. In 1971–72, their replacements, also known as the Senators, left the nation's capital for Texas, where they became known as the Rangers. In 1965–66 and 1967–68, respectively, the Braves and Athletics abandoned their new homes in Milwaukee and Kansas City, where they had been for fewer than 15 years, to move to Atlanta and Oakland. In 1970, the Seattle Pilots, after only one year in existence, eschewed Seattle in favor of Milwaukee.

Many teams did not move, but threatened to do that to gain leverage over their home cities. The Chicago White Sox, Cleveland Indians, and San Francisco Giants were all in that category; not coincidentally, all eventually got new stadiums as part of an incentive to keep them in their cities. The Giants received very few public funds for the construction of their new ballpark, but they were the exception. The White Sox, Indians, and the many other teams that had new stadiums built for them by their host cities benefited from the post-1957 climate in MLB, in which cities feared losing their teams, just as New York had lost the Dodgers and Giants. No elected mayor wants to be the person who let the White Sox leave Chicago or the Indians leave Cleveland.

The Dodgers and Giants also moved to cities with much stronger ties to Asia and Latin America than the other cities that had big league teams in the 1950s. The two most visible and important cities on the West Coast of the United States also had large, well-established Asian and Latino (primarily Mexican) populations. Relations between big league baseball and, for example, professional baseball in Japan changed when baseball moved significantly closer to Japan than it had for most of the twentieth century. The first Japanese player, Masanori Murakami, who played for the Giants in 1964–65, and the second, Dodgers pitcher Hideo Nomo, who made his National League debut in 1995, were both additionally valuable because they helped generate interest in their teams among their cities' large Japanese American populations. This also made it easier for those players to feel more comfortable playing in the United States.

It took more than 30 years after the Dodgers and Giants moved west for Japanese and other Asian players to have a significant impact on big league baseball; however, the role the Giants played in bringing Latino players into the big leagues was evident almost immediately. Again, the different geography and culture of the West Coast helped make this possible. Playing in San Francisco and Los Angeles, the Giants and Dodgers were very aware of the economic importance of Spanish-speaking fans. Moreover, baseball on the West Coast had always been slightly more diverse than the rest of the country—while the Pacific Coast League had always excluded African Americans, its policies toward Latinos and Asian Americans were not quite as discriminatory as the National and American Leagues in the pre-1947 period.

There is no way to know what would have happened to the Dodgers, Giants, or baseball in general if the two teams had not moved west when they did, or if they had moved to another region, like the South or Texas. Baseball almost certainly would have eventually expanded to the West Coast, but expansion teams would not have immediately excited fans in Los Angeles and San Francisco, many of whom had been longtime PCL fans with loyalties to the San Francisco Seals, Hollywood Stars, and PCL baseball more generally. Several years of bad teams in those two cities might have made it more difficult for big league baseball to become entrenched in the west.

If expansion had not happened by the mid-1960s, it is also possible that a western league would again have emerged to challenge MLB. Placing expansion teams in Los Angeles and San Francisco, rather than the wealthier, higher profile, and more successful Dodgers and Giants, would not have precluded that possibility. Fans in those two cities would not as easily have walked away from generations of loyalty to the San Francisco Seals, Hollywood Stars, or Los Angeles Angels (the PCL team) for an expansion team with no recognizable names and no real chance of competing in the National or American League. Nor were fans in those cities convinced that for most of the twentieth century they had been watching minor league baseball. For many of those fans, the PCL was just as important and competitive as the American and National Leagues were to fans in most second-division cities. Thus, creating a third big league, possibly based around PCL teams that broke their affiliations with their new big league partners, could have happened and changed big league baseball's trajectory. This is all just speculation that cannot be determined one way or the other, but it strongly suggests that baseball history since 1957 is deeply tied to the move of two historic franchises to new homes in California.

The spate of technological, demographic, and economic changes to American society that have influenced the direction of baseball since 1957 have little to do with the Dodgers and Giants leaving New York for the West Coast, but the presence of strong teams in Los Angeles and San Francisco helped baseball respond to these changes largely from a position of strength and wealth. Had, for example, MLB not had strong franchises in California, free agency would have raised a different and more complex set of challenges to the game, because it would have raised additional challenges to the hegemony of the National and American Leagues.

Regardless of our view of the Giants' and Dodgers' roles in forging modern big league baseball, following the move to the West Coast, they were undeniably teams that experienced momentous events in big league baseball. The first gay player, first free agent, most egregious alleged user of performance-enhancing drugs, most famous on-the-field baseball fight, oldest ongoing rivalry, and some of the most significant international baseball phenomena all happened to one or both of these two teams. It is an overstatement to say that the history of big league baseball since 1958 is the history of these two franchises, but if one were trying to understand the changes in baseball over the last 60 years, these two teams would be a reasonably good place to start. Similarly, much of the history of baseball in the first half of the twentieth century occurred in New York—and the Dodgers and Giants played a central role there as well.

THE OLDEST RIVALRY IN BASEBALL

The rivalry between the Dodgers and Giants is the oldest in professional sports. Even today it is among the most intense. The two teams have been competing with each other since 1891. For the first seven years of the rivalry, they were in neighboring cities, but shared a city for the next 60 years.[1] Whether they were separate cities or part of the same city, for 67 years the rivalry was between Manhattan and Brooklyn. For the last 60 years, the two teams have played in two cities in California that have also been rivals for a long time. In both eras, baseball was only part of the rivalry. In New York, this competition also drew upon the different cultures and identities of Manhattan and Brooklyn. In its West Coast iteration, the rivalry has also been about genuine regional loyalty. The mutual contempt between the two California cities runs deep. Any longtime San Franciscan will assure you that they live in the only real city on the West Coast, while pointing out the primary difference between Los Angeles and yogurt.[2] Longtime Angelenos, for their part, will argue that San Franciscans are forever feeling inferior since Los Angeles became the biggest and most important city on the West Coast decades ago.

No two teams in the history of big league baseball, or of any other major American sport, shared a league and a city for as long as the New York Giants and the Brooklyn Dodgers did. Moreover, because they did this at a time when there were only eight teams in each league, the two teams played each other 22 times a year for most of their shared New York history. This meant that the Giants and Dodgers each played 88 of their 154 games in New York City, making the rivalry very accessible, but also creating some statistical quirks.

For example, ask a baseball fan, even a very knowledgeable one, who hit the most big league home runs in New York City, and they might cite Yankees sluggers Babe Ruth, Mickey Mantle, or Lou Gehrig. The answer, however, is a much less known—but still great—New York Giants slugger named Mel Ott.

Ott's home ballpark for his entire career was the Polo Grounds. A left-handed batter, Ott took advantage of that field's short right field to hit 323 of his 511 career home runs there. He also hit 25 round-trippers as a visiting player in Brooklyn's Ebbets Field, thus eclipsing the 344 home runs Ruth combined to hit for the Yankees in the Polo Grounds, where the Yankees made their home in Ruth's first three years in New York, and Yankee Stadium. Ott, in addition to being probably the greatest hitter in New York Giants history, is an important footnote to the Giants–Dodgers rivalry. Ott managed the Giants from 1942 to 1948, the first six of those years as a player-manager. He was the Giants manager about whom Brooklyn Dodgers manager Leo Durocher famously said, "Nice guys finish last."

Before Ruth came to the Yankees in 1920, the New York Giants were considered the most successful team in baseball. They were also the most famous, arrogant, haughty, and visible team. John McGraw, their manager from 1902 to 1932, was one of the men most responsible for creating and refining the strategy that dominated baseball in the deadball era. The term "deadball" refers to how baseball was played before 1920. In those years, home runs were a rarity, as the game was centered around defense and pitching. Runs were scored by stealing bases, bunting, moving runners along, and making contact. Today that style of play is known as "small ball," but until the early 1920s, when Babe Ruth began to make his mark on the game, that was how baseball was played by every big league team.

THE GIANTS IN THE EARLY TWENTIETH CENTURY

During the first 30 years of the twentieth century, John McGraw was one of the most famous men in baseball. He had achieved some notoriety as a player in the late nineteenth century with the first incarnation of the Baltimore Orioles, who later became the Yankees, but really made his mark as a manager. Like many baseball personalities after him—from Babe Ruth, Casey Stengel, and Reggie Jackson through Derek Jeter and Joe Torre in the twenty-first century—McGraw benefited from playing for or managing a team that was based in New York.

McGraw was, even by the standards of baseball in the late nineteenth and early twentieth century, extremely competitive and, particularly during his playing days, not above doing whatever was necessary to gain even a minor advantage. As the third baseman for the great Orioles teams of the 1890s,

McGraw was known to occasionally grab a baserunner's belt as the runner led off of third base, making it impossible for that runner to get a good jump once the ball was put into play.

By the time he started managing the Giants, McGraw was 29 years old and had mellowed, if only a little. McGraw was a demanding, often difficult and impatient manager who was one of the best strategic thinkers in the game. He was also still stubborn enough to refuse to have his team participate in the 1904 World Series.

The year before, in 1903, the National League pennant-winning Pittsburgh Pirates had lost to the Boston Americans, who later became the Red Sox, in the first World Series between the champions of the National League and the newer American League. In 1904, McGraw's Giants won the pennant by 13 games, but refused to play against the Red Sox in the World Series because McGraw viewed them, and the American League in general, as somehow unworthy. The Giants won the pennant again in 1905, but by then McGraw had no choice but to have his team play in the World Series. They handily defeated the Philadelphia Athletics in five games. All four Giants victories were shutouts, with star pitcher Christy Mathewson throwing three in that short series. Joe "Iron Man" McGinnity pitched the other Giants shutout against the Athletics. For good measure, the only game the Athletics won against the Giants was a shutout by future Hall of Famer Chief Bender.

Lawrence Ritter and Donald Honig opened their acclaimed 1979 work on the early years of baseball by discussing McGraw: "John Joseph McGraw was a small-town boy who made it big as a runty 120 pound third baseman with the rough tough Baltimore Orioles in the 1890s. In 1902 . . . he was appointed manager of the last-place New York Giants, and in the next dozen years he clawed his way to five pennants and narrowly missed another. In subsequent years he argued bullied and schemed his way to five more." They also added that "Manager McGraw tolerated no back talk and quickly traded away players who resisted his absolute authority."[3] This description summarizes McGraw's style and personality as well as the centrality of McGraw and his Giants to baseball in the early twentieth century.

As a manager, McGraw was viewed as a brilliant tactician, but also as somebody who insisted on sound fundamentals and a hierarchical structure for the team, which started with him. For example, McGraw expected players to know how to bunt and to do so when he told them. Don Jensen writes that McGraw's "regular-season success was due to his knack for evaluating and acquiring players who fit into his system, which stressed good pitching, sound defense, and aggressive baserunning. McGraw bought, sold, and traded players more than his counterparts, grooming prospects for years before letting them play regularly. He also was an innovator, using pinch-runners, pinch-hitters and relief pitchers more than other managers."[4]

Despite his innovations, McGraw's conservative approach made him a slow convert to the power-oriented game that Babe Ruth pioneered in the late teens and early 1920s. Although, his Giants teams continued to play well into the new era—winning four straight pennants from 1921 to 1924—during McGraw's last eight full years with the team, when Ruth and Gehrig were setting home run records across the river in the Bronx, the Giants did not win even one pennant. That was, at the time, the longest period without a pennant in the team's history.

During McGraw's three decades leading the Giants, he managed 23 players who eventually made it to the Hall of Fame. Through the end of 2017, there were 220 players in the Hall of Fame. Thus, almost 90 years after he managed his last game, roughly 11 percent of the players enshrined in Cooperstown had played for McGraw. Among these players are some of the best players from the pre–World War II era including Mel Ott, Rogers Hornsby, and Frankie Frisch as well as less renowned Hall of Famers such as Ray Schalk, Fred Lindstrom, and Rube Marquard. Not all of these players were clearly deserving of Hall of Fame honors, but they benefited from their association with McGraw and, more importantly, former Giants second baseman Frankie Frisch, who led the Hall of Fame's veteran committee for many years.[5]

McGraw's most famous player, and the greatest of all the New York Giants, was Christy Mathewson. Mathewson was one of the best pitchers in baseball during the first part of the twentieth century, winning 373 games, including 372 with the Giants. His 2.13 career ERA is still the ninth lowest in baseball history. In 15 full seasons and parts of two others in the majors, all but one game of which was with the Giants, Mathewson won 20 or more games 13 times, exceeding 30 wins in four different seasons. He led the league in wins four times, ERA five times, strikeouts five times, and shutouts four times. He was part of the first class elected into the Baseball Hall of Fame in 1936.

Matty, as he was known as a player, was famous for his accomplishments on the field, but was also one of the first true celebrities of the nascent national pastime. At a time when baseball players were frequently drawn from the less educated ranks of the United States, and were frequently seen as being unrefined and vulgar, even thuggish, Mathewson, who had attended Bucknell University, conducted himself as a gentleman who was always mindful of the influence he had on young people. He was handsome, a reasonably religious Christian, and cut a very different image from most players of the era. McGraw, who had been a very roughly hewn player during his days with the Baltimore Orioles, had a background that contrasted sharply with that of his best player. This did not stop the manager and the pitcher from getting along very well both on and off the field.

Mathewson was one of the first great celebrities in baseball and was very much aware that he was a role model for many American boys. This is reflected in his book *Pitching in a Pinch, or Baseball from the Inside,* published in 1912, when Matty was at the very top of his game. In that work, he offered advice that was clearly meant to inspire America's youth both on and off the field: "It is in the pinch that the pitcher shows whether or not he is a Big Leaguer. He must have something besides curves then. He needs a head, and he has to use it. It is the acid test. That is the reason so many men, who shine in the minor leagues, fail to make good in the majors. They cannot stand the fire."[6] Ritter and Honig described Mathewson as "almost too good to be true any way you look at him. He was big, strong, handsome, intelligent, revered by his teammates, admired and respected by his opponents." This is a very uncritical description of the great Giants righty, but it is consistent with most other reports of Mathewson's character.[7]

John McGraw's Giants were unquestionably the most famous, most visible, and best team in the big leagues from 1903 to 1924, and remained the most visible and most famous for a few years after that. Despite that, they were also, after a fashion, a hard-luck team, losing six of nine World Series during this period. Indeed, three of the most famous plays in the early years of baseball history saw the Giants on the losing end of a bad break or clutch mistake by a player. The names Fred Merkle, Fred Snodgrass, and Heinie Zimmerman may not mean much to today's fans, although most reasonably attentive fans probably have encountered Merkle's name. However, those three players all were involved in key moments that did not go the way of the early New York Giants.

The Giants and Chicago Cubs were involved in a very close pennant race in 1908. In the first decade of the twentieth century, the Cubs, not the Dodgers, were frequently fighting the Giants for the pennant. In a key game between the two teams in late September 1908, Merkle was on first base with two outs and the winning run, in the person of Moose McCormick, on third. The next batter, Al Bridwell, hit a game-winning single, driving in McCormick. Merkle saw McCormick score and headed to the Giants clubhouse. Given the size and mood of the crowd, that decision was understandable, but the rules of baseball are clear that if the third out is made on a force play, any run that scores on that play does not count. That detail was not lost on Cubs second baseman Johnny Evers, who frantically called for the ball, amid the chaos of both teams and thousands of fans running onto the field, and touched second base. Merkle was ruled out. Due to the pandemonium on the field, the game could not be resumed so it was ruled a 1–1 tie. After the season ended, with the two teams both having 98 wins and 55 losses, the game was replayed. The Cubs won the rematch and the pennant.

That is the most generally accepted version of the events of that game, but in her 2007 book on the 1908 season and that game, Cait Murphy compares the play itself to "*Rashomon* . . . yield(ing) multiple narratives. There are tens of thousands of eyewitnesses, but they all see different things, mostly what they wish to see." Some, as Murphy argues, believe it was Cubs manager and first baseman Frank Chance, not Evers, who argued most vociferously for the call to go the Cubs way. The *New York Evening Mail* quoted none other than Christy Mathewson as saying, "Merkle touched the bag. I saw him do it." Another future Hall of Fame pitcher on that Giants squad, Joe McGinnity, said that he grabbed the ball and "flung that one out of sight" so that no Cub could get it. Evers later claimed that McGinnity did indeed throw the ball, but that Cubs pitcher Rube Kroh helped Evers recover it. In 1914, Hank O'Day, the umpire for that game, asserted that he called Merkle out even though nobody on the Cubs ever got the ball and touched second base.[8]

The 1912 World Series lasted eight games because Game Two ended after 11 innings with the Giants and Red Sox tied 6–6. There was no night baseball in those days so the game had to be stopped when it got too dark to play. Instead of resuming the game from that point, the next day, it was declared a tie. Thus, in the beginning of the eighth, and deciding, game of that World Series, the two teams were tied at three wins each and one tie. After the regulation nine innings of Game Eight, the Red Sox and Giants were deadlocked with one run each. An RBI single by Fred Merkle, only four years after his own famous mistake, put the Giants ahead by one run in the top half of the tenth.

The Giants starting pitcher, Christy Mathewson, was still in the game in the bottom of the tenth inning and needed to record three outs for the Giants to win the World Series. The first batter hit what by all accounts was an easy fly ball to Giants centerfielder Fred Snodgrass, but Snodgrass dropped it. That opened the door to a Red Sox rally in which they scored two runs and won the World Series. Snodgrass was viewed as a good defender and very solid hitter, whose slash line over the course of his nine-year career, .275/.367/.359, was good for that era, but he was only ever remembered for that one dropped fly ball.

Only five years later, the Giants found themselves on the wrong end of another strange play that cost them a World Series victory. In the 1917 World Series, the Giants' opponent was a very strong Chicago White Sox team. Among the White Sox players was Eddie Collins, one of the greatest second basemen ever, who was still in the prime of a career that ended with him hitting .333 with more than 700 stolen bases and more than 3,300 hits. Collins, who attended Columbia University, holds the record for hits and stolen bases for a graduate of an Ivy League university. That White Sox team also featured several of the players, including Joe Jackson and Eddie Cicotte, who would be banned from baseball for life for throwing the World Series two years later.

In the 1917 fall classic, however, the White Sox were playing to win. They beat the Giants in a six-game series, but the winning rally in the final game occurred because of a mental lapse by the Giants. Mental mistakes on the ballfields are always tough to accept—they are even more difficult for a team when they occur in the World Series, particularly when that team is managed by John McGraw, who was known throughout baseball for stressing fundamentals. In the sixth game, Eddie Collins scored the first run of the game on a fourth-inning rundown, when he alertly noticed that nobody was covering home plate following a ground-ball hit by White Sox centerfielder Happy Felsch. The speedy Collins broke for the unattended home plate, leaving Heinie Zimmerman, the Giants third baseman, helplessly to try to catch up with him. Collins won that race, and the White Sox went on to win the game and the World Series.

Merkle, Snodgrass, and Zimmerman were all maligned for the rest of their careers for their mistakes. This was probably unfair, particularly to Zimmerman, who chased Collins because nobody was covering the plate; however, those plays were among the most famous in baseball during the deadball era and further cemented the Giants' position as the most important team of that time. It is likely that the New York media had a role in this, as New York was the center of American media; things that happened to New York teams were celebrated more than events involving other teams.

THE EARLY DODGERS YEARS

The early years of the Brooklyn Dodgers, known as the Robins from roughly 1915 to 1930, were not as successful as those of the Giants. However, the team managed to win pennants in 1916 and 1920, losing in the World Series both times. In a nice twist of New York baseball fate, the first baseman on the Dodgers first pennant-winning team was Fred Merkle. The Dodgers did not do well in either of those two World Series. In 1916, they lost to the Red Sox four games to one. Perhaps the most memorable game of that series was a 14-inning 2–1 loss in Game Two. The Dodgers scored their only run in the first inning of that game, before Red Sox starting pitcher Babe Ruth shut them down for 13 straight innings. Those would be the first of 26 consecutive scoreless innings pitched by the Red Sox lefty, who later went on to bigger fame with another New York team in the 1920s. This record for consecutive scoreless innings lasted into the 1960s, before it was broken by Whitey Ford in 1961.

In 1920, the Dodgers lost the World Series to the Cleveland Indians five games to two. The Dodgers managed to split the first four games of that series; in Game Five, they trailed 7–0 going into the fifth inning. They rallied in the fifth when the first two Dodgers to bat, Pete Kilduff and Otto Miller, singled. With two men on and no outs, there followed the only unassisted triple play in World Series history: Clarence Mitchell hit a line drive toward Indians second baseman Bill Wambsganss, who caught the ball. He then alertly touched second to retire Kilduff, who had not returned to the base, before tagging Miller, who was caught between first and second. The rest of that World Series did not go any better for the Dodgers—and they did not make it back for another 21 years. More modestly than the Giants, the early success of the Dodgers nonetheless helped cement New York's position as the center of the baseball universe. Fourteen of the first 25 World Series, for example, featured at least one team from New York.

The great Dodgers players of that era included Burleigh Grimes, Zack Wheat, and Dazzy Vance. These players, while certainly among the best of their day, never achieved the level of fame as McGraw, Mathewson, or some other players on the Giants. The Dodgers' image as lovable losers and "Dem Bums" is a product of this period, when they simply could not compete with the Giants. By the early 1940s, that began to change, but the Dodgers narrative was set by then.

The years between their defeat in the 1920 World Series and their emergence as a perennial National League power beginning in 1941 were the nadir of the Dodgers' existence, but still extremely important in framing perceptions of the Dodgers. Between 1921 and 1940, the Dodgers won no pennants and finished as high as second or third place in an eight-team league only four times, while playing less than .500 baseball for 12 of those 19 years.

The late 1920s, when the Dodgers were known as the "Daffiness Boys," was the most memorable time during these two decades. Frank Graham in his 1945 history of the Dodgers described these years as "a jumble of misplays, of almost continual laughter, of incredible episodes on the field, in the dugout and in the office. They were the years in which the fans, not only in Brooklyn, but all over the circuit, gladly paid to see how many ways the Robins could contrive to lose ball games. They were, in all truth, the dizziest years a ball club ever had, for the Robins were now the Daffiness Boys."[9]

The Dodgers' incompetence on the field was only part of what helped make their image. There were many big league teams during the 1920s and 1930s, such as the Phillies or the White Sox (after several key players were banned from baseball for their activities in the 1919 World Series), who rarely contended, but few did it as colorfully, or in as big of a media market, as the Dodgers. During these years, the Dodgers were managed primarily by two men who were known, at the time, as clownish figures. Wilbert Robinson, who had guided the Dodgers to pennants in 1916 and 1920, continued as the Brooklyn skipper through the 1931 season. By the end of his 18 years managing the Dodgers, he was 67 years old and no longer known as a particularly savvy baseball man. He nonetheless remained popular with the players and the fans for his affability, and even goofiness. The latter was appropriate, perhaps even essential, given how bad the team was.

When Robinson died in 1934, *New York Times* writer John Kieran captured the complexity of Robinson, who was part clown, but also part astute baseball man, and was sufficiently important to the Dodgers that they were known as the Robins during several years of his tenure: "There may have been smarter managers than Uncle Robbie, but his record wasn't all that bad. . . . It is doubtful that baseball ever produced a more colorful figure than the esteemed Wilbert Robinson. Like Falstaff, he was not only witty himself, but the cause of wit in others. . . . A jolly old gentleman and as honest as the sunlight."[10]

Arthur Daley's 1951 description of Robinson captures the goofy nature of Robinson, but also the way he was perceived a few decades after he retired. By that time, his unserious side was the predominant part of his legacy. "There has probably never been a baseball manager quite like the Falstaffian leader of the Brooks during the era when the Daffiness Boys were in their heyday. He ran the team with musical comedy overtones. If it wasn't good baseball, at least it was an awful lot of fun."[11]

Harold Parrott's description of Robinson's later years as the Dodgers manager was less charitable toward the man who won two pennants in Brooklyn: "A little round man with a tummy that looked as if somebody had shoved in a pillow to make him pass for a department store Santa. . . . [He] was more of a habit than a manager. . . . Robbie couldn't remember his players' names, much less spell them."[12]

In his playing days, Wilbert Robinson had been a teammate, friend, and even business partner of John McGraw. The two had played together on the Baltimore Orioles, the best team of the 1890s, described as "the toughest, rowdiest, dirtiest, most foul-mouthed team in history, unhampered by rules, disdainful of umpires and authority."[13] McGraw played third base and Robinson caught. Off the field, the two were friends and shared business ventures such as a club and restaurant in Baltimore. Despite their friendship, McGraw and Robinson had very different temperaments. Robinson's biographers Jack Kavanaugh and Norman Macht describe the contrast between the two erstwhile friends and teammates: "On or off the field, McGraw was truculent, vituperative, foul-mouthed, ready to fight any time. He had the disposition of a man with a permanent pebble in his shoe. Robinson was by nature genial, lighthearted, a friend to one and all, though he could waddle into a brawl when needed."[14]

By the time Robinson took over the Dodgers, he and McGraw were no longer close. Graham described how, even during Robinson's first year at the Dodgers' helm,

> the presence of Robbie in Brooklyn intensified the rivalry between the Dodgers, or Robins, and the Giants. . . . [T]hey no longer were friends. . . . Robbie, eager to prove, to McGraw especially, that he was a capable manager, tried his hardest to beat the Giants. McGraw, writhing at even the measure of success Robbie had achieved and privately scornful of him as a manager, put added pressure on the Giants every time they went to Brooklyn, or played Brooklyn at the Polo Grounds.[15]

The feud between Robinson and McGraw began toward the end of Robinson's relatively successful stint as pitching coach for McGraw's Giants in 1912–13. Kavanaugh and Macht describe how, at a dinner following the Giants' defeat in the 1913 World Series, the two blamed each other for the Giants' loss in the final game. The argument culminated when "McGraw snarled, 'This is my party. Get the hell out of here,' and . . . Robinson showered McGraw with a glass of his beer on the way out."[16] The two did not reconcile until the early 1930s, when McGraw was almost at the end of his life.

In 1934, two years after Robinson retired following the 1931 season and was replaced by Max Carey, the Dodgers decided to bring in a new manager. The man Dodgers owner Stephen McKeever turned to was a 43-year-old former Giants and Dodgers outfielder named Casey Stengel. This seemed like a risky choice, as Stengel had never managed before. As a player, Stengel had been a solid hitter, posting a career slash line of .284/.356/.410, but there was more to Stengel than that. He had earned a reputation for being eccentric—though, given his skill at the plate and in the field, his eccentricities had been tolerated. Stengel had also played for both Robinson and McGraw and learned a lot from each of them. Given the success he enjoyed in his managerial career, Stengel's ties to these early great managers of New York teams demonstrate the continuity of the story of great baseball in New York.

To most baseball fans in the 1930s, Stengel was best known for an inside-the-park home run he hit in the top of the ninth inning of Game One of the 1923 World Series, giving his Giants a 5–4 win. The play was very dramatic in its own right, but became even more famous because Damon Runyon's column about it the following day remains among the best baseball writing ever.

> This is the way old Casey Stengel ran yesterday afternoon, running his home run home. . . .
>
> *His mouth wide open.*
>
> *His warped old legs bending beneath him at every stride.*
>
> *His arms flying back and forth like those of a man swimming with a crawl stroke*
>
> *His flanks heaving, his breath whistling, his head far back. . . .*
>
> People generally laugh when they see old Casey run, but they were not laughing while he was running his home run yesterday afternoon. People—60,000 of 'em, men and women—were standing in the Yankee stands and bleachers up there in the Bronx roaring sympathetically, whether they were for or against the Giants.
>
> "Come on, Casey!"
>
> The warped old legs, twisted and bent by many a year of baseball campaigning, just barely held out under Casey Stengel, until he reached the plate, running his home run home.
>
> Then they collapsed.[17]

Stengel's years managing the Dodgers were not successful. Over those three years, his teams finished in seventh, fifth, and sixth place, with an overall winning percentage of .453. Stengel was fired after the 1936 season, but was hired in 1938 to manage the Boston Braves. He was equally unsuccessful there, never finishing higher than fifth place in five full seasons and part of a sixth. After 1943, Stengel went to California, where he later managed in the Pacific Coast League. His career in the big leagues seemed to be over, but he resurfaced in 1949 with yet another New York team, the Yankees. He did a little better there, winning ten pennants and seven World Series, including five in a row, during his 12 years with the Yankees. Following his stint with the Yankees, by then in his 70s, Stengel was the manager of the New York Mets during their first four years.

As manager of the Yankees, Stengel had several advantages, including two of the best players ever, Mickey Mantle and Yogi Berra, in the prime of their respective careers, but he had also learned a few things over the years. With the Yankees, Stengel was a master of platooning, getting the most out of seemingly over-the-hill veterans and managing a pitching staff and in-game strategy in general.

Managing a Dodgers team that by the mid-1930s had little on-the-field talent—and not enough money to change that reality—had forced Stengel to innovate. While he did not succeed in turning those Dodgers teams into winners, he began to explore the tactics that later proved so successful with the Yankees. According to Steven Goldman, Stengel "searched restlessly for solutions that would be within his means to execute. With expensive acquisitions out of the question, that meant somehow making the current roster into something more than what it was. He grasped onto the idea that he might find a more potent lineup formula if he could move the players to positions other than those at which they had been fixed."[18]

That experimentation bore fruit in the 1950s with the Yankees, when Stengel effectively used players like Gil McDougald at second base, third base, and shortstop to ensure that powerful hitters Yogi Berra and Elston Howard, both natural catchers, could get more at-bats by also appearing in the outfield and, in Howard's case, first base.

NEW YORK AND BROOKLYN

The Dodgers and Giants began playing against each other in 1891, seven years before New York City in its current form was consolidated. Thus, the Dodgers–Giants rivalry grew up with the city of New York. The relationship between Brooklyn and Manhattan, even before the two cities merged into one, framed the Dodgers–Giants rivalry during the entire time they were in New York.

The Dodgers' identity reflected their home city and later borough. Brooklyn, for much of the twentieth century, was more modest, more working-class, and less glamorous than Manhattan, where the Giants made their home the entire time they played in New York. Today, neighborhoods like Williamsburg and

Fort Greene are where a new hip, urban, affluent America is on display. Other Brooklyn neighborhoods like Park Slope and Brooklyn Heights are home to as many upper-middle-class families as the Upper East Side or Upper West Side of Manhattan. Today visitors to New York from all over the country and the world will go to Brooklyn to shop, eat, or see a performance, but that was not the case 30—let alone 60, 80, or 100—years ago.

Brooklyn for many years was a patchwork of neighborhoods, reflecting the extraordinary ethnic diversity of the borough. There were Jewish, Italian, Irish, Polish, and African American neighborhoods. As the century went on, Latino, Caribbean, Russian, and various Asian groups built neighborhoods and communities in Brooklyn as well. Most of those neighborhoods were working class. Brooklyn had its own shopping districts, government buildings, and beaches, but it was always seen as less exciting, affluent, and glamorous than New York.

Scott Simon, describing the two boroughs at the time of Jackie Robinson's 1947 debut, captures both the real differences between Manhattan and Brooklyn as well as the not always accurate narrative that has been present for decades: "Manhattan was the borough of office towers and neon lights, while Brooklyn proclaimed itself the borough of well-attended churches, neatly tended trees and trolleys. Manhattan was Carnegie Hall, Gershwin and Toscaninni and Duke Ellington's Harlem. Brooklyn was Coney Island, stickball, half-sour dills, and doo-wop. . . . Manhattan was a destination. But Brooklyn was where the city lived."[19]

Robert Murphy wrote of the feeling of Brooklyn at the turn of the twentieth century at the time it was formally consolidated into New York City. Brooklyn at that time had a different image than what it would have in the mid- and late twentieth century, but was still defined by its relationship to Manhattan.

> It was a great city in size, but a lesser city in civic institutions; a great port and manufacturing city with a busy but contracted commercial center. It was great in spirit, proud of its accomplishments in municipal government and of a generally wholesome way of life. . . . Brooklyn took pride in the label "The City of Homes and Churches" . . . but no amount of pride would make it independent. For there Brooklyn stood, righteous yet self-conscious, beside a greater city.[20]

For most of the twentieth century, only the most intrepid tourists visiting New York went to Brooklyn. Movies and television shows were only set in Brooklyn if the creators of those shows wanted to depict either working-class families, urban blight, or specific ethnic communities, such as African Americans, Italian

Americans, Orthodox Jews, or (in the case of *Welcome Back, Kotter*) Puerto Rican Jews. During those years almost nobody from Manhattan saw Brooklyn as a destination for restaurants, theater, or the like. Despite this, or perhaps because of this, people from Brooklyn had a strong sense of identity—and the Dodgers were a big part of that identity.

The Dodgers were unique in the history of baseball because they were the only team affiliated with a place that was neither a city nor a state. Brooklyn, despite its enormous population, stopped being its own city in 1898; for the rest of the time the Dodgers were there, it was a borough, or constituent part, of the City of New York. This helped residents of that borough forge a stronger bond with their team.

For the last 70 or so years of the twentieth century, Brooklyn was the most populated of New York's boroughs. Data from the 1900 census shows that the population of Brooklyn was 1,167,000, less than two-thirds of Manhattan's population of 1,850,000. That ratio changed over the next 30 years, so that by 1930 Brooklyn had 2,580,000 residents, substantially more than Manhattan's 1,867,000. In every census taken since 1940, Brooklyn has had the highest population of any of New York City's five boroughs, with roughly one-third of the city's population residing there.[21] As Brooklyn's population grew in the early twentieth century, the character of the borough changed from a more rural alternative to Manhattan to a densely populated place that immigrants and first-generation Americans called home.

The Dodgers were a good fit for a borough that was growing quickly, but would not be in a position to catch up with Manhattan in influence or status until many decades after the team went west. This aligned nicely with the Dodgers position as the weaker of the city's two National League teams. Moreover, in the early 1920s the Yankees began to supplant the Giants as the best and most famous team in New York, and in the country as a whole. This relegated the Dodgers to being New York's third team for the next 15 years or so.

The Giants, in contrast, played in Manhattan. Although they played in the northern, more residential reaches of that island, they were always a New York team, not just a Manhattan team. The baseball geography of New York City during those years meant that residents of Manhattan were more likely to be Giants fans than Dodgers fans, but the bond was never as strong as it was for Brooklynites. Some of the evidence of this was clear in the decades following the move, as Giants fans did not bemoan the loss of their team with the intensity or emotion felt by Dodgers fans.

WASN'T THERE ANOTHER NEW YORK TEAM BACK THEN?

The Giants always had to share their northern Manhattan fan base with another team. The Yankees made their first home in Hilltop Park, located in northern Manhattan around 165th and Broadway, before sharing the Polo Grounds at 155th Street with the Giants. When the Yankees finally built their own stadium in 1923, they located that stadium in the South Bronx, only a short distance across the Harlem River from the Polo Grounds.

Since the move to the Bronx, the Yankees have made their home in a borough that, like Brooklyn, had a working-class identity and very diverse demographics for most of the twentieth century. Today, the Bronx, while much more stable and functioning than in the 1970s, when the word "Bronx" was shorthand for urban blight, has not enjoyed a renaissance comparable to what Brooklyn has experienced.

The Yankees, however, were never called the Bronx Yankees. They were always the New York Yankees, although they have long had the nickname "Bronx Bombers." In most of the baseball world, the Yankees have long been synonymous with wealth, arrogance, and a willingness to spend whatever money is necessary to win. In his 2016 book *Dodgerland,* a chronicle of the Dodgers and their Southern California home in the late 1970s, Michael Fallon offers a description of the Yankees that reflects this widely held view of the Bronx-based team: "The Yankees had long overtaken the Giants as the league's dominant team and now represented all the worst impulses in American society: the burning desire to win, even at the expense of fair play; the poisonous love of wealth and success above all else and the imperial urge to dominate."[22]

However, even today among residents of the Bronx, long the most embattled of New York's five boroughs, the Yankees are the local team, almost universally beloved. Nevertheless, the link between the borough and the team is not quite the same as what it was between Brooklyn and the Dodgers. Perhaps because they were named after a specific part of a bigger city, with its own identity, culture, demographics, and even accent, the old Brooklyn Dodgers were probably identified with their home more than any team in baseball history.

During the 34 years between the time the Yankees moved to the Bronx in 1923 and the Dodgers moved to Los Angeles in 1957, both teams made their homes in heavily working-class and very diverse outer boroughs, but the teams had different relationships to their respective boroughs. Both boroughs border Manhattan, New York's most famous borough, with Brooklyn lying to the south and the Bronx to the north. Both Brooklyn and the Bronx were largely rural in the nineteenth century and well into the early twentieth century.[23] During these years and into the midcentury, both boroughs were home to immigrants and their children from most parts of Europe, particularly eastern and southern Europe. The number of African Americans in both Brooklyn and the Bronx also grew considerably. Among all immigrant and ethnic groups, however, Italian Americans and Jews had the greatest influence on the culture and feel of both places, not least because of their enormous numbers.

The Bronx and Brooklyn during the middle of the twentieth century were vibrant and exciting places. Although they were, particularly in the eyes of outsiders, largely defined by not being Manhattan, they were both home to millions of hard-working people who were proud of their home boroughs and identified strongly with that home. Both boroughs were also fortunate enough to have a big league baseball team.

The Dodgers helped strengthen that identity, as being a Dodgers fan was something all Brooklynites shared, regardless of ethnicity or income—at least this is what we have been told repeatedly since the team left. The Yankees, according to this narrative, did nothing to foster or reflect a Bronx identity. The Yankees also never left the Bronx. This has relegated being a Yankees fan to a different role in Bronx nostalgia than being a Dodgers fan in Brooklyn nostalgia. Moreover, because the Yankees never left, they were still playing in the Bronx when the borough fell upon its hardest times. During those years, the bond between the Yankees and those fans who lived in the suburbs was tested. The proof that the Yankees and their fans passed that test is that the team is still there. Yankees fans, from the Bronx and elsewhere, never stopped going to see their team in the 1970s. That story does not fit conveniently into the narrative of the three New York teams so is not usually stressed, but it is pretty clearly the truth.

Another factor driving the different relationships the Dodgers and Yankees enjoyed with their home boroughs is that the Yankees, beginning in the late 1920s, were too big and famous to just be the team from the Bronx. In addition to being by far baseball's most successful team, the Yankees had stars—notably Babe Ruth, Joe DiMaggio, and Mickey Mantle—who were national celebrities and, in many respects, the face of the game for years. Ruth remains probably the single most famous baseball player ever. While all those players were beloved in the Bronx, they were also too big, and too celebrated, to represent just one borough. The Yankees quickly outgrew their new home borough and became the most famous team in America. They remain that way today. No team in baseball, and perhaps in all of sports is, as polarizing as the Yankees. Baseball fans everywhere either love them or hate them; in the Bronx, the view is still the former by a large margin.

The Brooklyn Dodgers never had a player who enjoyed a level of fame comparable to those players—or even to Christy Mathewson when he was the ace pitcher for the Giants. The only exception to this is Jackie Robinson. Robinson was one of the best known athletes in American history. He is also one of those unusual athletes who has become even more well known in the years since his death. Even when he was playing, Robinson was more famous for his role in integrating baseball, than for his play on the field. This is not to say he was not a great player. He was. He could hit, field, and run the bases at elite big league levels. However, segregation meant that he started his career late, at the age of 27. He also, oddly, spent the last four years of his career without a regular position, serving as a kind of super utility player. As good as Robinson was, his on-the-field performance was not comparable to that of Mantle, Mays, Mathewson, or Ruth.[24]

The Giants had already established themselves as the country's premier team, while the Dodgers had won two pennants of their own before New York's third team made it to the World Series. The Yankees teams of the first 20 years of the twentieth century had some good players. Jack Chesbro was the big league's last 40-game winner in 1904. Frank "Home Run" Baker, Roger Peckinpaugh, and Wally Pipp were all good hitters who played the infield well; and the great Wee Willie Keeler played for the Yankees for seven years at the tail end of his career from 1903 to 1909.

Until 1920, however, baseball in New York meant National League baseball. The Yankees were often an afterthought, occasionally pretty good, but almost never at the center of the city's baseball world. That changed in 1920, when the Yankees acquired Babe Ruth from the Red Sox and made one of the best left-handed pitchers in the game a full-time outfielder. In his first year with the Yankees, Ruth hit .376 and set a record, which he would later break, with 54 home runs. He also led the league in runs, RBIs, walks, slugging percentage, and on-base percentage. The Yankees, however, finished in third place that year.

Ruth led the Yankees to American League pennants in each of the following three years. The Yankees' opponent in the World Series in 1921–23 was the New York Giants. This was the first time the World Series was played entirely in New York, and thus the first "Subway Series." However, in 1921–22, although all of the games were accessible by subway, one could not travel between the two ballparks by subway because the entire World Series was played in the Polo Grounds, the home field of both the Giants and the Yankees in those days. It was not until 1923 when the Giants–Yankees World Series was played in two different ballparks. However, even then, taking the subway from the Yankees' new home, Yankee Stadium, to the Polo Grounds was possible, but would have required a detour south as the two parks were on opposite sides of a river with no convenient subway routes between them.

Beginning in 1921, the Giants–Dodgers rivalry took on an additional dimension as the Yankees started their almost half century of being by far the best team in the American League. Thus, during the remaining 37 years that the two National League teams played in New York, the rivalry between the Giants and Dodgers became even more complex, as the Yankees were often waiting in the World Series for whichever of the teams managed to win the National League pennant. During those 37 years, there would be 13 Subway Series, including all the times the Dodgers won the pennant. Moreover, both the Giants and the Dodgers struggled to beat the Yankees in the World Series, as the Yankees triumphed in ten of those 13 Subway Series.

IS BROOKLYN STILL IN THE LEAGUE?

The Dodgers struggled throughout the 1930s. The Giants may have been overshadowed by the Yankees during that decade, but they were nonetheless a very good team, winning three pennants and finishing in second place twice. They were led by Carl Hubbell, their ace left-handed pitcher known for his devastating screwball and for striking out five future Hall of Famers in a row in the 1934 All-Star Game. The Giants also had two of the best hitters in the league, Bill Terry, a lifetime .341 hitter who was the last National League player to post a .400 batting average over a full season, and Mel Ott, a slugging outfielder who, when he retired, had hit more home runs than any player in National League history.

For fans of the Dodgers the decade was very frustrating. The Dodgers of the 1930s were not just bad, but they were laughably bad. This was the era of Babe Herman's comically bad baserunning. Graham describes the famous game in the late 1920 when

> there was a runner on first base when Babe [Herman] hit a screaming drive to right center and, rounding first base, headed for second. Running head down, he failed to note that the man who had been on first base, thinking the ball would be caught, whirled sharply as Herman neared second base, and charged back, with the result that he wound up on first base and Babe on second. Thus,

not only had a runner passed another on the base line but two runners had passed each other going opposite directions.[25]

During his last years managing the Dodgers, the rotund Wilbert Robinson had become something of a comic figure, better known for his rapport with the media than for his strategic acumen or the teams he put on the field. The highlight for the decade for the Dodgers was not a pennant or World Series victory, but most likely two games at the end of the 1934 season.

On the morning of September 29, the Giants and Cardinals had identical records of 93–58 and were tied for first place in the National League. The Dodgers, for their part, had locked up sixth place in the National League and had a 69–81 record with two games left to play. Casey Stengel's Dodgers traveled uptown to the Polo Grounds for the final two games of the season to play a Giants team that included future Hall of Famers Bill Terry, Mel Ott, Travis Jackson, and Carl Hubbell. The Dodgers won both those games, while the Cardinals won their two games against the Reds, and the Giants were eliminated.

Those wins were undoubtedly especially sweet for the Dodgers and their fans because in January 1934, as spring training was about to begin, Giants player-manager Bill Terry was asked whether he thought the Dodgers would pose a threat to the Giants' pennant hopes. His less than diplomatic response was "I was just wondering whether they were still in the league."[26] Those words were remembered by the Dodgers throughout the season and proved very embarrassing for Terry when the season was over. It is, however, a good demonstration of the asymmetry of the Dodgers–Giants rivalry in that period that the highlight of the 1930s for Dodgers fans was not winning a pennant, but simply knocking the Giants out of the race. The rivalry would never be that imbalanced in favor of the Giants again.

The bad times wound down with the decade. In the third game of the 1940 season, Leo Durocher, the Dodgers manager and shortstop, gave himself the day off. He started a rookie in his place. From that day until the Dodgers left Brooklyn, they would be the most successful team in the National League, winning seven pennants before moving to Los Angeles. There were many great and famous players on those teams, including Jackie Robinson, Roy Campanella, Duke Snider, Gil Hodges, Don Newcombe, Clem Labine, Dixie Walker, and others. However, the heart and captain of all those teams, and the only player to play in every one of the 44 World Series games the Dodgers played during that period, was Pee Wee Reese. When Reese replaced Durocher at shortstop on April 23, 1940, the Dodgers stopped being lovable losers. They finished in second place in 1940, won the pennant in 1941, and were a good team for all their remaining years in Brooklyn.

HOW NEW YORKERS FOLLOWED BASEBALL

For much of the early twentieth century, baseball was largely understood and experienced through the printed word. Television was not part of American life in any meaningful way until after World War II. Although some baseball games were broadcast on the radio as early as the 1920s, it was not until the mid-1930s that the three New York teams began to regularly broadcast their games on the radio.

There were, however, many newspapers in New York that covered baseball in great depth. These included general circulation newspapers like the *New York Times, Daily News, New York Post, New York Mirror, New York Tribune,* and the *New York Globe.* There were also Italian, Yiddish, and other non-English language newspapers that covered baseball. The Communist Party–affiliated *Daily Worker* had a sports section and used its platform to advocate for integrating baseball. The *Brooklyn Daily Eagle* catered to Brooklynites, following the events in their home borough, including the Dodgers. There was no equivalent newspaper in the Bronx dedicated to providing a similar service to Yankees fans in that borough.

In addition to the large number of newspapers in New York, the quality of writing was very high. For example, the description of Casey Stengel's inside-the-park home run in the 1923 World Series, cited earlier in this chapter, was written by Damon Runyon. Runyon is better known as a chronicler of New York City, through both fiction and nonfiction, not just baseball. His most famous book, *Guys and Dolls,* was the work on which the famous musical play by the same name was based. Other writers of that era such as Ring Lardner Jr. and Grantland Rice wrote primarily about sports, but did it with impressive literary style.

The printed word was particularly important during this period not only because there was no television and little radio, but also because attendance at games was frequently very low. Table 5 shows that between 1903 and 1945, the Dodgers drew fewer than 500,000 fans 22 times, or slightly more than one-half of the years in question. The Yankees fell below this modest threshold roughly one-third of the time. The Giants, probably due to their Manhattan location

Table 5. Attendance for New York Teams, 1903–45

Attendance Measure	Dodgers	Giants	Yankees
First year drawing more than 1,000,000	1930	1945	1920
Total years drawing fewer than 500,000	22	4	15
Total years drawing more than 1,000,000	4	1	9

Source: Baseball Reference (2018), https://www.baseball-reference.com/.

and greater fame, only drew fewer than 500,000 fans four times in this period. Moreover, the Dodgers and Giants drew a million or more fans only four times and once, respectively, over these years. The Yankees, however, drew one million or more fans nine times, all in the years from 1920 to 1930, when Babe Ruth was the best player in baseball and hitting home runs for the Yankees. Overall, there were several years during the first half of the twentieth century when all three New York teams combined to draw fewer fans than either the Yankees or Mets regularly do in a single twenty-first-century season.

The Dodgers, in particular, struggled to draw fans. In 1916, a season in which they won the pennant, they drew only 447,747 fans. Two years later, in 1918, the Dodgers drew an appallingly low 83,831 fans, only slightly more than 1,000 fans a game. From 1934 to 1937, they never topped 500,000 in a season. For their part, the Yankees went nine consecutive seasons, 1910–18, drawing fewer than 500,000 fans. However, after adding Babe Ruth in 1920, they never dropped below that number again. Since 1920, the Yankees' worst year for attendance was 1935, when they only drew 657,508 fans. That may have been partially because Ruth, the player who had been the biggest drawing card in the history of the game, had left the Yankees for the Boston Braves in the 1934–35 offseason.

These numbers are further evidence that during the period when baseball was most successfully imprinting itself on American culture generally and on the story of New York City specifically, big league baseball, at least as measured by attendance, was not a mass phenomenon. It is also not surprising that during the deep Depression of the 1930s attendance was down. With widespread unemployment and growing poverty, few people even in baseball-crazy New York had the disposable income to buy tickets to baseball games.

This data reinforces the notion that while baseball was always a business, and usually characterized by ownership exploiting labor, it was not "big business" until much later. However, measuring the impact of the Giants and Dodgers and their role in the identity of the various parts of the city—or the impact of baseball in American culture more generally—simply by looking at revenue and attendance figures is misleading. It does not capture how many people in New York talked or argued about the two teams, how passionately they wished for their team to win, or how much they hated the rival team. This was the context in which the Giants–Dodgers rivalry evolved. The rivalry was intense for most of the prewar period, but is now largely remembered for providing background to the final 11 years the two teams played in New York.

NEW YORK IN THE 1950S

The decade or so immediately following World War II was when New York reached the apex of its economic and cultural preeminence. The United States was the world's only major country that had not been decimated economically, militarily, or physically during World War II. The country was growing rapidly while becoming wealthier and more powerful than most of its European allies or foes. New York was the core of that economic engine and the capital of American finance, banking, insurance, advertising, fashion, theater, and art. It was the largest, wealthiest, and most important city in the country at the height of the American century.

Martin Shefter summarized the wealth and influence of New York during this period:

> During the decades following World War II, when American power was at its peak, elites and institutions based in New York exercised enormous political, economic and cultural influence both at home and abroad. Wall Street lawyers and bankers played a central role in fashioning the politics of containment, collective security and liberal internationalism that the United States pursued in the international arena. Corporations headquartered in the metropolis brought American products, and extended American business methods, throughout the world. Finally, New Yorkers exercised predominant influence in many areas of American cultural life.[1]

According to the 1950 census, the population of New York City was 7,982,000 in 1950, meaning that just short of one in 20 Americans lived there at that time. In the 65 years since, New York City's population has grown by 568,000,[2] but New York's population today constitutes a significantly smaller proportion, just under 2.7 percent, of the entire U.S. population.

New York in the 1950s was a city of affluence, but also of good working-class, frequently union, jobs. It was no longer quite the city of immigrants that it had been for most of the early part of the twentieth century. The white middle- and working-class people who would in following decades leave New York for the suburbs and warmer parts of the country to the south and west still, in large part, lived and worked in New York.

By the 1950s, the immigration that had defined New York in the early twentieth century had more or less ebbed, at least until the post-1980 period of immigration remade the city once again. The city, while still diverse, with huge Jewish, Italian, and Irish populations, many of whom were by that time second- and even third-generation Americans, as well as substantial African American populations and smaller communities of people from most corners of the globe, was not as racially diverse as it became in the late twentieth century. Latinos and Asian Americans represented much smaller proportions of the population. According to the 1950 census, the city was slightly more than 90 percent white.[3] The proportion of foreign-born New Yorkers was still a healthy 23.6 percent, but that group was aging and not being renewed by more immigration the way it had been in the prewar years, or would later in the century.[4]

It is dangerous to generalize too much about New York at any time, including in the 1950s. During that decade, like pretty much every decade for several centuries, New York was in a period of transition. While immigration from eastern and southern Europe had slowed considerably during the postwar period, the 1950s was the decade when the stirrings of New York's transition to a majority nonwhite city first began in earnest, as African Americans continued to come to the city from the South and also as Latinos, primarily in those years from Puerto Rico, began to move to New York in significant numbers.

During the 1950s, an estimated 470,000 Puerto Ricans came to the mainland of the United States. A very large majority of those people settled, at least initially, in New York City. That is more than twice as much as during any other decade of the twentieth century.[5] A 1957 New York City planning document states that, "for the past 3 years, the average (number of Puerto Ricans migrating to the United States) has been slightly under 40,000." The report also anticipated that 32,000 Puerto Ricans would be coming to New York each year from 1958 to 1960. That estimate turned out to be a little bit low.[6] According to the U.S. Census, New York City was 85 percent white in 1960. This was still a big majority, but it was the beginning of a steady decline of the city's white population that would accelerate in following decades.[7]

The growing Puerto Rican population in New York was a source of some racial strife and tension. This is familiar to many today from the 1957 musical *West Side Story*, which was a mid-twentieth-century version of *Romeo and Juliet* set in a part of Manhattan's West Side that had been predominantly Irish and Italian, but into which Puerto Ricans were moving (the same area is today home to Lincoln Center). Less famously, Lenny Bruce captured the feeling of a city of white people giving way to one of Latinos—and the fear that caused in many white people—in a routine he performed in the late 1950s and early 1960s. The punch line was that an elderly Jewish couple comes home to find, in Bruce's words, "the Puerto Ricans stashed a joint in the Mezuzah."

The impact of these new New Yorkers was, of course, not just felt in Broadway musicals and the offbeat ramblings of troubled comic geniuses. The changing demographics of New York City, more specifically New York's transition from being an overwhelmingly white city to a majority nonwhite one, is one of the most central New York stories of the last half of the twentieth century; and it began in a real way in the 1950s. That story ended up having a very significant impact on the fate of baseball in New York during the 1950s. Demographic changes also contributed to white flight from the city into both the surrounding suburbs and other parts of the United States. As white New Yorkers left the city, they brought with them their loyalty to New York teams and to New York baseball of the 1950s more generally.

NEW YORK BASEBALL'S GOLDEN AGE

The late 1940s through the mid-1950s was also the period when New York City baseball reached its greatest heights. It is hard to overstate the extent to which baseball revolved around New York in the ten years from 1947 to 1956. There were great players on other teams in other cities during this period, most notably Stan Musial and Ted Williams as well as Robin Roberts and Warren Spahn, but New York was where the action was. During this ten-year period, teams from New York won 16 of 20 pennants and nine of ten World Series. Between 1949 and 1956, all but four of 46 World Series *games* were played in New York, including 23 in a row from Game Three of the 1950 World Series through Game Two of the 1954 World Series. Between 1949 and 1958, at least one New York team was in the World Series every year. Players from New York won 13 of the 20 regular-season Most Valuable Player (MVP) awards between

1947 and 1956, including three each for Dodgers catcher Roy Campanella and Yankees catcher Yogi Berra.

The number of World Series teams and MVP awards only provides a partial indication of New York's preeminence in the baseball world in the ten years between 1947 and 1956. The Dodgers, Giants, and Yankees were all good teams with some good and even great players, but their impact went beyond that. At least five New York players from this period—Yogi Berra, Joe DiMaggio, Mickey Mantle, Willie Mays, and Jackie Robinson—in addition to being among the greatest players ever, achieved a level of fame that exceeded their on-the-field accomplishments. All five of these players transcended being simply baseball stars and became American heroes.

Berra, who died in 2015 at the age of 90, became so famous for his malapropisms and unique wisdom that his record as a ballplayer, which included the three MVP awards, being a key part of a record-setting ten World Series–winning teams, and earning recognition as one of the two or three greatest all-around catchers ever, is frequently overlooked, particularly by younger fans. In his later years, fans also became aware of Berra's record as a war hero during the invasion of Normandy in World War II.

DiMaggio was a great ballplayer, but on paper certainly not as good as contemporaries Ted Williams or Stan Musial. DiMaggio was the superior fielder, but retired with a lower batting average and fewer home runs, hits, runs, and RBIs than either Musial or Williams. This was in part due to his shorter career, but DiMaggio's career OPS+, a rate statistic that would be improved by a shorter career that did not include the decline phase, was 155. That is an excellent number, but lower than Musial's 159 or Williams's 190.[8] Over the course of his career, DiMaggio accumulated 78.1 WAR, compared to Musial's 128.1 and Williams's 123.[9] However, neither of those two superior players married Marilyn Monroe, and no famous songwriter ever wondered aloud where they had gone, as Paul Simon did about DiMaggio.

Mantle and Mays were the two best players in baseball for most of the 1950s and 1960s. For a generation of influential baby boomers, these two men became, and remain, baseball icons. Mantle was a player of such extraordinary skill, boyish good looks, and All-American background, complete with an alliterative name, that if he had not existed, some hackneyed writer of baseball fiction would have had to invent him.

Mays is now generally regarded as the second greatest ballplayer ever, behind only Babe Ruth, but now in his 80s is appreciated as a national treasure as well. For example, at the start of the 2009 All-Star Game, President Barack Obama threw out the first pitch. The left-handed throwing president, known as more of a basketball fan, made a pretty decent throw for a middle-aged man who had never been much of a baseball player. It was later learned that he had received a little bit of private coaching on Air Force One from Mays. In 2015 Obama awarded Mays the Presidential Medal of Freedom.

One of the most famous Americans of the twentieth century, Robinson is recognized as a national hero who made a substantial contribution to the civil rights movement and to our country's long journey toward becoming a more democratic state. Almost no athlete in American history has made as much of an impact off the field than Robinson did.

The four most remembered baseball moments during the 1947–56 period all occurred in New York. In 1947, Jackie Robinson played his first game for the Dodgers in Brooklyn. Bobby Thomson hit his famous "shot heard 'round the world," which gave the Giants the 1951 pennant, in the Polo Grounds. That park was also the location of Willie Mays's famous catch off the bat of Vic Wertz in the 1954 World Series, which is recognized as the greatest catch in World Series history, although probably not of Mays's career. Two years later, Don Larsen pitched the only perfect game in World Series history at Yankee Stadium. Thomson's home run and Larsen's perfect game both came at the expense of the Dodgers, so those events involved a second New York team as well.

One way to appreciate the gap in baseball during this period between New York and the rest of the country—or at least the gap in how we weight these places differently in our collective baseball memory—is to look at the most memorable baseball events that neither occurred in New York nor involved a New York team. Probably the most remembered non–New York event of this era occurred on August 19, 1951, only a few weeks before the shot heard 'round the world, when the St. Louis Browns sent Eddie Gaedel, a little person who stood three feet seven inches tall, to the plate as a pinch-hitter. This was a stunt by Browns owner Bill Veeck, seeking to draw some attention to his hapless team. Gaedel, as might be expected, walked.

There were other important moments in this period that had great bearing on the game, but went largely unnoticed at the time and are rarely celebrated today. One of these also involved Veeck and occurred on July 5, 1947. About six weeks after Jackie Robinson played his first game with the Dodgers, with one out in the top of the seventh of an Indians–White Sox game, Indians player-manager Lou Boudreau sent Larry Doby up to pinch-hit for pitcher Bryan Stephens. Doby struck out, but became the first African American player in the American League.

Another significant event, although one that like Doby's debut is not generally recognized as such, occurred on April 14, 1953, when the Milwaukee Braves hosted the Cardinals. That was the Braves' first game in their new Milwaukee home after moving from Boston, and represented the first movement by a big league franchise in over half a century. Before the decade was finished more than a quarter of all big league teams had relocated.

The 1948 American League pennant race, which ended with a dramatic one-game playoff in which the Indians beat the Red Sox, is no longer remembered except by older Indians and Red Sox fans. Even that year the Yankees narrowly missed catching Boston and Cleveland, ending the season only 2½ games behind the pennant-winning Indians.

There was some great baseball in the 1950s outside of New York, but it is not remembered well and the most exciting moments were largely concentrated in New York.

Thus, from 1947 to 1956, New York was the undisputed capital of baseball, but that was at least as much because of the great Yankees teams of the era as because of the Giants–Dodgers rivalry. Despite the exciting 1951 pennant race, when the Giants came from 13 games back to force a playoff that they won on the strength of Bobby Thomson's famous home run, the two New York–based National League teams rarely found themselves together in a close pennant race in the 1947–56 period. When the Giants won their other pennant of this period, in 1954, the Dodgers managed to finish second, but fully eight games back. The Giants finished in second place, 4½ games behind Brooklyn, in 1952, but did not finish close to the Dodgers when the Brooklyn squad won pennants in 1947, 1949, 1952, 1955, or 1956.

While the Dodgers–Giants rivalry was strong during these years, the Yankees had few rivals in the American League. Although the Indians managed to win pennants in 1948 and 1954, the Yankees won the American League pennant all the other years between 1947 and 1958. They won the World Series eight of those 12 years as well. Yogi Berra, Joe DiMaggio, Whitey Ford, Phil Rizzuto, and Mickey Mantle were among the players who starred for those teams, but they also had a Hall of Fame manager, Casey Stengel, and numerous very good, but now largely forgotten players like Moose Skowron, Gene Woodling, Gil McDougald, Allie Reynolds, Vic Raschi, Eddie Lopat, Bobby Brown, and Hank Bauer. These were the Yankees that Dom Forker described as the "Men of Autumn," to contrast their success in the World Series with that of the now more beloved, but less successful Brooklyn Dodgers.[10]

The Dodgers' identity in the 1950s was forged mostly in relation to a Yankees team that managed to beat them with surprising regularity in the World Series during this period. Roger Kahn describes the Dodgers appeal as "stirred by the high deeds and thwarted longings of The Duke, Preacher, Pee Wee, Skoonj and the rest. The team was awesomely good and yet defeated. Their skills lifted every-man's spirit and their defeat joined them with everyman's existence, a national team, with a country in thrall, irresistible and unable to beat the Yankees."[11]

The extent to which the whole country was actually enthralled with the Dodgers, rather than with their own local teams, is not clear. This perception, although perhaps revealing the provincialism of New Yorkers, was real for many New York baseball fans of the era and is an insight into how baseball in the 1950s has come to be remembered.

Moreover, the most lasting and powerful impressions of the Brooklyn Dodgers, a team that in one iteration or another played in Brooklyn for more than 70 years, were those that were forged in their last 11 years in their home borough. As Andrew Paul Mele argues in the introduction to his *Brooklyn Dodgers Reader,* "The real legacy of the Brooklyn Dodgers was built over the last decade of their existence. . . . Between 1947 and 1957, they won six pen-nants, lost twice in the last inning of the last game, and won the only world's championship Brooklyn would ever see."[12]

In 2007, the Museum of the City of New York hosted an exhibition about baseball in New York from 1947 to 1957. The introduction described the ex-hibit as a "look at the eleven seasons when New Yorkers lived and experienced baseball in their town in a way never to be repeated again."[13] The exhibition reflected the truism that the 1950s—or at least the first eight years of that de-cade—were a special time for New York baseball. In a companion essay to Ken Burns's famous documentary *Baseball,* George Will, in an otherwise typically conservative, grumpy, and backward-looking piece of writing, notes:

> The fifties were the last decade when America suffered from the defect of vision known as New York–centrism. New York seemed to be the center of the universe in culture generally and baseball especially. The nation's gaze was about to turn, south toward Washington, and west, where the course of empire was taking the population—and a couple of New York's baseball teams. But in baseball, until 1958, the fifties belonged to three boroughs: the Bronx, Manhattan, and Brooklyn. Yankee Stadium, the Polo Grounds, and Ebbets Field seemed almost to have cornered the market on glory.[14]

Harvey Frommer also expressed much of what made the 1950s a special time for baseball in New York City: "Through the long and steamy summer nights and in the blaze of its days, from early spring to the winds of autumn, baseball dominated New York City. The deeds and personalities of the Dodgers, the Giants and the Yankees transformed the huge metropolis into a small town of neighborhood rooting."[15] Frommer also sought to place New York City baseball in a broader postwar context. "For a city eager for entertainment after the lights went on again after the darkness of World War II, the Dodgers, the Giants, the Yankees, their rivalry, their successes, their innovations, their stars, attracted the fanatical attention of millions."[16]

During these years, the feeling that New York was the center of the baseball universe was made even stronger because so many of the key actors had ties to more than one New York team. Casey Stengel, who managed the Yankees from 1949 to 1960, had been a star outfielder for the Dodgers and Giants and had also managed the Dodgers. Leo Durocher managed the Dodgers from 1939 to midway through 1948, with 1947 off because he was suspended. A few days after being fired from that job, he was hired by the Giants, which he managed until 1955. Durocher had started his playing career with the Yankees and ended it with the Dodgers. Sal Maglie was a star pitcher on Durocher's pennant-winning Giants teams in 1951 and 1954, but pitched for Brooklyn in 1956 and 1957 and for the Yankees in the last half of 1957 and in 1958. Johnny Mize was the Giants top slugger from 1942 to 1949, with 1943 to 1945 off due to military service; however, when the Yankees needed an extra bat for the 1949 stretch run, they bought him from the Giants. He was a valuable pinch-hitter and first baseman for the Yankees as they won five consecutive World Series beginning in 1949. There were limits to the ties between New York teams as well: Following the 1956 season, Jackie Robinson decided to retire at age 37 rather than accept a trade to the Giants.

The decade between 1947 and 1956 was an extraordinary time for baseball in New York City. "With three major league teams—the Yankees, the Brooklyn Dodgers, and the New York Giants—at least one of whom played in the World Series every year except 1948; two National League teams in an intense rivalry; and seven landmark subway series, New York was the undisputed baseball capital of the nation."[17] Additionally, books about baseball in the 1950s have titles like *The Ten Best Years of Baseball*,[18] *New York City Baseball: The Last Golden Age, 1947–1957*,[19] and *Brooklyn's Dodgers: The Bums, the Borough, and the Best of Baseball, 1947–1957*,[20] demonstrating the lasting impression that New York baseball of that era has made.

New York in the 1950s was, due to its story lines, great players, memorable moments, and championship teams, a very special time and place for baseball, but there was something else that made this period so memorable. For example, the decade's—and perhaps century's—most famous baseball moment occurred when a team from Manhattan beat a team from Brooklyn for the National League pennant and a chance to play a team from the Bronx in the World Series. Often overlooked in that New York baseball moment is that the man who hit that home run had grown up in another of the five boroughs, Staten Island. The demographic changes to which Will alluded had not yet shifted the country's economic and power center south and west from New York. Television was becoming more widespread so that people all over the country could see weekly television broadcasts that frequently featured the New York teams because they were usually among the best teams. Similarly, the World Series was first televised in 1947, and over the next decade, as the fall classic was being watched by fans all over the country, it was always New York teams who were in the World Series, frequently representing both leagues.

After the 1950s, New York never again occupied the center stage of the baseball world as unambiguously and enduringly as it did during those years. Since the Dodgers and Giants moved west, there has only been one Subway Series. The 2000 World Series was celebrated with great fanfare in New York, but unless you are a Yankees fan, it cannot be considered a great or memorable World Series. There have been many exciting players in New York in the last 60 years, including Tom Seaver, Dwight Gooden, Reggie Jackson, Derek Jeter, and Mariano Rivera, but there has never been as much baseball talent concentrated in New York as there was between 1947 and 1956. Today there are 30 big league teams, almost twice as many as the 16 that existed in the 1950s. This all but ensures that baseball cannot be dominated by a small handful of teams the way it was in the 1950s.

WHY IS ALL THIS STILL REMEMBERED?

New York in the 1950s was also an exceptional place because of the enormous amount of influential literary, cultural, and other figures who came of age in that time and place and then went on to make an impact on the United States during the last third or so of the twentieth century. Much of the cultural history of the mid- to late twentieth century and early twenty-first century in the United States was created by people who spent at least some of their formative years in New York in the 1950s. Some of these people left the city while still young, while others continued to live there well into adulthood. This includes people like Martin Scorsese, Woody Allen, Billy Crystal, Don DeLillo, Larry David, Robert De Niro, Doris Kearns Goodwin, Bernie Sanders, Paul Simon, and Barbara Streisand.

This group skews notably white with substantial Italian and Jewish representation, but that is also part of the story of New York and the United States during the decades following the Dodgers' and Giants' departures. As these groups moved from the city for other parts of the country, the city's demographic makeup changed, but the broader American culture, particularly in literature, film, and academia, was increasingly influenced by people who had grown up in New York, but, in many cases, left for elsewhere in the United States.

Many who were part of the midcentury New York diaspora brought New York baseball culture to their art. Larry David's television program *Curb Your Enthusiasm* has included frequent references to Mickey Mantle, as well as to Joe Pepitone who played for the Yankees during the 1960s. Paul Simon and fellow son of the borough of Queens Art Garfunkel asked America where Joe DiMaggio had gone in their 1967 song "Mrs. Robinson." Woody Allen grew up in Brooklyn, but was a Yankees fan.[21] Baseball of that era made its way into Allen's movies like *Manhattan,* through references to Willie Mays, as well as *Radio Days,* referencing World War II–era baseball.

For every Billy Crystal or Larry David who publicly reveres Mickey Mantle, for every Paul Simon who sings about Joe DiMaggio as a symbol of America's lost innocence, or for every Woody Allen who posits that Willie Mays is one of the answers to the question of "why life is worth living,"[22] there has been—well, nobody of similar cultural stature rhapsodizing about Ted Williams's sublime swing and service to his country, Stan Musial's consistent slugging, or Warren Spahn's excellent pitching, during those years.

Don DeLillo's 1997 tome *Underworld* begins with a 60-page fictional description of the 1951 Bobby Thomson game between the Dodgers and the Giants. The long passage includes a section about what happened to the home run ball and a long meandering and imaginary conversation between J. Edgar Hoover, Jackie Gleason, Frank Sinatra, and Toots Shor, who, in DeLillo's novel, all attended this game together. This introduction is intended to set a tone for 1950s New York and for much of the following decades. It also brought that moment to life for thousands of readers, many of whom were baseball fans, yet without previous knowledge of that seminal game in 1951.

DeLillo describes the view from the radio booth as the game is beginning:

When you think about the textured history of the teams and the faith and passion of the fans and the way these forces are entwined citywide, and when you
think about the game itself, live-or-die, the third game in a three-game playoff,
and you say the names Giants and Dodgers, and you calculate the way the
players hate each other openly, and you recall the kind of year this has turned
out to be, the pennant race that has turned the city to a strangulated rapture,
an end-shudder requiring a German loan-word to put across the mingling of
pleasure and dread and suspense, and when you think about the blood loyalty
. . . the love-of-team that runs across the boroughs and through the snuggled
suburbs and out into the apple counties and the raw north, then how do you
explain twenty thousand empty seats?[23]

DeLillo, who grew up in the Bronx in the 1940s and 1950s, expertly hints at
the end of 1950s New York baseball. It is unlikely that many baseball fans today
are aware that the Polo Grounds was more than one-third empty on October
3, 1951. Only 34,320 fans were at the ballpark that day, despite its capacity of
55,000.

Toward the end of that section, set in 1951, DeLillo, with the benefit of hindsight, captures the lasting impact of the game. "And the fans at the Polo Grounds
today will be able to tell their grandchildren—they'll be the gassy old men leaning
into the next century and trying to convince anyone willing to listen, pressing
in with medicine breath, that they were there when it happened."[24]

The impact that the writers, filmmakers, television personalities, and musi-
cians from a specific generation of New Yorkers made on American culture,
while significant, can be overstated. However, it was not just the likes of Paul
Simon, Don DeLillo, and Woody Allen who accomplished this, but also the
hundreds of thousands of lesser known New Yorkers who spent at least some
of their formative years in that city between 1947 and 1956 before leaving to
make their mark in the arts, business, academia, or politics in other parts of
the country. Many of those people, scattered around the country, continued
to talk about the baseball of their youth well into the twenty-first century.

I was raised by one of these people. My mother lived in New York City,
although in Manhattan, not Brooklyn or the Bronx, for the first 31 years of her
life before moving to San Francisco around 1971. For most of my childhood,
discussions by former New Yorkers, whom my mother met and befriended in
San Francisco, about what New York had been like in the 15 to 20 years following
the end of World War II was part of the background noise of my home life and
frequently included some chatter about the "golden age" of New York baseball.

For many of those members of the late twentieth-century New York diaspora, who were born either shortly before or during the first stirrings of the
baby boom, the Brooklyn Dodgers, Mickey Mantle, Yogi Berra, Casey Stengel, Willie Mays, and the shot heard 'round the world were not just baseball
memories, but were shorthand for youth, innocence, and a New York City that
by 1970 or so no longer existed—and had been replaced by one that was less
familiar, more dangerous, and demographically different from the New York
of their memories.

Many of these people moved into positions of influence, but not quite
fame at colleges, universities, publishing houses, finance and real estate firms,
magazines, the film industry, and similar professions. This allowed them, in
small ways and not always consciously, to contribute to the perception that the
1947–56 period in New York was a very special time and place for baseball.

BASEBALL OUTSIDE OF NEW YORK

The 1950s, which for baseball began on April 15, 1947, when Jackie Robinson
played his first game for the Dodgers, is frequently described as baseball's
golden age.[25] For baseball in New York, the reasons for this are clear, but for
the rest of the country this is much less apparent. Philadelphia and St. Louis,
for example, made it through the decade with a total of one pennant, but each
city lost one of their teams. Boston also lost a team, as the Braves moved to
Milwaukee only four years after winning the pennant. Teams like the Washington Senators and the Detroit Tigers rarely contended during these years and
were unable to impede the dominance of the Yankees in the American League.

Baseball in the 1950s was in many other respects not a golden age. Robert
Murphy describes baseball in the early 1950s as "a troubled game. . . . Each year
after a peak of almost 21 million in 1948, total attendance had declined. By '52
it was down to 14.6 million, and the following year it would be a quarter million less than that. . . . Through the mid-fifties, voices rose to address a game
'in crisis,' raise questions about its 'survival' and offer various solutions."[26]

The unimpressive attendance figures were only part of the problem. For
example, although Jackie Robinson struck a very significant blow against
apartheid in baseball and American society more broadly, the first ten years
after Robinson started playing for the Dodgers were hardly easy for an initially small cadre of African American and dark-skinned Latino ballplayers.
African American players encountered racism on the field and from fans; if

they played for a team that trained in Florida, they also had to cope with the de jure segregation of the Deep South during spring training.

The first group of dark-skinned Latinos who began their careers in the 1950s, including Cubans like Orestes Minoso and Puerto Ricans like Roberto Clemente, confronted an additional form of racism. Minoso, like many other early Latino players, was given a nickname, Minnie, that Roberto Gonzalez Echevarria described as a "kind of offense, in this case both to historical accuracy and to . . . dignity." Echevarria argues that giving Latino players these kinds of undignified nicknames was a reflection of the attitudes the media and baseball hierarchy held toward Latino ballplayers in this era.[27] Adrian Burgos Jr. writes that as the first dark-skinned Latino player in the big leagues, Minoso, whose career started in 1949, "dealt with beanballs, bench jockeying from opposing teams, and jeers from fans who remained opposed to integration."[28]

Clemente was not given an insulting nickname, but instead frequently had his first name shortened and anglicized in the media, and even on his baseball card, simply to Bob. Clemente's experience with the media also reflects the difficulties the first group of dark-skinned Latino players faced. Burgos notes that "the sportswriter's goal of creating good copy meant emphasizing for readers the lines of racial and cultural difference." Frequently this meant reporting quotes by Latino players, like Clemente, using broken English and exaggerated phonetic spellings of English spoken with a Spanish accent.[29] Additionally, throughout his career, Clemente was portrayed as somehow deficient as a competitor and as somebody who sought to get out of the lineup whenever he had a minor injury. John Rosengren writes that when Juan Marichal, the great Giants pitcher from the Dominican Republic, began his career in 1960, "he was confronted by the range of stereotypes about Latin players—that they didn't hustle, didn't mind losing, quit when behind, feigned injuries, and perhaps most damaging, were hot-blooded, quick-tempered types prone to violence."[30]

Baseball, like many other American institutions in the 1950s, was essentially conservative. The economic structures of the game were still weighted very heavily toward ownership. Challenges to the reserve clause, which bound players to their teams, were still years away, so owners held all the power in contract negotiations. While there was something homey and nice about star players working in the offseason, this was also an indication that the industry was not financially strong and that, when it was, players were not getting their fair share.

The stories of players like Gil Hodges, who sold cars in Brooklyn, or future Hall of Famers Phil Rizzuto and Yogi Berra of the Yankees, who worked in clothing stores during the offseason, evoke a more innocent and modest time, but they also cover up an ugly side of the game. Late in the evening of January 28, 1958, or early on the following morning, star Dodgers catcher Roy Campanella was in a terrible car accident while driving home to Glen Cove, Long Island. The accident left Campanella paralyzed from the waist down for the rest of his life, ending his playing career. Campanella was 36 at the time of the accident and winding down his playing days, but had enjoyed a great career, including three MVP awards and eight All-Star selections. When the accident occurred, Campanella was driving home from a liquor store he owned and operated in Manhattan. It is not hard to wonder whether a better compensated Campanella might have been home earlier that evening, not worrying about his business in Harlem.

On the field, baseball in the 1950s had some great moments, particularly for the New York teams, but it was also a time of poor attendance, teams that were permanently out of contention, and a brand of play on the field that was not always exciting. Bill James, in an essay on how baseball was played in the 1950s, writes that

> the baseball of the 1950s was perhaps the most one-dimensional, uniform, predictable version of the game which has ever been offered to the public. By 1950, the stolen base was a rare play, a "surprise" play. In the first seven years of the decade no team stole a hundred bases in a season. . . . In the early 1950s, every team approached the game with the same essential offensive philosophy: get people on base and hit home runs.
>
> I wouldn't state it for a fact, but it is possible that the attendance problems of the early fifties were in some measure attributable to this. . . . Perhaps this was exciting baseball if your team was the Yankees or the Dodgers or (early in the decade) the Giants. . . . [T]hose three teams . . . truly did play an exciting aggressive game of baseball as did few other managers.[31]

James is one of most astute observers of baseball ever to write about the game, so his words should be recognized as very credible. His description of 1950s baseball as slow is borne out by the numbers. In 1950, for example, Dom DiMaggio led the American League with 15 stolen bases. That would be a bad month for later speedsters like Maury Wills, Lou Brock, Tim Raines, or Rickey Henderson.

One way to understand this is to examine the impact that Jackie Robinson had on big league baseball when he came to the Dodgers, not just because he was African American, but because of his baserunning. This passage by Rick Swaine captures Robinson's prowess on the bases:

It was running the bases, however, where Robinson's star shined brightest. He was a dynamo on the basepaths—fast, clever, daring, and rough. He was the most dangerous baserunner since Ty Cobb, embarrassing and intimidating the opposition into beating themselves with mental and physical errors. He created havoc by taking impossibly long leads, jockeying back and forth, and threatening to steal on every pitch. His mere presence on base was enough to upset the most steely-nerved veteran hurlers.

Robinson revived the art of stealing home, successfully making it nineteen times in his career. At the age of thirty-five in 1954, he became the first National Leaguer to steal his way around the bases in twenty-six years, and a year later he became one of only twelve men to steal home in the World Series.[32]

Swaine did not overstate Robinson's baserunning prowess, but the context in which the groundbreaking Dodger stole his bases is also important. Robinson, despite what was said about his baserunning, never stole even 40 bases in a season, topping 30 only in his 1949 MVP campaign. This may have been more of a reflection of how his managers did not quite know how to use a weapon like Robinson, rather than of his baserunning ability; however, it is evidence that baseball remained a pretty slow game even after Robinson joined the Dodgers.

Perhaps because of the homogeneity of strategies, the years 1947 to 1956 were not ones of great individual accomplishment, other than in slugging home runs. The most bases anybody stole in a season during these years was 40 by Willie Mays in 1956. Only three pitchers won 25 or more games in a season: 28 by Robin Roberts in 1952, 27 by Don Newcombe in 1956, and 25 by Mel Parnell in 1949. Strikeouts were down as well. Only one pitcher, Herb Score, topped 250 in a season, with 263 in 1956, but his career was cut short by a line drive off the bat of Gil McDougald the following year. During that ten-year period, the 200-strikeout mark was met or exceeded only three times—twice by Score and once by Bob Turley.

In some respects, the notion that the 1950s in general were the golden age of baseball has less to do with baseball itself and is more a product of postwar demography, specifically the huge baby boomer generation. Many people perceive baseball to be at its best when they were between about 9 and 12 years old. For older baby boomers, this included the second half of the 1950s. Additionally, there is a conservative, or at least nostalgic, aspect to this belief. In the 1950s, baseball was covered in the sports pages, not the business section; baseball players looked like ordinary people; salaries were more modest; there was no designated hitter; and pitchers were much more likely to finish the games they started. All of this changed as, beginning in the 1960s, a new brand of ballplayer emerged. This new brand of baseball player was more likely to speak his mind and demand his share of baseball's revenue. Older fans who did not like this began to see 1950s baseball as the last era of the baseball they knew and loved.

There is an uglier aspect of this perspective, one expressed by longtime television commentator Andy Rooney in a 2007 column: "I know all about Babe Ruth and Lou Gehrig, but today's baseball stars are all guys named Rodriguez to me. They're apparently very good, but they haven't caught my interest." Rooney expressed a racist sentiment, but also revealed a truth for older white men for whom a game played by Latinos is less compelling or relatable. For these baseball fans (Rooney, for example, was born in 1919), the 1950s represent a time when they could pronounce the names of almost every player, and the players with very few exceptions all spoke English; in their minds, this was a golden era exactly because they identified with it and felt part of it.[33]

The period 1947–56 in New York specifically cannot be dismissed so easily. Clearly something special was going on in New York at that time. For ten years New York was at the center of the baseball world. Not only did New York teams win much more than their share of pennants and World Series, but New York was home to some of the best baseball stories of the era. The integration of baseball, the two players who came to define baseball for millions of baby boomers, the only perfect game in World Series history, the most famous single play in the game's long history, and the greatest catch in World Series history all occurred in New York during these years.

These great moments notwithstanding, the best players of the era were not playing in New York. The two best players in the big leagues from 1947 to 1956, according to WAR, were Stan Musial with 75.6 WAR and Ted Williams with 61.6 WAR. Jackie Robinson was a close third with 61.5. Thus, while Williams and Robinson were essentially tied, Williams and Musial were the clear leaders in the American and National Leagues, respectively. Williams led all American League players in WAR during this period by a substantial margin. Indians center fielder Larry Doby was second with 46.8 WAR. Additionally, Williams missed most of 1952 and 1953 because he was serving in the Korean War. Had he played those two seasons, he would have outpaced Robinson by a substantial margin for the years in question.

Williams and Musial, two of the greatest players ever, hit with their typical excellence throughout the 1947–56 golden age. Musial's .336/.427/.589 with 300 home runs and 387 doubles over those ten years marked him as a slugger consistently able to put up MVP-caliber numbers. During those years, he was named MVP once and finished second in MVP voting three times. Williams only hit 253 home runs because he missed two seasons for military service, but his .344/.488/.634 slash line, sustained over eight seasons in a ten-year period was even better than Musial's, and represented a torrid decade of hitting by one of the greatest hitters ever. During those eight seasons, Williams won one MVP award and finished in the top five in MVP voting an additional five times.

From 1947 to 1956, these two players of historic greatness were in the prime of their careers and were the best players in their respective leagues. However, they are almost completely left out of the popular histories and recollections of the period. Almost all baseball fans are aware of Williams's career of extraordinary hitting, which lasted more than 20 years and bridged his military service. Similarly, most fans know that Williams hit .406 in 1941 making him the last player to hit .400 or better in a season. More studious and literary fans may remember Williams's home run in his last game, in 1960 at Fenway Park, made famous by John Updike's profile of the event in *The New Yorker*:

> Like a feather caught in a vortex, Williams ran around the square of bases at the center of our beseeching screaming. He ran as he always ran out home runs—hurriedly, unsmiling, head down, as if our praise were a storm of rain to get out of. He didn't tip his cap. Though we thumped, wept, and chanted "We want Ted" for minutes after he hid in the dugout, he did not come back. Our noise for some seconds passed beyond excitement into a kind of immense open anguish, a wailing, a cry to be saved. But immortality is nontransferable. The papers said that the other players, and even the umpires on the field, begged him to come out and acknowledge us in some way, but he never had and did not now. Gods do not answer letters.[34]

There is, however, very little written about Williams during the 1947–56 period that has become part of the baseball lore from that era. The only exception is the recognition of Williams's extraordinary contribution in the military, as he fought in both World War II and Korea. Thus, the greatest hitter of this golden age is best known for going to Korea, rather than for anything he did with his bat during this period.

There is also no single moment involving Stan Musial from this ten-year period that is remembered today. For that matter, there is no significant moment or event from his entire career that is remembered today. Musial may be the most forgotten truly great player of the modern era. Musial won three MVP awards in his career; finished in the top ten in MVP voting every year from 1948 to 1957; was selected to the All-Star team in 20 seasons, including every year from 1946 to 1963; was easily elected to the Hall of Fame with 93.2 percent of the votes the one and only time he was on the ballot; and, for the more quantitatively inclined, was eleventh in all time WAR. However, he is not well remembered today outside of St. Louis, where he played his entire career.

In books about baseball in the 1950s, particularly those focused on New York, Musial appears periodically, making a cameo in a story that is ultimately about other teams and other players. In the middle of a Dodgers pennant drive, the Cardinals come to Brooklyn, and Musial drives in a bunch of runs in a short series, or the Giants visit St. Louis and manage to escape with two wins, despite Musial slamming the ball all over the yard for the series. He appears in accounts of 1950s pennant races like Robin Williams appears in the later seasons of *Happy Days*—stealing the show, but in no way central to the plot. Even Musial's nickname, "The Man," was given to him by Dodgers fans who, according to the legend, would moan, "Here comes that man again!" whenever the slugging Musial came to bat against the Dodgers.

To the extent Musial is remembered for anything specific in this period it is something he did not do. On May 6, 1947, the Cardinals traveled to Brooklyn to play the Dodgers for their first meeting of the year. Several members of the Cardinals proposed refusing to play against the Dodgers because Jackie Robinson, who was in the first months of his career, was going to be on the field. That idea ended when the team's best player, Musial, told his teammates he wasn't hearing it and that he intended to take the field against the Dodgers, regardless of what his teammates wanted.[35]

The simplest explanation of why Musial and Williams are no longer remembered for how well they played in the 1947–56 era is that neither team won a pennant during this period. Musial's Cardinals and Williams's Red Sox played against each other in the 1946 World Series, with the Cardinals beating the Red Sox in a memorable seven games; however, following that series, neither team won another pennant until after Musial and Williams had both retired, the Cardinals in 1964 and the Red Sox in 1967. The Red Sox contended in 1948 to 1950, but then fell out of contention altogether until their 1967 pennant. The Cardinals were the best team in the National League, and indeed all of the big leagues from 1942 to 1946, but between 1947 and 1963, which was Musial's last season, the Cardinals only came within five games of a pennant once.

Williams's Red Sox were similarly absent from the World Series during the last decade or so of their greatest slugger's career. The Red Sox did not make it back to the World Series until 1967, when they again lost to the Cardinals. The Red Sox lost a close pennant race in 1948, when they dropped a one-game playoff to the Indians after finishing in a tie during the regular season. In 1949, they lost probably the most dramatic Yankee–Red Sox pennant race until 1978, as they finished one game back after losing the last two games of the season to the Yankees.

Even in New York, the extent to which 1947–56 was a golden age for all three teams is not clear. For the New York Giants, despite winning two pennants and one World Series, their last ten years in New York were not close to being their most successful ten-year span. For example, from 1915 to 1924, they won five pennants and two World Series; from 1905 to 1914, they won four pennants and one World Series. Four times from 1947 to 1956, the Giants finished in the second division—meaning they came in fifth or worse in an eight-team league. Moreover, during their last three years in New York, they never reached 850,000 in attendance, despite their 1954 championship season.

Following their 1954 championship season, the Giants began a period of decline, leading up to their departure for the West Coast. Frommer argued that "in 1954, the Giants had the spotlight of the baseball world on them. In 1955, the Yankees and Dodgers took it away, transforming the 'Jints' into the stepchild of New York City baseball. It was a year of utter bliss in Brooklyn. . . . For fans of the Giants there was a sense that the team was coming apart."[36]

Frommer summarized the state of the Giants when they moved to San Francisco in 1958, writing that "the players still wore 'Giants' across their uniform chest, but the franchise was struggling for an identity. It was a maudlin finale for the sports organization that once had been the apogee of New York City baseball."[37]

Frommer's comments are significant because they reflect both the status of the Giants relative to the other two New York teams at the tail end of that city's greatest baseball era and also the myopia that has come to characterize descriptions of the move. The Giants of the late 1950s had the game's best player, a head start on scouting in the Dominican Republic, and a farm system that was about to become one of the most productive in baseball history. Describing those early San Francisco Giants as having no identity tells us more about the perspective of the analyst than about the team itself.

Struggles on and off the field notwithstanding, the Giants' last decade or so in New York could possibly be described as their golden age for two reasons—one play and one player. If we can manage to look past the scintillating brilliance of this one play and this one player, the Giants' footing in New York in the 1950s begins to appear tenuous indeed.

The play, vividly described by DeLillo and many others, was Bobby Thomson's shot heard 'round the world in 1951. This one play, simply by the force of its drama and excitement, and its occurrence in a pennant-deciding game against the Dodgers—with the winner going on to play the Yankees in the World Series—sealed the position of the Giants in the legends surrounding New York City baseball of the era.

While Bobby Thomson provided the one dramatic moment, the man on deck when that home run was hit was the best player of his generation, the most complete player in the history of the game, and probably the best ever other than Babe Ruth. Willie Mays, known as the "Say Hey Kid" because of his habit of using the phase "Say Hey" when speaking to somebody whose name he was not sure about, was a player of unparalleled talent, grace, and skill. As a member of the New York Giants, he ensured that team would remain in the national spotlight and would contend even when he was not surrounded by great players. Mays is part of the golden age of New York not just because of his performance on the field, but because of his off-the-field persona. For example, as a rookie he lived in a boardinghouse in Harlem near the Polo Grounds and was known to occasionally play stickball with children from the neighborhood. This is, in some respects, a nice story, but it is also a reminder of the racial politics of the era.

Mays's reputation as a player has withstood the test of time. However, the extent to which he belongs to New York's golden age of baseball is debatable. He played his first game in 1951, four years after Jackie Robinson's debut with the Dodgers. He also missed most of the 1952 and 1953 seasons due to military service, so was really only a full-time player for the New York Giants for five years. Mays belongs more to the San Francisco Giants, for whom he played 2,095 games, than to the franchise's New York iteration, where he only played 762 games.

During New York's golden age of baseball, the Giants were clearly the city's third team. Among the three New York teams, the Giants finished third in attendance every year from 1947 to 1957, except for 1948 and 1954. In those two years they drew slightly more fans than the Dodgers did. They never outdrew the Yankees during those years and frequently trailed them in annual attendance by a margin of well over 500,000.[38]

THE GOLDEN AGE STUMBLES

In many respects, the pinnacle of baseball in New York in the 1950s was reached on October 4, 1955. On that day, the Dodgers finally won the World Series, as Johnny Podres threw a complete-game shutout to defeat the Yankees 2–0 in Game Seven. For many of the more than 62,000 fans who filled Yankee Stadium that day, it would have been difficult to believe that in less than two years both the Dodgers and Giants would have played their last home game in New York.

The 1955 World Series was played against the backdrop of the early rumblings of the Dodgers' departure. In a *Daily News* story about the Dodgers' World Series victory the day after the final game, Brooklyn borough president John Cashmore is quoted as offering his congratulations to the Dodgers, while simultaneously urging the Dodgers "to turn a 'deaf ear' to other cities who would lure the team away from Brooklyn."[39] Cashmore was probably primarily concerned about New Jersey trying to lure the Dodgers away. In 1956 and 1957, the Dodgers were actively exploring ways to get out of Brooklyn to a place that was more lucrative and played 15 games in Jersey City.

Thus, the biggest irony about what was allegedly the greatest period for baseball in New York history was how quickly it ended. The period of time between Jackie Robinson's first game with the Dodgers and the Dodgers' first game in Los Angeles was 11 years. From Don Larsen's perfect game in Game Five of the 1956 World Series to the Dodgers' last game in Brooklyn and the Giants' last game as a New York team was less than a year.

This golden age of New York baseball lasted fewer years than a typical career of a good ballplayer. Yogi Berra, for example, played his first game with the Yankees in late 1946, a few months before Jackie Robinson first played for the Dodgers, and played his last big league game in 1965, several years after the Giants and Dodgers had moved west. Berra played those last games of his career with the Mets, the successor New York team of the Dodgers and Giants. Ted Williams and Stan Musial were both established stars by the time Jackie Robinson began his career with Brooklyn and were still great players when the Dodgers and Giants began playing in Los Angeles and San Francisco.

The speed with which the Dodgers and Giants left New York and the extremely short time between being a championship team and leaving the city, a period of two years for the Dodgers and three for the Giants, contributed to the surprise and rancor that Dodgers and Giants fans in New York felt about the decision to move—and to the belief among these fans that owners Horace Stoneham, and particularly Walter O'Malley, were criminals who had betrayed the fans and, in the case of O'Malley, the entire borough of Brooklyn. The Giants and Dodgers were not like the Philadelphia Athletics, St. Louis Browns, or Washington Senators, teams that had been bad on the field for years before leaving their longtime home city.

Teams do not, however, abandon their longtime homes overnight, so the roots of the decisions by the Giants and Dodgers to move west started several years before 1958, their inaugural season in California. These initial discussions and explorations grew out of poor attendance, particularly given the quality of the teams, demographic changes in central Brooklyn and northern Manhattan, as well as the clear opportunity California represented for the right big league team or teams.

4

BASEBALL ON THE WEST COAST

WE HAD BIG LEAGUE BASEBALL HERE LONG BEFORE
THE GIANTS AND DODGERS

The Dodgers' and Giants' departure from New York for Los Angeles and San Francisco is often understood to be synonymous with the introduction of big league baseball to the West Coast. While the Dodgers and the Giants were the first major league teams to make their home on the West Coast, it is an oversimplification to claim that they were the first big league teams—that is, if big league is understood to mean high-level baseball viewed as the best around by those who played for and followed the teams.

During much of the first 50-plus years of the twentieth century, "big league" is precisely how fans on the West Coast thought of the Pacific Coast League (PCL). When I began attending Giants games at Candlestick Park, less than 20 years into the Giants' tenure in San Francisco, it was not difficult to find older fans who would remind me that San Francisco had big league baseball before the Giants and Dodgers moved west. The veracity of this assertion is open to interpretation, as the National and American Leagues were more stable, had a broader reach, and featured a level of play that was, in general, higher than that of the PCL. Nonetheless, the perceptions, at least among baseball fans of the era, were real. Additionally, for most of the years before the Dodgers and Giants moved to California, baseball on the West Coast included semipro ball, barnstorming teams from Japan, and big leaguers barnstorming there during the offseason.

The quality of West Coast baseball, and the loyalties fans held to teams in the PCL in particular, made it even more important that the first major league teams in Los Angeles and San Francisco were established teams with well-known and popular players. When the Dodgers and Giants arrived in

California, the presence on their rosters of players like Willie Mays, Duke Snider, Pee Wee Reese, and others made it easier to overcome residual loyalty to PCL teams such as the San Francisco Seals or Los Angeles Angels. Particularly in San Francisco, it was difficult to persuade these fans to swap loyalties from the PCL even to established and well-known big league teams. It is less likely that hapless expansion teams, like the early New York Mets, would have been able to ease fans' transition from the PCL to the National League.

It may be difficult to imagine today that an expansion team in Los Angeles or San Francisco in the late 1950s or early 1960s would have failed to win over a sufficient fan base; however, in the 1950s and 1960s, many franchise moves, including the initial relocation of the Athletics (to Kansas City in 1955) and the Braves (to Milwaukee in 1953), did not work out. Within 15 years, both teams had relocated again, this time to their current host cities. Some expansion teams, like the Seattle Pilots and expansion Washington Senators, did not last even that long in the cities to which they moved.

The question of what would have happened if MLB had placed an expansion team in Los Angeles in the 1960s is not an entirely hypothetical one. The Los Angeles Angels joined the American League in 1961, along with the second-phase Washington Senators.[1] The Angels were a typical expansion team, although probably better than most. After finishing eighth, in a ten-team league, in 1961, they finished a surprising third in 1962. However, between 1963 and 1977, they only finished above .500 four times and did not make a postseason appearance until 1979.

The Angels began their tenure playing in Wrigley Field in Los Angeles, a ballpark that only had capacity for about 20,500 fans; however, even given that, they drew only 603,510 fans during their first year, an average of under 8,000 per home date. The Angels moved to the much bigger Dodger Stadium, capacity 56,000, the next year, and drew over 1.1 million in their second year. However, the next three years' attendance was well under one million. This led the Angels to move farther south and east to Anaheim, where they have remained since 1966.

It is difficult to assess the extent to which Angelenos welcomed the Angels, because the Dodgers were already in Los Angeles when the expansion Angels were created. It is likely that had the Dodgers not been there, the Angels would have drawn more fans, at least initially. It is also the case that because the Dodgers were so much better from their arrival until 1979, when the Angels finally won their first AL West division crown, they were always the favorite team of Los Angeles baseball fans. However, it also remains true that the during their first decade or so, the expansion Angels rarely drew well and had almost no players who were very popular, with possible exception of Dean Chance, who was, briefly during the early 1960s, the third-best starting pitcher in Southern California.

An interesting contrast can be made between the Angels and another expansion team that was placed in a city that already had one team. The Mets drew more than 900,000 fans in 1962, their first year, but then drew more than 1,000,000 every year until 1979. There is no question that the Mets won the hearts of New Yorkers more quickly, and more enduringly, than the Angels did with regard to Angelenos. The reason for this is obvious—after losing the Dodgers and Giants, New Yorkers were anxious to have another National League team. That, however, is precisely the point. The MLB brand was much stronger in post–Dodgers and Giants New York than it was in post-PCL Los Angeles or San Francisco.

BASEBALL AND THE WEST

Today, when baseball is described as our national pastime, it is implicit that the baseball in question is MLB. We see this, for example, before World Series games when video montages are presented that show images of today's stars all the way back to the almost mythic figures of the early twentieth century like Ty Cobb, Walter Johnson, Christy Mathewson, and, most of all, Babe Ruth. Major League Baseball has a very impressive history and is wise to continue to use that history to strengthen its brand. That history is, to a great extent, MLB's comparative advantage relative to the NBA or the NFL. However, baseball became America's national pastime not because of 16 teams playing in front of largely empty stadiums for half a century or so. Rather, it rose to national prominence because it was played everywhere, from sugarcane plantations in Hawaii to cotton fields in the Deep South; from the inner cities of the Bronx and Brooklyn to the sand dunes of what are now the Richmond and Sunset districts of San Francisco; from the Old West of Montana and Wyoming to staid New England towns.

Although there were no National League or American League teams on the West Coast, baseball was still as popular and widely played there as in the Northeast and Midwest in the decades before the Dodgers and Giants moved west. Additionally, because of the warmer weather, the West Coast was then, as it is now, a fertile source of baseball talent. Young players there are able to play on fields year-round, making it easier to hone their skills at things like judging fly balls and hitting live pitching in game situations. The number of top MLB players from baseball's early years who came from the West Coast, especially California, is extraordinary. The Yankees dynasty of the 1920s and 1930s included some key players from San Francisco, many of whom were Italian American. Slugging second baseman Tony Lazzeri and Joe DiMaggio, although separated by a few years, grew up in the same neighborhood in San Francisco and attended the same high school, Galileo.[2] When DiMaggio traveled east for his first spring training with the Yankees, he drove there not just with Lazzeri, but also with Lazzeri's double-play partner, Frank Crosetti, another Italian American with roots in San Francisco.

In addition to DiMaggio and his brothers Dom and Vince, other early baseball stars from the San Francisco area included Lefty Gomez, Ernie Lombardi, Joe Cronin, and Ping Bodie (born Francesco Stephano Pezzolo). San Francisco was not the only part of the West Coast that sent star players to the big leagues. Ted Williams was from San Diego; Earl Averill hailed from the state of Washington; and numerous stars such as Joe Gordon, Bobby Doerr, Duke Snider, and Eddie Mathews had roots in Southern California. In addition to these well-known stars, numerous lesser-known players from the West filled big league rosters during these years.

Many of the top baseball players from the West made their way east to play in the major leagues. Others such as Lefty O'Doul, Ernie Lombardi, or Babe Pinelli either went back and forth between the PCL and American and National leagues or played in the PCL for a few years before or after their major league careers. Still other PCL players, good enough to play in the major leagues, stayed in the West, either by choice or because the opportunity to go east did not present itself.

In addition to players, many managers moved between the PCL and the big leagues. Casey Stengel managed the Oakland Oaks from 1946 to 1948 after managing the Brooklyn Dodgers and Boston Braves. He left the Oaks following the 1948 season to return to New York and manage the Yankees. One of Stengel's best players on the Oaks was a local boy from Berkeley whom Stengel brought to the Yankees in 1950, during Stengel's second year managing the team. Billy Martin and Stengel remained extremely close until Stengel was unable to prevent Martin from being traded away from the Yankees in 1957. The two were not on speaking terms for most of the next two decades, but reconciled shortly before Stengel's death in 1975. By then Martin had returned to the Yankees, hired to take Stengel's old job midway through the 1975 season.

Stengel's successor in Oakland was Chuck Dressen, who had managed the Cincinnati Reds from 1934 to 1937. Dressen left Oakland after two seasons to manage the Brooklyn Dodgers. The two former Oaks skippers ended up managing against each other during the 1952 and 1953 World Series. After managing the Dodgers for three seasons, Dressen would go on to manage the Senators, Braves, and Tigers. The most famous of all PCL managers was Lefty O'Doul. Splitting his playing days between the PCL and the big leagues, O'Doul was a Hall of Fame–quality hitter, hitting .349/.413/.532 during parts of 11 seasons with the Yankees, Red Sox, Giants, Phillies, and Dodgers. He managed in the PCL for 23 years, mostly with the San Francisco Seals, and won more games than any other manager in that league.

It is easy to envision the PCL as a kind of West Coast alternative to the National and American leagues—a league where top-caliber players, though on balance perhaps not quite as good as those in the big leagues, competed in front of loyal fan bases in games and leagues that mattered and were viewed as essentially big league. This characterization has a fair amount of truth to it, but is also an oversimplification.

The PCL is better understood as part of the broader universe of baseball that coexisted alongside the National and American Leagues throughout most of the first half of the twentieth century. The PCL was probably the best organized of all the entities in that constellation, offering a quality of play rivaled only by the best Negro League teams. It was, therefore, a hybrid of a minor league, developing players for the National and American leagues, and a top-tier in-dependent league. The PCL was better organized, with more continuity and record keeping, than almost any league outside the National and American Leagues, but it was not quite a third major league. Dennis Snelling, the author of the most comprehensive history of the PCL, noted:

> Its teams frequently outdrew major league franchises year after year, especially in relation to the population of the cities it represented. Players repeatedly spurned offers to play in the major leagues because they wanted to remain in the PCL. . . . Before it was relegated in the 1960s to the role of a farm system for the established major leagues, the Pacific Coast League was unlike any other minor league in the history of the game. . . . The players were older—many were major league veterans who knew how to play the game. And they cared about winning.[3]

As proud and durable as it was, there was still less stability in the PCL than in the American and National Leagues during the first half of the twentieth century. Some teams like the San Francisco Seals, Los Angeles Angels, and Portland Beavers endured throughout the history of the PCL, going back to the 1890s. Other teams, like the Mission Reds (1926–37) and the Vernon Tigers (1909–25), did not last quite as long. Similarly, the length of the season also varied over the years. In some years, some teams played 170 or more games. In 1905, for example, the Seals played 225 games. In some years, the two best teams in the PCL met in a championship series; in other years, the team with the best record was determined to be the champion, based simply on its record.

The PCL's relationship with the major leagues was always complicated. Although for most of its history it was an independent league, PCL teams occasionally had relationships with big league teams. For example, the San Francisco Seals were independent for most of their history, but between 1936 and 1957 had affiliations at various times with all three New York teams and the Boston Red Sox, for a total of five of those 22 years. The Hollywood Stars, another prominent PCL team, central to the story of the Dodgers and Giants, was affiliated with the Giants, Dodgers, White Sox, and Pirates for 13 of the years between 1941 and 1957. Even then, being affiliated with a big league team did not mean the same thing for a PCL team in the 1940s that it means for a minor league team today. These PCL teams still had a fair amount of independence, even with regard to player decisions, but it was still understood that the top players on the PCL team could be taken by the big league partner at any time and that no other big league team could make a claim on those players. It was only in 1959, a year after the Giants and Dodgers moved west, that all the teams in the PCL were affiliated with big league teams, thus losing any meaningful claim on true independence.

Although the PCL quickly became a fully affiliated minor league after the Dodgers and Giants moved to California, other options had been explored in the relatively recent past. Immediately following World War II, discussions of formalizing the PCL's status as a third major league began to receive significant interest and attention. Michael Lomax asserts that the impetus for this came following the failed attempt by the St. Louis Browns in 1941 to move to Los Angeles.[4] The timing of the Browns' efforts could not have been much worse, as Pearl Harbor was bombed a few days before a key league vote was scheduled. The attack changed the other teams' thinking, particularly with regard to travel and making any big changes as the country moved toward war.

Lomax states that PCL owners voted unanimously to become a third major league in 1946, but ultimately did not get the support from the two existing major leagues that it needed. The impetus for the PCL's decisions reflected both that baseball on the West Coast was an excellent product and that new means of transportation, like the jet plane, made regular games between teams on the West Coast and in the rest of the country more possible than before. However, there was also a recognition that, for these same reasons, the West Coast was becoming an increasingly attractive and feasible destination for

National League and American League franchises looking for a new and more lucrative home. Ultimately, the PCL proposal got little support from either existing major league.

The PCL's efforts to become a third major league were largely defensive. The failed attempt by the Browns to move to Los Angeles was a clear signal to the rest of the PCL that the stability that had defined the major leagues for the last half century was winding down and that, although the Browns failed to gain approval for their move to Los Angeles, other major league teams would try a westward move in the future. Thus, for the PCL, the 1950s were an up-or-out moment, where they would either become a third major league or be pushed out of Los Angeles, San Francisco, and perhaps other cities by big league franchises moving west. Once the PCL failed at the former, the latter became inevitable.

Debating whether or not the PCL was legitimately a major league is something of a mug's game because it defines the terms of the debate in a way that does not reflect the reality of the baseball environment for much of the 1900–1957 period. During these years, when taken as a whole, the quality of baseball was better in the National and American Leagues than in the PCL. The Giants and Athletics and later Yankees and Cardinals were clearly better than the Seals, Angels, or Stars, just as Ty Cobb, Babe Ruth, and Stan Musial were better than Brick Eldred, Frank Shellenback, Brooks Holder, and other PCL stars of the era—but that is not the point.

More relevant than this technical—and, from the point of view of the PCL, unwinnable—argument about which league had better baseball is the fact that the PCL had authentic fans, stories, players, and lore that, in the eyes of those who played and watched the league, represented the baseball story on the West Coast. Dick Dobbins captured this seemingly contradictory sentiment well in the opening words of his 1999 oral history of the PCL, *The Greatest Minor League*: "The old Pacific Coast League was a grand minor league. Alas it was still a minor league. . . . [A]n excellent brand of baseball had been played on the west coast for almost a century, [but] it was still not major league baseball. But PCL fans knew in their hearts that the league had been 'major league' for years."[5]

In the twenty-first century, the word "baseball," at least in the context of professional sports, has largely come to mean the major leagues—that is, baseball affiliated with the National and American Leagues. When we say, for example, that Ty Cobb has the highest batting average in baseball history, or that Lefty Grove was the best left-handed pitcher in baseball in the early 1930s, it is clear that we are referring only to the American and National Leagues, despite what we know about who was excluded from those leagues. However, this was much less clear earlier in the twentieth century. Today, it is easy to see that the Pittsburgh Pirates have been part of the same league, playing in the same city for over a century, and that team has one of the longest continuous histories of any team in baseball; however, in 1930 it was not apparent that the Pirates would be around 80 years later and the San Francisco Seals would not. This was even less apparent in 1910. Moreover, while now it seems inevitable that the Federal League, Negro Leagues, and PCL would all fail, it was much less certain at the time. History, it is often said, is written by the winners; the history of baseball is no exception.

This is significant, because it helps us understand how the PCL was viewed by its fans and players when it was most popular. A player on the Seals or the Los Angeles Angels in the 1925–50 period, or a fan of one of those teams, may well have thought that the Seals or Stars were very comparable to the Chicago White Sox, Philadelphia Phillies, or other big league franchises that struggled to draw fans and win games during those years. From our perspective today, this does not seem to have ever been the case. After all, the Seals no longer exist, and the White Sox and Phillies are both playing ball and both won the World Series in the last 20 years; however, fans 80 years ago could not have known how those teams and those leagues would evolve.

Thus, the history of big league baseball is the history of baseball now because many of the other streams dried up. With that knowledge, it is easy to tell the story of how the PCL stream, for example, was always weaker and more threatened, regardless of whether or not that was the case at the time. Fans of the PCL during the first half of the twentieth century did not see it this way. They probably rarely, if ever, thought about what the future of the PCL, or baseball on the West Coast in general, would be half a century later. Rather, they simply enjoyed the highest quality of baseball they could experience on a regular basis. They cared about the outcomes, followed their favorite players, and enjoyed baseball as much as any big league fan. That is not quite the case with baseball outside of the big league level today.

WERE THE SEALS A SPECIAL CASE?

It is an ironic coincidence that while the Giants' departure from northern Manhattan never elicited anger and heartbreak comparable to the Dodgers' departure from Brooklyn, the San Francisco Seals are more remembered and celebrated than any other PCL team. Lefty O'Doul, who managed the Seals from 1935 to 1951 was very famous in his hometown of San Francisco until he

died in 1969. His eponymous restaurant was located in downtown San Francisco until early 2017 and for many years was usually packed when the Giants
were playing an important game. It is still possible to see baseball fans in San
Francisco, even ones who were born long after the Seals played their last game,
wearing Seals caps or jackets. Overall, the Seals have been remembered longer
and more fondly than any other PCL team of their era.

During the years the Seals were the marquee franchise of the PCL, their
primary rivals were not either of the teams from Los Angeles, but the Oakland
Oaks who played across San Francisco Bay. The Seals–Oaks rivalry was usually
one-sided as the Seals were generally the better team. The most intense PCL
rivalry was between the two Los Angeles teams. In his history of the PCL,
Snelling maintains that "the rivalry between the Los Angeles Angels and Hollywood Stars was without equal anywhere. No college or professional sports
rivals played with more fire and intensity than those two minor league baseball
teams did during the 1940s and 1950s."[6] The assertion that the Stars–Angels
rivalry was more intense in the 1950s than the Dodgers–Giants rivalry in New
York is not provable, but Snelling's larger point that PCL teams competed aggressively and cared a lot about the outcome is clearly true.

One of the reasons the Seals are remembered so well is that over the course
of the pre-1958 history of the PCL, the Seals were the best team in the league.
Between 1903 and 1957, the last year before the Dodgers and Giants moved
west, the Seals won 14 PCL championships, more than any other team. It also
helped the Seals' legacy that the most famous PCL player ever was a San Franciscan who played with the Seals before going to the Yankees. Moreover, after
retiring from baseball in 1951, Joe DiMaggio continued to make San Francisco
his home, most of the time, until his death in 1999. For generations of San
Franciscans, Joe DiMaggio was a living reminder of the city's proud pre-Giants
baseball history. During these years, DiMaggio was an admired local celebrity,
whose name could frequently be found in the newspapers, particularly in the
columns of Herb Caen, San Francisco's most famous newspaperman.

For his part, Lefty O'Doul played and managed, or both, for the Seals for
a total of 20 years. This created a strong bond between the city and O'Doul,
who was a colorful and compelling figure. Irwin Herlihy, who was a Seals fan
as a boy and young man describes the importance of O'Doul to the Seals:
"Through it all there was only one hero for me, that is until 1951 [O'Doul's last
season managing the Seals]. Lefty O'Doul was Mr. San Francisco baseball. To a
young man he was everything you could want in a hero."[7] Having the Seals so
strongly identified with O'Doul, who continued to be a major baseball figure

after the Giants arrived, in part because of his work with baseball in Japan, made it possible for San Francisco baseball fans to learn about and appreciate the Seals long after they had stopped playing. Additionally, because O'Doul was one of the few PCL stars who left the major leagues to return to the PCL despite his ability to hit well wherever he played, his story, which after a while was only known in San Francisco, was seen by many San Francisco baseball fans as evidence that the PCL was indeed a very good league and the Seals a very good team. O'Doul was so well liked in San Francisco that in the early 1960s he was rumored to be the next manager of the Giants.[8] O'Doul's memory, and thus indirectly that of the Seals, is kept alive at the new Giants' ballpark, where a bridge (over McCovey Cove), plaza, and entrance are all named after the famous Seal.

Although, by the time the Giants got to San Francisco, their new hometown was clearly the second biggest and most important city in California, that was not the case for all of the history of the PCL. Los Angeles only exceeded San Francisco's population for the first time in the 1920 census, and then by only 70,000. By 1930, however, Los Angeles had almost twice the population of San Francisco.[9]

Population figures aside, for most of the first half of the twentieth century, San Francisco was recognized as the financial and cultural capital of the West Coast. It was also understood to be the more cosmopolitan of the two cities. In the late nineteenth and early twentieth centuries, when baseball's popularity was beginning to accelerate, San Francisco, following the boom started with the Gold Rush of 1849, emerged as a center of commerce and industry on the West Coast. Richard Walker describes San Francisco's centrality and importance to the global financial sector during this time:

> In the third quarter of nineteenth century, San Francisco's gaggle of *nouveaux riches* were kings of all they surveyed, reigning over an extractive empire stretching to Alaska, Mexico, and Hawaii. With 150,000 people by 1870 and 350,000 by the end of the century, the city held about one-fifth of the populace of the entire West Coast and climbed to seventh largest city in the country. . . . San Francisco used its mercantile network, transportation system, and financial clout to bring the western U.S. under its hegemony. . . . San Francisco became the financial hub of the West, with an overwhelming concentration of depository and correspondence banks, insurance and underwriting companies, stock exchanges, and brokerage houses.[10]

The late California historian Kevin Starr wrote of the San Francisco of the 1890s as having a "dawning ambition to become a center of world trade and a busy point of arrival and departure for international traffic."[11] Nobody would have said that about Los Angeles at the end of the nineteenth century

San Francisco maintained this position until well into the twentieth century, despite falling behind Los Angeles in population by the 1920s. Additionally, in the years before World War II, when automobile travel was not as widespread, San Francisco's relative density helped develop a stronger fan base for the Seals, as most San Franciscans could either walk or get to Seals Stadium relatively easily by public transportation.

In 1946 Lefty O'Doul's Seals won the PCL by four games, winning 115 of 183 games. That team drew more than 670,000 fans for the season. This was a PCL, and minor league, record that lasted until the 1980s. There were many big league teams that as late as the 1970s, including the Giants in 1972 and 1974 to 1976, did not draw that many fans over the course of the slightly shorter big league season. The 1946 Seals drew more fans than either the Philadelphia Athletics or St. Louis Browns that year, although the Athletics averaged more fans per game.[12] The owner of that Seals team, Paul Fagan, also instituted a $5,000 minimum salary for that team. That was the same as the major league minimum at the time.[13] The postwar years were not the only era when PCL attendance was comparable to that of the American and National Leagues. Almost a quarter century earlier, in 1922, the Seals won another league championship, this time over the course of a 199-game season. They won the league by four games, winning 127 and losing 72. Their attendance that season was 426,021, more than that of four of the 16 teams. On a per game basis, the Seals drew better than the Phillies and Braves in 1922.[14]

Because the Seals had been such a good team for generations, and because San Francisco's population did not grow nearly as fast as that of Los Angeles in the years following World War II, the Seals lingered longer in the memories of San Francisco baseball fans than that of either the Stars or Angels did for Los Angeles baseball fans. One additional piece of evidence for this was offered by Jerry Cohen, the owner and founder of Ebbets Field Flannels. Ebbets Field Flannels sells caps, T-shirts, sweatshirts, and other memorabilia largely from teams that no longer exist, including Negro League and PCL teams. In response to a question, via email, about which PCL team is the best seller, Cohen responded, "The SF Seals far outsell any other PCL team."[15]

The enduring legacy of the Seals helps keep the memory of the PCL alive,

but it also overshadows some of the other great PCL teams, most notably the
Los Angeles Angels. Keeping the memory of the Angels alive is more difficult
for a number of reasons. First, since 1961 there has been a big league team
called the Los Angeles Angels, California Angels, and various odd combina-
tions of Los Angeles and California, but always the Angels. On the one hand,
this creates continuity between the PCL and the American League, but it also,
particularly with the passing of time, makes it more difficult to single out the
legacy of the PCL Angels.

Additionally, there are no figures of the stature of Lefty O'Doul or Joe
DiMaggio who were strongly identified with the Angels and remained that
way after the Angels ceased to exist, as those two famous players did with the
Seals. Several well-known big leaguers played for the Los Angeles Angels of
the PCL, including Sam Crawford, a Hall of Fame outfielder, longtime Tigers
teammate of Ty Cobb, and still the all-time triples leader. Crawford, however,
was not from California, but from Wahoo, Nebraska—and was known as
Wahoo Sam when he was playing. He played four years with the Angels from
1918 to 1921, after the conclusion of his big league career. He hit very well during those years, with batting averages ranging from .292 to .360, but he was
never a true Angeleno the way the DiMaggio brothers or Tony Lazzeri were
real San Franciscans. Another former PCL Angel was Gavvy Cravath, one of
the great sluggers of the pre–Babe Ruth deadball era. Cravath was a Southern
Californian, but he played his last game with the Angels in 1907. Other former
Angels include people like Jimmie Reese, Jigger Statz, and Tommy Lasorda, but
none of them had a deep connection to the team, although Lasorda continues
to be strongly identified with Los Angeles baseball.

The gap in how the Seals and Angels are remembered also probably has
something to do with the two cities themselves. While both San Francisco and
Los Angeles are highly transient cities, with large populations of immigrants
from other countries and migrants from other parts of the United States, San
Francisco grew less rapidly during the middle of the twentieth century, so
Seals fans and their children were a bigger part of San Francisco from, say,
1980 or so to 2000 than comparable fans of the PCL Angels in Los Angeles.
Additionally, while it is true that in the American gestalt the West represents
the future and the East the past, and there is less focus on local history in
either city than in places like New York or Boston, it is also probably the case
that there is a greater awareness of history in San Francisco, at least during
the first decades after the two teams moved west.

The Angels, nonetheless, have an impressive legacy. They were almost always a strong and contending team, winning ten PCL championships. They are better remembered than most teams that have not played a game in close to 60 years, and the official Minor League Baseball website recognizes the 1934 Angels as the greatest minor league team ever.[16]

THE END OF THE PCL

The PCL has never exactly gone away. It is currently a fully affiliated minor league, with 16 teams in 14 states including Texas, Florida, Oklahoma, and many other states that are very far from the Pacific Ocean. Because there are now big league teams in West Coast cities from San Diego to Seattle, the PCL has been forced inland. There are PCL teams today in West Coast states California and Washington, but the cities in which they play, Sacramento and Tacoma, are not on the coast. The PCL's move eastward has occurred gradually with West Coast cities being phased out as they acquired big league teams.

The last season of the PCL as an independent, albeit mostly affiliated minor league was 1957, the year before the Giants and Dodgers came to California. It is easy to presume from this that it was the Dodgers and Giants moving west that facilitated the collapse of the independent PCL, but the causality is actually reversed. The decline of the PCL, beginning in about 1947, made it more possible for the Giants and Dodgers to move west.

In 1946, the first full season of baseball since the end of World War II, when the Seals were again PCL champions and set the attendance record for minor league baseball, reflected a boom time for the PCL. That boom was surprisingly short-lived. In that regard, the PCL, like the Giants and Dodgers on the other side of the country, went from new heights of popularity to facing very grave problems at a surprising speed.

The postwar boom, which included a continued population shift to California, unprecedentedly widespread affluence, and growing cultural import, also saw the slow collapse of the PCL. There were several reasons why this happened, but three stand out as the most significant: the rise of television, the integration of MLB, and the decline of barnstorming.

The 1950s were the decade when television went from being a new invention that was not widespread and only found in a few homes to being very widespread and found in most American homes. In Theodore White's book about the 1960 presidential election, *The Making of the President, 1960,* the first of the now-familiar postelection books of campaign journalism, he described television in the 1960s. He wrote about television's impact on that election, but the core analysis is more broadly applicable:

> Ten years earlier (in 1950) of America's then 40,000,000 families only 11 percent (or 4,400,000) enjoyed the pleasures of a television set. By 1960 the number of American families had grown to 44,000,000, and of these *no less than 88 percent, or 40,000,000, possessed a television set.* . . . By the summer of 1960 the average use of the television set in the American home was four or five hours out of the twenty-four in each day. . . . [I]t is now possible for the first time to answer an inquiring foreign visitor as to what Americans do in the evening. The answer is clear: *They watch television.*[17]

As television grew, it became an increasingly important medium for experiencing baseball. While in the 1950s baseball was not televised anywhere near the extent it is today, there was still much more baseball on television than ever before. Programs like *Game of the Week*—broadcast on CBS and ABC during the 1950s and for many years announced by Dizzy Dean, who was eventually joined by Pee Wee Reese—as well as the World Series brought the major leagues into the homes of Americans for the first time.

For fans on the West Coast, the growing importance of television, and baseball on television, meant that big league baseball was no longer an abstraction that they could only read about and occasionally hear on the radio—for example, during the World Series—but it was something they could see on at least a weekly basis. As good as the PCL had always been, by the 1950s the National and American Leagues were offering a superior product. Television made that conclusion apparent to fans on the West Coast. This gradually weakened perceptions of the quality of baseball in the PCL and undermined enthusiasm for those teams, which was reflected in the declining attendance figures.

James Walker and Robert Bellamy describe how baseball on television in general, and the *Game of the Week* more specifically, weakened minor league baseball throughout the country:

> Focusing on one major contest per week made each game special . . . offering quality MLB games that eroded local allegiances to minor league teams. The TV game of the week coincided with a major transformation of MLB that would bring franchise relocation . . . and then expansion. . . . From 1953 to

1965, the game of the week's first era, Major League Baseball became much more major, and Minor League Baseball much more minor.[18]

Although baseball in the 1950s was generally televised only once a week during the regular season, meaning that direct competition between major and minor league games only occurred on that day, fans who watched big league baseball on television could not help becoming more interested in the story lines, pennant races, and teams in the big leagues than they had been in previous decades. This made it more difficult for West Coast fans to continue to follow with great interest the teams and players of the PCL.

The remaining two major factors that contributed to decreasing interest in the PCL, the integration of big league baseball and the decline of barnstorming, are related. The PCL, like the National and American Leagues, had been segregated at the time Jackie Robinson broke in with the Dodgers; like the big leagues, it began to desegregate after 1947.

Jackie Robinson's impact on both baseball and the entire country was, of course, extraordinary. He made us a better country and struck a blow against the institutional racism that treated millions of African Americans unfairly. He also deepened the connection between baseball and American culture as he brought the nation's struggle with racism and segregation into the forefront of the baseball world. Robinson also made big league baseball into a better, more competitive, and more exciting game. This was in part because Robinson was both an excellent and an exciting player. His aggressive baserunning was something that had not been seen in the big leagues in decades. However, Robinson's larger impact was realized as more top African American players followed him into the big leagues, primarily the National League. By the mid-1950s, players like Willie Mays, Roy Campanella, and Larry Doby had, along with Robinson, established themselves as among the very best players in baseball. Frank Robinson, Henry Aaron, and others followed shortly after that.

Jackie Robinson grew up in Pasadena, near Los Angeles. Frank Robinson, one of the best African American players half a generation younger than Jackie Robinson, grew up in Oakland. Many of the best African American players in the decades since the 1950s, including Ozzie Smith, Eddie Murray, Rickey Henderson, and Barry Bonds, have also been from California. Smith and Murray were teammates at Locke High School in South Central Los Angeles. Nonetheless, in the 1950s, as today, the African American population was not concentrated on the West Coast, except in a few cities, but rather in the South, the Northeast, and scattered areas of the Midwest. For African American players growing up in these parts of the country, the big leagues were a distinctly more attractive option than the PCL, especially since it was not widely known by anyone (regardless of race or ethnicity) outside of the West Coast. Thus, the National League, which was ahead of the American League in welcoming nonwhite players, benefited much more from the desegregation of organized baseball than the PCL did. This further widened the gap in quality of play between the big leagues and the PCL.

The desegregation of the big leagues also opened the door to dark-skinned Latino players, who had previously been excluded because of baseball's apartheid. This meant that by the mid-1950s a number of excellent players from the Caribbean were making their marks in the big leagues, such as Roberto Clemente from Puerto Rico and Orestes Minoso from Cuba. Caribbean baseball culture had long been in relatively close proximity to the big leagues of the East Coast—close enough for some major league teams to conduct spring training in Cuba, the Dominican Republic, and Puerto Rico in the 1940s and 1950s—and players from these islands were more aware of the National and American Leagues than of the PCL. This also helped move top talent to the big leagues and expand the gap between the big leagues and the PCL.

Integration of MLB not only dramatically improved the quality of play at the big league level, but had an effect on other baseball structures as well. The most obvious of these was that, once the big leagues began to draw top African American players, the Negro Leagues declined into irrelevancy. More accurately, the decline that had begun in the World War II era accelerated.[19]

The integration of big league baseball was the first step in the postwar development of baseball that gradually brought more of the top talent in the world to the big leagues. A result of this was that other forms of baseball became less popular and ultimately either were folded into big league baseball, like the post-1957 PCL, or disappeared entirely, like the Negro Leagues. Barnstorming more or less went the way of the Negro Leagues and gradually faded away during the 1950s. The best big league players no longer barnstormed in the winters, in part because fans in remote places began to have access to televised baseball.

The impact of all this on the PCL was that baseball, in the minds of postwar Americans, became associated with MLB. The ability to see big league players on television regularly in the 1950s, and the better quality of play and players on the field, made MLB more attractive to fans even as far away as California or Oregon. As MLB got stronger and drew more of the best players, independent leagues no longer operated at a distance—either literally or figuratively—from the big leagues; where a generation ago they had the space to cultivate their own fans and draw great players, they were now having to compete with the

National and American Leagues. The Negro Leagues became home to players who were either too old or not quite good enough to play in the big leagues. The PCL, with its not quite big league–not quite minor league status, did not fit in well into this postwar baseball framework, either. It didn't help that, beginning in the mid-1940s, so many PCL teams were affiliated with big league teams, making it less likely for the best players on the West Coast to stay long in the PCL before heading east to the major leagues. Thus, over time, fans lost interest in the PCL, and the cycle of low attendance and low salaries was fed by a poorer quality of play.

WEST COAST BASEBALL BEYOND THE PCL

The PCL, like the National and American leagues, was segregated for most of its existence. On the West Coast, this meant that not only were African Americans excluded, but most Mexican Americans—Ted Williams was a major exception—and Asian Americans were excluded as well.[20] Given the large Japanese American population of California, this was a significant policy that affected many ballplayers.

The Negro Leagues, which were such an important part of the American baseball landscape in the years until Jackie Robinson first played for the Brooklyn Dodgers, however, were not a presence on the West Coast. This was partially due to demographics. In the early twentieth century, the African American population of the West Coast was small compared to the Deep South or growing cities of the Northeast and Midwest. In 1930, for example, there were only 81,000 African Americans in California out of a total population of more than 5.5 million. By 1950, that number had grown to more than 450,000, but by then the Negro Leagues were in decline.[21]

Geography also prevented the Negro Leagues from having teams in California. The African American population of the state was concentrated in Los Angeles and the Bay Area, so those would have been the natural places for Negro League teams. However, there were no significant African American populations anywhere outside either of those regions. Therefore, the almost 400 miles between Los Angeles and the Bay Area would have been the shortest distance these teams would have traveled. Beyond that, the teams would have had to travel as far afield as Texas and perhaps Denver or Portland to find other sizable African American communities. For an institution that relied almost entirely on buses for transportation, this would not have been possible. During the years the major leagues were segregated, African American players from California who wanted to compete at the highest level had to go east to play for Negro League teams.

In a case of extraordinarily bad timing, the one attempt to create a viable Negro League on the West Coast occurred in 1946, only one year before Jackie Robinson's rookie year with the Brooklyn Dodgers. The league was called the West Coast Baseball Association and consisted of only six teams, the Fresno Tigers, Los Angeles White Sox, Oakland Larks, Portland Rosebuds, San Francisco Sea Lions, and Seattle Steelheads.[22] A combination of logistical problems, involving things like securing continued access to ballparks, and lack of interest, as reflected in low attendance, doomed the league to failure before the first season was over.

Among the two most famous players who appeared in that league were Sam Jones and Lionel Wilson. Jones was a pretty good pitcher, who went on to win 21 games and finish second in the Cy Young balloting in 1959, while playing for the Giants in only their second year in San Francisco. He pitched in one game for the Oakland Larks in 1946. Wilson was a left-handed pitcher on that same Larks team, who also only played in one game. Wilson never played organized baseball after 1946, but he stayed in Oakland and eventually served three terms as mayor of that city between 1977 and 1991.

Racial politics on the West Coast have always been different than the rest of the country because of the demographic differences. While the West, in general, always had fewer African Americans than the Deep South, Northeast, or even Midwest, most of the country's Asian Americans and Mexican Americans were, at least for the years the Dodgers and Giants were playing in New York, concentrated in the West and Southwest. Thus, the story of baseball in Los Angeles and San Francisco, and in California more generally, cannot be fully told without looking at how these groups—excluded from the National and American Leagues as well as the PCL—played baseball in the pre–Jackie Robinson era.

Japanese Americans were unusual among immigrant groups to the United States in that for them playing baseball was not just a way to prove themselves as Americans, but also to create links with their country of origin. Accordingly, baseball was extremely popular and important for Japanese American immigrants on the West Coast. For these Japanese Americans the outlet for this passion for baseball was a network of town teams, semipro teams, and other baseball clubs that played against each other and against white, African American, and Mexican American teams in California and throughout the West, particularly in the years before World War II. These teams were not organized in the way the PCL or other leagues were, but they nonetheless had high levels of play, were very competitive, and were followed very closely by Japanese American baseball fans.

During World War II Japanese Americans were interred in camps throughout the West and even parts of the South. This was one of the most shameful episodes in American history, as American citizens were rounded up and put in camps for no reason other than the country from which they had immigrated. Even this human rights abuse and the terrible conditions inside the camps could not dislodge a love of baseball from Japanese Americans. In the camps, there were baseball teams and competitive leagues. A few players and teams were allowed to travel outside the camps for games, while the games inside or adjoining the camps drew enormous crowds as the people who were interred were desperate for entertainment and distraction.

Most reasonably informed baseball fans know that big league players and teams barnstormed to Japan beginning in the late 1920s. This helped popularize the game in Japan and later helped rebuild United States–Japan relations following World War II. However, it is less well known that Japanese teams came to the United States and were part of the fabric of semipro, barnstorming, and other informal baseball settings. These teams came mostly to the West Coast, as it was closer and there were large Japanese American communities who were enthusiastic about seeing these players and could provide them with help and support.

California is far enough away from the Caribbean that players from the Dominican Republic and Cuba were never a big part of baseball on the West Coast until the Dodgers and Giants moved there. However, there has been a large Mexican population in California since before California was part of the United States. Most Mexican Americans were also excluded from the PCL, but they played baseball, too. Most of this was centered around Los Angeles, but teams from the city also competed against Mexican teams, both in the United States and in Mexico. According to Francisco Balderrama and Richard Santillan in their history of Mexican American baseball in Los Angeles:

> Regardless of their age, players and the Los Angeles community prized baseball as a venue where Mexican athletic talent and skill were tested against African Americans, Japanese Americans, and Anglo Americans, especially for the amateur and semiprofessional teams. . . .
>
> Baseball has been a foremost presence in the lives of Mexican Americans since the early twentieth century. . . . [B]aseball contests and teams involved nearly the entire community and often had important social, political, and

cultural dimensions. Along with family and religion, baseball was an institutional thread uniting the community.[23]

AFTER THE WAR

During the first years of the twentieth century, the concentration of big league baseball teams in the original 11 major league cities was logical both demographically and logistically. In 1910, for example, each of the six largest cities in the United States had at least one team. Those cities combined were home to 12 of the 16 big league teams. The largest city without a team was Baltimore, which at that time had the seventh most people of any city in the country. The smallest city that year with a big league team was Washington, D.C., the sixteenth largest city in the country, with a population of just over 331,000. San Francisco was the eleventh largest city in the country, and the most populous on the West Coast. Los Angeles was seventeenth with just under 320,000.[24]

By 1950, that had changed. There had been no franchise movement in the intervening 40 years, but Los Angeles, with no big league team, had become the fourth largest city in the country. The six largest cities were still well represented, with eight teams. However, Cincinnati, with just over half a million people, was the eighteenth largest city in the country and the smallest city with a big league team.[25]

During the first decade of the twentieth century, when the American League was emerging as a partner to the National League, and the two together were beginning to form what is now known as MLB, the logic for teams being concentrated in the Northeast and Midwest was clear. Big league baseball would look totally different, and probably would have collapsed altogether, if it had sought to be national from the beginning. The travel alone would have been an enormous obstacle that would have made it necessary to structure the leagues differently.

Thus, the de facto structure of parallel big leagues in different parts of the country was a reasonable one, probably the only reasonable structure for the game in these early years. This was reinforced not only by high-level independent leagues like the PCL, but also by the sprawling Negro Leagues network that provided some of the very best baseball in one region, the South, where there were no big league teams.

It is easy, and mostly pointless, to imagine that organized baseball might have developed very differently. The ultimate dominance of the National and

American Leagues was neither preordained nor guaranteed. It is possible that these regional leagues might have been strengthened, leading to some kind of an annual tournament between the winners of the National League, American League, national Negro League, PCL, and perhaps even champions from the Mexican and Caribbean leagues. In 1945 or so, this may have even looked like the most likely option. At that time, the PCL was seeking to become a third major league, and the integration of the major leagues, and American society as a whole, while only a few years away, did not look inevitable at all. It is also possible that the Giants and Dodgers could have moved west to anchor a new independent PCL with teams in Seattle, San Diego, another in Los Angeles, and a few other cities on the West Coast. This league then could have been a formidable third major league. None of these possibilities seem realistic now, and they may have never been. However, few baseball people in 1925, 1935, 1945, and perhaps even 1955 would have seen the National League and American League as each evolving into leagues with 15 teams, representing cities in every corner of the United States and one city in Canada.

The PCL, various semipro Japanese American and Mexican American teams, barnstorming big leaguers coming to California in the offseason, and even the short-lived West Coast Baseball Association are all part of the West Coast baseball tradition that ultimately gave way to MLB's dominance in the West and all of the United States. These institutions created the kind of love for the game that made it easier for the Giants and Dodgers once they got to the West Coast. Although they had been in decline for years, the Giants and Dodgers' move west was also what finally finished off these institutions.

5

THE MOVE

The departure from New York of the Giants and Dodgers was a rupture in the fabric of big league baseball that also had a significant impact on New York City and the psyches of thousands, perhaps millions, of New Yorkers. The question of why the Dodgers and Giants left, and the impact of that move on New York has been explored extensively.[1] This chapter will touch on some of these issues, but primarily describe the debates around the move west.

Understanding the debates is important because it helps explain attitudes that affect the historiography of the move even to this day. The extreme nostalgic feelings that can still be encountered in Brooklyn, and the persistent view that the cause of the Dodgers' departure lies with powerful outside forces, have their roots in a specific understanding of why the Dodgers and Giants left.

In the bigger picture, different interpretations of why the Dodgers and Giants left New York have bearing on broader questions of urbanism and racial politics in midcentury New York and America. The Dodgers and Giants were just baseball teams—albeit in the way that Bob Dylan or Leonard Cohen were just songwriters. These two teams were also powerful and influential cultural and business institutions, which made decisions in the late 1950s that reveal a lot about America and the urbanism of that time.

The debate, indeed most of the analysis about the move in general, has always focused primarily on what was occurring in New York, as if San Francisco and Los Angeles were just accidental cities into which the Giants and Dodgers more or less randomly fell. That approach leaves out a big part of what was happening at the time. This chapter will also explore the role of some of the political community forces in Los Angeles and San Francisco that were part of the courting and winning of the Dodgers and Giants.

THE DEBATE

From the New York perspective, the story of why the Dodgers and Giants left New York is one with many potential villains and no heroes. The two individuals most often described as the villains in this story are Walter O'Malley, the owner of the Dodgers, and Robert Moses, the New York City Parks Commissioner, who for decades was an extremely powerful behind-the-scenes force in New York City politics and land use.[2] O'Malley and Moses make great villains. By the late 1950s, both were older, wealthy men who looked the part. O'Malley was a big, affluent-looking man, frequently seen with a cigar in his mouth and a smile on his face. Moses cut a very different profile. He was a prototypical permanent government type. Despite never holding elected office, he had been in and around government in New York for decades. Although he had been credited with building much of modern New York City, by the late 1950s criticisms around the racial impact of his work and his undemocratic style were beginning to be more frequent.

Every Brooklynite of that era knew that if you were stuck in a room with Hitler, Stalin, and Walter O'Malley and had only two bullets, the right thing to do was to shoot O'Malley twice. This was gallows humor that was not exactly fair to O'Malley. However, a more challenging question for Brooklynites might be what to do if Robert Moses were in that room as well and you had only one bullet. Obviously this joke is somewhat in poor taste and can only be taken so far. Moses was an autocratic and insensitive official, and O'Malley broke the hearts of many fans of the old Brooklyn Dodgers, but neither committed genocide or were brutal dictators. Neverthless, the joke reflects the need many felt to find somebody to blame for the Dodgers' departure. The strong need for a villain in this story is in part a way to deflect attention from the failure of the people of Brooklyn to support the Dodgers. That is the third angle in this debate—that Dodgers and Giants fans simply stopped supporting their teams and left O'Malley and Stoneham little choice but to head west. Again, all these narratives focus more on the Dodgers than on the Giants, but many of the same issues pertain to both.

Concerning O'Malley and Moses, Paul Hirsch writes,

Few men in sports history have been vilified to the extent Walter O'Malley was when he moved the Brooklyn Dodgers to Los Angeles in 1957. Over recent decades, New York City Parks Commissioner Robert Moses has begun to share some, if not all, of the blame for the Dodgers' move. Countless trees have died supporting the contention that either O'Malley ripped the franchise from the bosom of a borough that has never recovered its identity or self-esteem, or that Moses did not understand the value of keeping the Dodgers in Brooklyn and was unnecessarily obstinate when it came to reaching a mutually satisfactory agreement with O'Malley to keep the team in the city.[3]

In broad strokes, the blame-O'Malley argument is that the Dodgers owner betrayed the people of Brooklyn, ripping a good team out of the borough for no reason other than personal avarice. Implicit in this story is the view, which may in fact be accurate, that Brooklyn was a special place and that the Dodgers had a particularly intense relationship with the people of Brooklyn, more so than those of other places with their teams. O'Malley, according to this story, had a good thing in Brooklyn, but could not resist the greener, and more lucrative, call of Southern California. This story line tends to view Horace Stoneham as a more or less hapless dupe of O'Malley, willing to move his Giants to the less lucrative, and chillier, destination of San Francisco, to ensure the success of O'Malley's plan.

Moses is a less obvious villain, but his role in the departure of the Dodgers and Giants stems from his alleged unwillingness to agree with the teams about constructing new stadiums. Robert Caro, in his extraordinary biography of Robert Moses, *The Power Broker*, describes how Moses

rammed through, over the opposition of protesting neighborhoods, approval for new expressways, for two great new bridges, the Throgs Neck and the Verrazano . . . killed, over the efforts of Brooklyn Dodgers owner Walter O'Malley, plans for a City Sports Authority that might have kept the Dodgers and Giants in New York, and began happily to plan the housing projects that he had wanted on the sites of the Polo Grounds and Ebbets Fields all along.[4]

Caro's biography of Moses is one of the great works of biography in the twentieth century. Through the biography of Moses, an extraordinary man who was very important and influential, but never particularly well known outside of New York, Caro tells the story of New York through much of century and explains how the city came to look and feel the way it does. He offers nuanced and compelling descriptions of important New Yorkers like Al Smith, Franklin Roosevelt, and several mayors, most prominently Fiorello LaGuardia. Even today, anybody seeking a good understanding of New York, or of urban policy making more generally, would do well to read Caro's masterpiece. *The Power Broker*, however, is not a short book. It has 1,159 densely packed pages as well as notes, an index, maps, and photos. In that book, which can hardly be described as laudatory toward its subject, Caro only mentions O'Malley, the Giants, or the Dodgers in the passage just quoted. Horace Stoneham is not mentioned at all. There is reason to believe that if Moses was really the primary reason why the two teams left, Caro would have spent more time on the question in his comprehensive biography, or would have made sure that the material he wrote in earlier drafts made it into the final published version of the book.

Robert Murphy's 2009 work on the Dodgers and Giants' departure from New York, however, offers a good explanation of how Moses came to be seen as a major villain in this story.

> Caro's tome effectively demonized Moses for decades, and it influenced authors discussing the death of the Brooklyn Dodgers. Moses, being the man in the middle of all New York capital projects, is a central character in the story of the Dodgers' and Giants' departure, and the issue of their staying or leaving, at least on the Brooklyn side, was far more important than Caro's meager treatment of it indicated. It is fair to conclude that with all the power he embodied, he could have done more to keep the teams in the city, but not to suggest that he had no interest or made no effort to help them do so.[5]

The intensity of the debate over whether O'Malley or Moses is more at fault for the Dodgers and Giants' departure—and the more general need to find somebody to blame—has been used by several generations of Brooklynites (primarily) and other New Yorkers to avoid looking more closely at the extent to which they are responsible for the two teams' departure for California.

In the 1950s, despite the growing popularity of television and baseball's growing experimentation with televising more games, most teams still relied substantially on selling tickets to generate revenue. As noted earlier, attendance in general was down across baseball during this period. This contributed to franchise moves in the early 1950s as well as to the consistent allure of the West Coast for the Giants and Dodgers.

Table 6 provides an overview of some attendance figures from 1947 to 1957. In 1947, the Dodgers and Giants ranked second and third in attendance. The Yankees ranked first in attendance that year, as they did in every year from 1949 to 1952.[6] In 1947, the three New York teams combined to draw 5,587,526 fans.

Table 6. Attendance for New York Teams, 1947–57

Season	Giants (Rank)	Dodgers (Rank)	Yankees (Rank)
1947	1,600,793 (3)	1,807,526 (2)	2,178,937 (1)
1948	1,459,269 (6)	1,398,697 (5)	2,373,901 (2)
1949	1,218,446 (7)	1,633,747 (4)	2,283,676 (1)
1950	1,008,878 (9)	1,185,896 (5)	2,081,380 (1)
1951	1,059,539 (7)	1,282,628 (4)	1,950,107 (1)
1952	984,940 (8)	1,088,704 (4)	1,629,665 (1)
1953	811,518 (10)	1,163,419 (4)	1,537,811 (2)
1954	1,155,067 (5)	1,020,531 (8)	1,475,171 (2)
1955	824,112 (12)	1,033,589 (8)	1,490,138 (2)
1956	629,179 (15)	1,213,562 (4)	1,491,784 (2)
1957	653,923 (15)	1,028,258 (10)	1,497,134 (2)

The number in parentheses following the total attendance figure for that year is the ranking of the Giants or Dodgers across the major leagues. There were 16 big league teams during these years. Sources: Ballparks of Baseball, "1940–1949 Ballpark Attendance" (2017), http://www.ballparksof baseball.com/1940–1949-mlb-attendance/; "1950–1959 Ballpark Attendance" (2017), http://www .ballparksofbaseball.com/1950–1959-mlb-attendance/.

In that year slightly more than 28 percent of all fans who attended big league games did so in New York City.

The Yankees' solid attendance rankings during these years, never falling below second place, or 1,475,000 annual attendance, demonstrate the complexity of the problem facing the Giants and Dodgers. The Yankees' ability to draw relatively good crowds contrasted with the Dodgers and particularly the Giants at a time when the Bronx, Brooklyn, and northern Manhattan were all undergoing demographic changes. The Yankees during these years were the best team in baseball, winning nine pennants and seven World Series in these 11 years, but the Dodgers had great teams too and went to the World Series six times in this period. The Yankees continued to lead, or come close to leading, the big leagues in attendance throughout this period, while the Dodgers and Giants never ranked higher than they did in 1947.

The data also suggests that attendance in these years was bad throughout big league baseball. It is no surprise that a pennant-winning team with colorful stars like Mickey Mantle and Yogi Berra, playing in New York City, regularly led the American League in attendance; however, in several of these years, they drew only around one and a half million people. Baseball could have continued like that, as it had been for years, but it would have remained a much smaller and less moneyed industry and would have quickly fallen behind other sports, like football and basketball.

From 1953 through 1957 the Milwaukee Braves led the big leagues in attendance every year. They had some very good teams in those years, finishing second three times, third once, and winning the pennant in 1957. They had two future inner-circle Hall of Famers, Eddie Mathews and Warren Spahn, for all five of those years. A third, Henry Aaron, joined the Braves in 1954. The Braves, during these years, were an excellent team, with several high-profile and exciting stars, but that is not the primary reason why they drew so well.

The Braves' remarkable attendance was largely due to big league baseball being new to Milwaukee in 1953, the year the Braves moved there from Boston. This could not have been lost on O'Malley and Stoneham. It could also not have been lost on these two men that Milwaukee was smaller than Los Angeles or San Francisco and much closer to other big league cities—Chicago is fewer than 100 miles from Milwaukee—than either of the West Coast cities were. If the Braves could draw so well in Milwaukee, these men must have thought, imagine what the Giants and Dodgers could do on the West Coast.

There was also another side of the Braves' success in Milwaukee. After they stopped winning in the late 1950s, attendance began to fall; by 1966 the team had moved to Atlanta, meaning they had only made it 13 years in Milwaukee. Few could have foreseen such a scenario for Milwaukee in the early 1950s, but that experience was something that would resound in later years for the Giants. Interestingly, as early as 1954, one former big leaguer and San Francisco Seal, who was also a native San Franciscan, foresaw this concern for a major league team in San Francisco. When asked about the possibility of the Giants coming to his hometown, Dom DiMaggio commented: "San Francisco would support a big league team even if it didn't win for the first three years. After that, the shine would be off. . . . After a while even the ushers wouldn't show if the team stayed in eighth place every year."[7]

While the Dodgers and Giants regularly trailed the Yankees, and later the Braves, in attendance, the two teams confronted different economic realities during this period. With the exception of 1954, when the Giants won the pennant over the second-place Dodgers by five games, the Dodgers outdrew the Giants every year during these years. Moreover, they were in the top 25 percent of all teams for attendance in six of these 11 years and only fell into the lower half for attendance in 1957, when they were understood to be leaving Brooklyn at the end of the season. The Giants, however, were a different story. Beginning in

1952, their attendance was low, with the one exception of their pennant-winning 1954 season. Their inability to draw well in the year immediately following their World Series victory made it clear that they were struggling.

These attendance figures suggest that as the 1950s went on, New York was no longer well served by having three big league teams. This did not mean that the departure of both the Giants and Dodgers to the West Coast was inevitable. For example, the Giants could have moved to a city not quite as far away as California, with the Dodgers remaining in Brooklyn. Had the city moved faster to get the Dodgers a new place to play, that might have happened.

The attendance numbers demonstrate the extent to which Giants fans more or less abandoned their team sometime in the early 1950s, while the same was not quite as true for their cohorts in Brooklyn. Attendance only reveals part of the environment in which the Dodgers and Giants had to make decisions. Despite drawing reasonably well during the 1950s, changes in Brooklyn were making it apparent that the Dodgers were approaching difficult times if they intended to stay in their borough. Thus, although Walter O'Malley still had a viable business in Brooklyn in these years, any reasonably astute business-person could have seen that keeping the team in Ebbets Field was not a good long-term plan. O'Malley did not wait until his problems reached the level of those of the St. Louis Browns, who drew a total of fewer than 1.2 million over the course of their final three seasons combined before moving to Baltimore, or the Boston Braves, who drew a total of fewer than 1.8 million their final three seasons in Boston before moving to Milwaukee.

O'Malley, Moses, and indeed the people of Brooklyn, including those who had recently left the borough for the suburbs, were all being influenced by the same battery of changes in New York. The postwar boom had drawn people out of overcrowded urban neighborhoods into the suburbs. This meant that a trip to see the Giants or Dodgers play represented an investment of time and money that was made more difficult because, naturally, older urban ball-parks like Ebbets Field and the Polo Grounds did not have sufficient parking. Additionally, the changing demographics of the neighborhoods of northern Manhattan and central Brooklyn meant that many white fans were no longer comfortable going there. Suburbanization, problematic infrastructure, crime, and racism came together by the mid-1950s to make it clear that the Giants and Dodgers could not continue in their longtime home fields.

Doris Kearns Goodwin, who grew up rooting for the Brooklyn Dodgers and was saddened and upset by their departure, captures this dilemma well in her memoir *Wait Till Next Year,* when she recounts how she used to keep score while listening to or watching the Brooklyn Dodgers' games.[8] She would then describe the events of the game to her father after he returned home to Long Island from work every day in New York. Goodwin's family lived in Rockville Center, Long Island, at the time. The story is a sweet one, although perhaps a little treacly, about the bond baseball brought to one father and daughter, and it offers some insight into how a well-known historian first encountered the challenge of telling a compelling story about events that had already occurred. However, it is difficult to encounter Goodwin's description without thinking that one of the reasons the Dodgers eventually left Brooklyn was precisely because people like the Kearns family had moved out of the borough.

CHANGE AND STABILITY IN NEW YORK

Cities are constantly changing, few more than New York. Anybody who does not believe this should simply approach a native New Yorker over the age of 40, ask them if much has changed since they were younger, and be prepared to listen for several hours. New York today is much safer and more affluent than it was 25 years ago. Lower-income and high-crime neighborhoods of 25, or even 15, years ago are now home to expensive lofts, organic grocery stores, bespoke haberdashers, and the like. Immigrants from places like the former Soviet Union and Central America have made their mark on the city during these years as well.

The 1950s may have seen New York at the height of its influence, wealth, and importance, but that moment came and went very quickly. By the mid-1950s, the demographic, economic, and cultural forces that have been a big part of the story of New York for the last 60 years or so were beginning to emerge. Movement of Puerto Ricans to New York began in earnest in these years. These were the first Latinos to move to New York in large numbers, but many more followed, from places such as the Dominican Republic and, more recently, Mexico and other parts of Central America and the Caribbean. It may be difficult for any New Yorker under 60 to believe, but in the 1950s there was not a lot of Spanish spoken in New York. Yiddish was a much more useful language in New York back then. Today, on the other hand, Spanish is ubiquitous in New York, while the only New Yorkers who speak Yiddish are a handful of Orthodox Jews, some very old Jewish people, and a smattering of younger Jews interested in learning their grandparents', or great-grandparents', language.

New York's economy was still very strong in the 1950s, but the movement of middle-class families to the suburbs and the beginnings of the shrinking of the city's manufacturing jobs contributed to declining tax bases that made it harder to address the problems of crime, education, and infrastructure that dogged New York for most of the last third or so of the twentieth century.

Although New York has long been a city with enormous numbers of immigrants, who have contributed to the cultural vitality of the city, that immigration had ebbed quite a bit by the middle of the last century. The proportion of foreign-born New Yorkers peaked in the 1910 census, when 40.79 percent of all New Yorkers had been born outside the United States. This is an astounding number, but not one that is unimaginable to today's New Yorkers. In 2013, for example, the proportion of foreign-born New Yorkers was 37.2 percent, the highest since 1910. That number has fluctuated a great deal during the century between 1910 and 2013. The period when New York City had the lowest proportion of foreign-born residents was between 1950 and 1970, when it ranged from 18.2 to 22.6 percent.[9] During those years, immigration had slowed and most of the foreign-born population was made up of older European immigrants from earlier in the twentieth century.

This is significant because it suggests that the years leading up to, and immediately following, the Dodgers and Giants' departure from New York were, with regard to demographics, unusually stable, even stagnant. This was almost certainly understood by businesspeople like O'Malley and Stoneham, who saw middle-class New Yorkers and their jobs leaving the city to be replaced by lower-income nonwhites, whom the owners and many fans—not without racist sentiment—viewed as undesirable and even dangerous. From the vantage point of the late 1950s, when New York was entering a period of multi-decade economic decline, few could have foreseen the dramatic increase in immigration beginning in 1980, as well as other developments that have led to the economic rebirth of the city in recent years.

THE CALL OF THE WEST

Much of the debate around the departure of the Giants and Dodgers has focused on questions such as whether or not the two teams were economically viable in New York, what the demographic changes in the neighborhoods around Ebbets Field and the Polo Grounds meant for the two teams, or the why the city could not build new ballparks for the two teams. These questions are important but they also overlook a very important set of questions about what was occurring in San Francisco and Los Angeles during the years leading up to the move.

Dodgers owner Walter O'Malley (*left*), celebrating a Brooklyn Dodgers victory with manager Walter Alston, later took the team to Los Angeles and made it one of baseball's most successful franchises. (Courtesy National Baseball Hall of Fame and Museum)

Giants owner Horace Stoneham brought his team to San Francisco, but success did not come easily to the team in their new home. (Courtesy National Baseball Hall of Fame and Museum)

When Jackie Robinson played his first game with the Brooklyn Dodgers in 1947, he changed baseball, and America, forever. (Courtesy National Baseball Hall of Fame and Museum)

Willie Mays was one of the greatest players ever and was one of the game's biggest stars for the San Francisco Giants when they moved west. (Courtesy National Baseball Hall of Fame and Museum/McWilliams)

The great Dodgers lefty Sandy Koufax, posing with four baseballs after tossing his fourth no-hitter. (Courtesy National Baseball Hall of Fame and Museum)

Juan Marichal was the first great Dominican player in the major leagues and remains the best pitcher in San Francisco Giants history. (Courtesy National Baseball Hall of Fame and Museum)

Steve Garvey was the face of the Los Angeles Dodgers during much of the 1970s and early 1980s. (Courtesy National Baseball Hall of Fame and Museum)

Barry Bonds was a wonderful all-around player, who became the face of the performance-enhancing drug scandal in the 1990s and 2000s. (Courtesy National Baseball Hall of Fame and Museum/Yablonsky)

By the early 1950s, after Pacific Coast League (PCL) attendance had peaked around 1946, San Franciscans and Angelenos remained loyal to the Seals and Angels, but were increasingly aware that they too were big league cities who deserved major league franchises. By 1953 or 1954, there was a growing interest in both cities in getting an MLB team. Some even viewed this as inevitable. This view was concisely stated by Los Angeles mayor C. Norris Poulson who declared that "it is absurd to envision a population center of this size without Major League Baseball."[10]

When the 1950s began, there had been no big league expansion in half a century, so the two West Coast cities did not entertain the idea of getting an expansion team in the early and middle years of that decade. Instead, rumors circulated around some of the big league teams with the worst attendance problems, like the Philadelphia Athletics or St. Louis Browns, about possibly moving west. However, it was not just the struggling teams that were rumored to be on the move. The Giants and Dodgers were parts of these discussions from the mid-1950s on. Even the Yankees, a team that still plays in the same borough where it played in 1923, were briefly rumored to be on the move, with Los Angeles the most likely destination.

Bill Leiser began a 1954 column in the *San Francisco Chronicle* with the observation that "smart commentators are writing that the New York Yankees may be prepared to move to Los Angeles." Leiser was bearish about this possibility, closing the column by tempering the rumor. "We'd say there is a far greater chance the Giants of the National League will move out of New York. . . . There'll be serious talk of the Giants moving long before there's a serious threat of the Yankees moving."[11]

The Yankees were the most successful team on and off the field in the mid-1950s and had been for decades. It is very unlikely that the powerful Yankees ownership team of Del Webb and Dan Topping ever gave much thought to moving, but it is significant that there was talk of this, at least in the San Francisco and Los Angeles media. Confidence was so strong in the West Coast during these postwar years that it did not strike civic boosters as absurd that the Yankees would uproot to a new city, because they might make even more money than they were making in New York. That is, in fact, exactly what the Dodgers did a few years later.

The two mayors usually credited with bringing the Giants to San Francisco and the Dodgers to Los Angeles, respectively, are George Christopher, who became mayor in 1956, and C. Norris Poulson, who took office in 1953. San Francisco began advocating for a major league team while Christopher's predecessor,

Elmer Robinson, was in office; however, according to Robert Garratt, "[Christopher's] tenacity, persistence and tact had much to do with convincing Stoneham that San Francisco would be an attractive choice."[12] Moreover, Poulson and Christopher tried to work together to bring big league baseball to California. Garratt further observed that "both mayors knew their chances of bringing Major League Baseball improved considerably with two teams on the West Coast."[13]

San Francisco and Los Angeles had to persuade the Giants and Dodgers that moving west was a sensible and lucrative idea, but this was the easy part of the work. The demographic and economic data spoke for itself. In the years immediately following World War II, San Francisco and Los Angeles were growing in population and booming economically. Moreover, both cities had long and impressive baseball histories. However, there were other obstacles closer to home for the leaders of San Francisco and Los Angeles hoping to bring big league baseball to their cities.

First, neither city had a ballpark that would be a good long-term home for a major league team. Seals Stadium and Wrigley Field of the PCL were able to suffice for a few years, but they were a far cry from the larger, modern ballparks surrounded by ample parking that both teams wanted. Additionally, despite the PCL being in decline, there was a great deal of residual affection for the Seals in San Francisco and Angels in Los Angeles. Some fans wanted these teams to become part of the two existing major leagues. Others still wanted the PCL to become a third major league. However, as the 1950s went on, it became increasingly apparent that neither of these outcomes was possible.

As discussions about the Giants and Dodgers moving to new homes on the West Coast became more serious, it became increasingly clear that to fans of the Seals and Angels this would mean the end of their teams. From today's perspective, it may seem obvious that swapping a minor league team for a big league team, especially a star-studded one like the Dodgers or one for whom Willie Mays played center field, was a clear upgrade, but this was less apparent at the time. Loyalty to existing PCL teams ran deep and multigenerational. Additionally, the move would disrupt existing big league loyalties for West Coast fans. For example, many fans of the Seals may have already had a favorite big league team that was not the Giants; for them, becoming Giants fans required shaking off two team loyalties and replacing them with a new one.

As late as the summer of 1957, when the discussions with the Giants were very far along, a "Save the Seals" organization sought, ultimately unsuccessfully, for a ballot initiative, asking voters to choose between the PCL and the Giants.

Elmer Norton, the vice president of the group, explained their reasoning. "Substitution of a 'poor' Giants team for a 'good' Seals team; there is little difference between the PCL and major league competition; and pay TV [thought to be part of the Giants arrangement] is outrageous."[14]

CANDLESTICK POINT AND CHAVEZ RAVINE

The task of building, funding, and locating space for stadiums raised a different set of questions in each West Coast city, questions that New Yorkers like Stoneham and O'Malley had not previously confronted. Seals Stadium was understood to be the likely temporary home for the Giants if they were to move to San Francisco, but this was never going to be a permanent solution. The ballpark worked for the PCL, but was simply too small to be anything more than an interim home for a big league baseball team. Even after the city built additional seats, Seals Stadium still had a capacity of just under 23,000 during the time the Giants played there. The field itself, however, was about the right size for a big league ballpark of the era. It was 410 to straightaway center, 340 down the left field line, 385 to right, 375 to left center, and 397 to right center. It played as a slight pitcher's park during the two years the Giants made it home.

Seals Stadium, however, had one big positive—its location. It was at the corner of 17th and Bryant in San Francisco's Mission District. While that was very much a blue-collar neighborhood, which within a few decades would have its share of crime and violence, it was also centrally located and well served by public transportation. Equally importantly, it was relatively warm. A New Yorker like Horace Stoneham could be forgiven for not understanding San Francisco's complex system of microclimates, but that would quickly prove to be a costly mistake for Stoneham and the Giants.

Native San Franciscans, or anybody who spends a substantial amount of time there, grow to know the city's quirky weather patterns and how they contrast with those of cities on the East Coast or in the Midwest. It never gets as cold in San Francisco as it does in winter on the East Coast or in the Midwest. The temperature rarely dips below freezing, and it only snows once every few decades, but there is much more to the weather than that. In San Francisco, seasonal variations in weather are mild and often unpredictable, but the climate can change a lot over the course of the day, and from neighborhood to neighborhood.

Seals Stadium was located in a part of town that was warmer than most. It was far enough east that the fog from the Pacific Ocean did not get there during the day most of the time. It was also far enough inland that it did not get the chilling breezes from San Francisco Bay. Seals Stadium was, therefore, in many respects an ideal ballpark for a high-level minor league team in San Francisco. It was just not quite big enough for a big league team.

Like San Francisco, Los Angeles did not have an MLB-ready venue to host a new baseball team. Unlike the Giants, however, the Dodgers did not spend their first years in Los Angeles in a minor league baseball facility that was not quite big enough. Wrigley Field—the home of the PCL Los Angeles Angels—would have been the natural place for them if the Dodgers had wanted to pursue that route.[15] Instead, the Dodgers played their first four seasons in Los Angeles at the Los Angeles Memorial Coliseum. The Coliseum was an enormous stadium that had been used primarily for college football and occasionally for other huge events. Don Zminda provided a good description of the venue:

> With a seating capacity of over 90,000, the Los Angeles Memorial Coliseum was the largest ballpark ever to regularly host major league games. It was also one of the strangest. Games at the Coliseum could contain 250-foot home runs to left, 440-foot flyouts to right, and fielders staggering to pick up the ball in the park's combination of single-decked seats, bright sunlight, and white-shirted fans (some of them movie and television stars).[16]

The Coliseum had enough capacity and parking for big league baseball, but the dimensions were not right, so it was not a long-term solution for the Dodgers.

The lack of adequate modern baseball facilities was one of the major reasons the Giants and Dodgers were leaving New York, so it was apparent they were not moving to California, or anywhere else, unless new state-of-the-art stadiums would be built for them. Although San Francisco and Los Angeles, and both of their mayors, badly wanted MLB teams, building new and adequate stadiums for them proved difficult.

The early 1960s were the first years of a spate of stadium construction for big league teams that would grow to include new stadiums for expansion teams, like the Mets and the San Diego Padres, as well as new facilities for teams that were not moving, like the Cincinnati Reds and the Philadelphia Phillies. Today most of these stadiums are collectively viewed as the worst in big league history. They were anonymous, impersonal, multi-use buildings that offered little to baseball fans, but that is not how they were seen at the time.

Ballparks built before World War II—of which two, Fenway Park in Boston and Wrigley Field in Chicago, are still in use today—were built primarily in urban areas that were accessible either by foot or by public transportation. These ballparks often only had capacity for 30,000 or 40,000 fans. Ebbets Field had a maximum capacity of between 18,000 and 35,000, depending on renovations, from the time it was first used in 1913 to its last season in 1957. Most of these older ballparks did not have sufficient parking or room to build parking lots.

When the Giants and Dodgers began to think more realistically about moving west, one of their primary concerns was to have modern stadiums with big capacity and enough parking. Access to public transportation was much less of an issue. This raised very different political, geographic, and practical challenges for San Francisco than for Los Angeles. San Francisco is, and was, not only much smaller than Los Angeles, but also much more compact. San Francisco is only 49 square miles, about one-tenth the size of Los Angeles. San Francisco is also bound by water on three sides and mountains on a fourth. San Francisco is part of a much bigger Bay Area region, but Mayor Christopher and others had no intention of seeing the Giants find their home in the East Bay or down the peninsula after working so hard to bring big league baseball to the city.

By the late 1950s, the 49 square miles that constitute San Francisco were already relatively densely settled. Its 1960 population of 740,316, while down from 1950, would not be exceeded until the year 2000.[17] The city did not have the tall apartment buildings particularly in the southeast part of the city that are seen today, and several of the industrial areas south of Market Street were not very residential, but there was not a lot of obvious room to grow or build a stadium.

Open spaces in San Francisco included the Presidio and Golden Gate Park, but the former was a military base that continued to be used in that capacity until the end of the Cold War, and the latter a beloved urban park, so building a ballpark in either of these places was not a real possibility. Kezar Stadium, home at that time of the 49ers football team, was probably not big enough for the Giants. Moreover, its location just south of Haight Street in the eastern part of Golden Gate Park was already a congested residential neighborhood with limited parking. It is intriguing, however, to imagine how San Francisco in the late 1960s and later might have been different if the Giants had made their home more or less in the middle of Haight-Ashbury.

There were some areas that made sense as possible sites for a new ballpark. One of these was Candlestick Point, located in the southeast corner of the city, close to the airport and with good highway access from Highway 101 and even Highway 280, the major ways into and out of San Francisco from the south. Candlestick Point is one of a handful of small peninsulas jutting out into San Francisco Bay from southern San Francisco. It is near the neighborhoods of

Hunter's Point and Bayview, which were both lower-income African American areas at the time, but because fans were going to get there by car the Giants' ownership was less concerned about the neighborhood. Horace Stoneham was instead very concerned about parking. The absence of sufficient parking was one of the issues that Stoneham believed had hurt the Giants' attendance in New York. He wanted ten thousand parking spaces adjacent to any new ballpark. There was enough space at Candlestick Point to ensure this.

Candlestick Point had been a major shipbuilding hub during World War II that drew migrants, particularly African Americans, to San Francisco and the Bayview–Hunter's Point neighborhood. However, shipbuilding was no longer a major engine of employment in the area by the time the Giants moved west.

Candlestick Point, like many parts of San Francisco, was built substantially on landfill. Buildings built on landfill are particularly vulnerable to earthquakes, a genuine hazard in most of California. Fortunately, when the biggest earthquake in more than 80 years hit the Bay Area in 1989, shortly before the start of a World Series game at Candlestick Park, there were no deaths at the sold-out ballpark.

It is not known for certain how Candlestick Point got its name. According to Alex Bevk of Curbed San Francisco, "There's lots of debate on how Candlestick Point got its name. Some say it's because of the long-billed Curlew shorebird that was nicknamed candlestick. Others say it's because an early U.S. Coast Guard survey named it after a rocky outcropping. Those versions are boring, so we prefer the bit of lore claiming that the burning of abandoned sailing ships resembled lighted candlesticks as they sank into the bay."[18]

Candlestick Point was in many ways the ideal location for a ballpark. It was accessible by highway; close to the rest of the city, but not in the middle of a residential neighborhood; and had ample space for parking. The ballpark that was built there, Candlestick Park, or the 'Stick, was a prototype for the new era of multi-use stadiums. The Oakland Raiders football team played there one season when it first opened. The San Francisco 49ers called Candlestick home from 1971 to 2013, playing there for years after the Giants moved to their new ballpark in Mission Bay. The Beatles famously played their last concert together at Candlestick Park in 1966. Candlestick was easily accessible for fans in cars from most of the city, the peninsula, and even from the East Bay because the Oakland Bay Bridge fed onto Highway 101, although those fans, for the most part, stopped coming when the A's arrived in Oakland in 1968.

The construction of a new ballpark at Candlestick Point did not create major problems with the community in the area. Wade Avery, writing on the San

Francisco history website FoundSF, argued that the new ballpark was viewed very positively by the community at the time.

> However, in August of 1958 the community saw an opportunity to grow it hadn't seen in over a decade, the construction of a new stadium for the San Francisco Giants baseball team right in the BVHP [Bayview–Hunter's Point] community. The park, which was initially designed to hold 43,000 spectators, injected life into a community that had begun to struggle with employment following the downturn of the slaughterhouse and shipbuilding industries. On April 12, 1960, Candlestick Park opened its gates and with it came hope that the stadium would lead to more jobs and development in the area around the stadium.[19]

Candlestick was completed in time for the 1960 season, meaning that San Francisco had found a permanent home for the Giants before Los Angeles did the same for the Dodgers. This was a source of pride for many San Franciscans, for whom the rivalry with Los Angeles had always been more than just baseball. The ballpark was built quickly, but the process was not without scandal, political intrigue, and a whiff of corruption.

> A closer look at the events leading to the planning and building of Candlestick will show a different picture, one that suggests tension, confusion, shenanigans (if not duplicity) underhandedness and backroom dealings between City Hall and the builder. Candlestick was trouble from its conception, long before any dirt was moved, plans sketched or pilings sunk. Pressure to open for the 1960 season, exerted by the city and the Giants, produced cost-overrides and corner-cutting that would greatly affect both the pace and workmanship in the stadium's construction.[20]

These construction-related problems would be a harbinger of problems that the Giants would have with Candlestick Park during all of the 40 years they called it home. There were two problems that were immediately apparent regarding Candlestick Park. The first, and often overlooked, problem is that from the beginning the ballpark was never well served by public transportation. That could be said for San Francisco in general, a city whose residents have long been very dependent on their cars.

There is some irony here, because one of the initial reasons both the Giants and Dodgers left New York, and locations that were relatively easily accessible by subway, was because they wanted ballparks with more parking. There was enough parking at Candlestick Park, but that did not help people, notably children and the elderly, who did not want to, or could not, drive to Giants games. Additionally, as traffic in the Bay Area grew more congested between the 1960s and the 1990s, the absence of decent public transportation became a more glaring problem.

There was never rail service to the 'Stick. The little cable cars might have climbed halfway to the stars on Russian Hill, but they never came anywhere near Candlestick Park. The San Francisco Municipal Railway, known to all as Muni, sought to resolve this problem by running a network of buses to the ballpark on game days. The buses, known as the ballpark express, would take fans from various parts of the city on express routes to the game for a higher fare than normal. They were erratic and slow moving, but they got fans to the game most of the time.

Public transportation has long been inadequate in San Francisco. Despite the city's progressive politics, which would suggest a commitment to decent public transportation, the city's topography and vulnerability to earthquakes have raised particular challenges with regard to, for example, underground metros and the like. Additionally, San Francisco is not immune to the car culture that helped define postwar California. For years, visitors to San Francisco who have heard about the city's cosmopolitan, even European, reputation have been surprised to see the extent to which San Franciscans rely on their cars. This began to change in the early twenty-first century, when cycling began to become more common in the hilly city and then later as popular private car services such as Uber and Lyft began to make an impact on San Francisco.

In a 2015 overview of public transportation in San Francisco, Peter Hartlaub wrote, "San Francisco is among the most beautiful spots in the world, but it's an exceptional nightmare from a transit point of view. In addition to the obvious problems with the hills, early settlers were forced to deal with swamp-like conditions to the east, sand dunes to the south and west and corrupt politicians in every crevice of the city."[21]

By midcentury, the swamps were no longer a problem, but the hills and earthquakes remained. San Francisco opened its first underground light rail line in 1980, the N Judah, using some of the same tunnels that were built for the Bay Area Rapid Transit (BART). This line began to take commuters from downtown all the way to the Outer Sunset, the westernmost neighborhood in the city, but this was decades after, for example, the New York City subway had begun operation. The N remains one of only a small handful of San Francisco light rail lines that have even some of their routes underground. None of these went to Candlestick Park, although most go to the Giants new home in the South Beach neighborhood.

The other problem that plagued Candlestick Park for almost 40 years was the weather. The legend now is that the 'Stick was the coldest, windiest, and most unpleasant place to watch a game in big league history. That is not entirely true. Candlestick was a beautiful place for a day game. It was often sunny, but rarely too hot; while there was generally a breeze, it was rarely too strong or cold.

Night games at the 'Stick were an entirely different experience. With the wind chill, the temperature could easily drop into the 40s or 30s. Even hardened San Franciscans, who didn't need Mark Twain to tell them how cold their summers were, generally were not prepared for that. Night games at Candlestick were sufficiently cold that fans huddled in clothes that were more suited for winter in New York than a summer baseball game, sipping lukewarm coffee or hot chocolate, often leavened from flasks tucked into their coats, hoping for a quick Giants win. The cold made going to a game an unpleasant experience for fans, but the wind also added color, and created problems, on and off the field. The perhaps apocryphal story of Stu Miller being blown off the mound by a gust of wind in the 1961 All-Star Game may be the best example of this, but there were many more quotidian cases, such as hot dog wrappers, napkins, and other forms of ballpark detritus blowing around in mini-whirlwinds all over the field, distracting fans and players alike.

Social critic and lifelong Giants fan Greg Proops offered this fond and affectionate, but also realistic, remembrance of Candlestick Park: "In Candlestick . . . I saw on the field, a fox, a skunk, not at the same game, dogs, cats, birds. It was the windiest park in the history of mankind. Peanut shells in your Coke . . . from the third inning on . . . that was from someone else. . . . The hamburgers there were rock hard. . . . There was no beef in them, only sawdust colored black."[22]

The wind and cold weather at Candlestick made it a very unpleasant place for fans, but also unappealing for players, particularly power hitters, who did not like seeing the wind turn home runs into fly outs. Additionally, infielders and outfielders found it more difficult to do simple things like catch high fly balls in the windy environs of the 'Stick. One result of this was that good hitters often did not want to come to the Giants. This problem became more acute after free agency in the 1970s. The weather also kept revenues down, as the Giants always struggled with attendance. Thus, there were many good players whom the Giants could not afford, but who did not want to play in San Francisco anyway. That is not exactly a good formula for a successful baseball team.

The Dodgers, who played at the Los Angeles Memorial Coliseum for four seasons before moving to the brand-new Dodger Stadium for the beginning of the 1962 season, where they have remained ever since, ended up with a much better ballpark that the Giants did, at least until the Giants moved in 2000. However, the Dodgers had a much more difficult time getting the ballpark built and encountered much more opposition from residents of Chavez Ravine, the area where Dodger Stadium now stands.

Jerald Podair argues that the fight over building Dodger Stadium, of which the residents of Chavez Ravine were only one consideration, was emblematic of a broader debate about the future of Los Angeles in the 1960s. He argues that supporters of the proposed stadium "envisioned Dodger Stadium as an important step in revitalizing Los Angeles's lackluster downtown area and as one of the central amenities that marked the emergence of a sophisticated and modern city. Stadium critics rejected the idea that a great American city required a central core studded with civic monuments."[23]

The fight over the construction of Dodger Stadium, according to Podair, also "became the locus for an argument between those who envisioned Los Angeles as an everyday city of neighborhoods and services and others who saw it as a modern, growth-focused city with a vibrant central core featuring civic institutions that announced themselves to the nation and the world."[24]

Thus, while the construction of a new stadium for the Dodgers was essential to the success of Walter O'Malley's initial decision to move the Dodgers west, it also was an important issue for the city of Los Angeles itself during a period of growth and prosperity, but also transformation.

Chavez Ravine, a canyon north of downtown Los Angeles, had been home to a Mexican American neighborhood, actually several Mexican American neighborhoods, for most of the twentieth century by the time the Dodgers moved west. Chavez Ravine was, in many respects, a great location for a ballpark. It was centrally located, close to major thoroughfares, but with space for a lot of parking. Access by public transportation was not good, but that was never a major issue for the Southern California ballpark. Chavez Ravine was also a canyon that required a lot of work, leveling hills and the like, before the ballpark could be built.

The initial negotiations around Chavez Ravine were complex. O'Malley wanted 350 acres. The City of Los Angeles did not want to sell O'Malley quite that much. Moreover, they did not own that much of the area and would have to seize some of the surrounding homes and neighborhoods through eminent domain. After months of negotiations, by late 1957, Walter O'Malley and the City of Los Angeles reached an agreement.

If the Dodgers were to come to Los Angeles, they would receive approximately three hundred acres of land at Chavez Ravine for which the city would commit $2 million for grading and the county another $2.7 million to construct access roads. In return the Dodgers would give the city Wrigley Field, valued at over $2.5 million, develop and maintain for twenty-five years a forty-acre public recreation area at Chavez Ravine, and pay an estimated annual $350,000 in property taxes. The city and the Dodgers agreed to share oil and mineral rights, although no such resources had been found at Chavez Ravine.[25]

This was a very good deal for O'Malley and the Dodgers. It is also evidence that, at least at the leadership level, Los Angeles was much more committed to luring the Dodgers than New York had been to keeping them. O'Malley had not asked New York to build a stadium for them, but simply to make the land available at a good price. Los Angeles was willing to do much more than that.

While O'Malley and the Dodgers may have been happy with the commitment of their prospective new city, they may have been puzzled and a bit frustrated when they learned only a few months after making this agreement that politics in California did not work quite the way that it did in New York City. New York was, and remains, a city with a powerful chief executive and a legislature that is usually either dominated by the mayor or unable to do much to stop him. Some may be tempted to think of the New York City Council as a rubber stamp, but that is inaccurate. As Henry Stern, who served in that legislative body for about a decade, pointed out, "a rubber stamp leaves an impression."

When the Dodgers and Giants played in New York, the Board of Estimate, which was declared unconstitutional in 1989, had influence over land-use matters, but was controlled by eight elected officials—three citywide and five borough presidents. There was, and still is, nothing in the political life of New York that compares to the initiative and referendum process that has long existed in California and that threatened to stop the Dodgers from building a ballpark in Chavez Ravine.

In late 1957, opponents to the Chavez Ravine deal gathered enough signatures to place an initiative on the June 1958 ballot. The initiative, known simply as Proposition B, asked, "Shall the Ordinance authorizing and approving the contract set forth therein between the City of Los Angeles and the Brooklyn National League Baseball Club, Inc. and authorizing the execution thereof, be adopted?"[26]

The opposition to the proposed stadium at Chavez Ravine originated from several different places. Some viewed the agreement as a giveaway, where the city was giving the Dodgers valuable land and getting little in return. Many of the people who felt that way wanted the Dodgers to come to Los Angeles, but just not on those terms. A piece of campaign literature for the "no" side urged voters to:

> VOTE NO on "B"—Unless you want to GIVE MILLIONS OF YOUR TAX DOLLARS . . . and MILLIONS OF DOLLARS OF CITY OWNED LAND . . . to a private commercial team for BARS, HOTELS, RESTAURANTS, AMUSE-MENT PARK, APARTMENT HOUSES, STORES, SHOPPING CENTERS,—as well as baseball. . . . Why spend millions of your tax dollars and make a gift of this fabulously valuable land to a private, profit making Corporation?[27]

The piece also listed five members of the Los Angeles City Council who were "in favor of a major league baseball [team] in Los Angeles, but ALL recommend a NO vote on 'B.'"[28]

Some of those who opposed the deal had their own financial interest. For example, leading the opposition to Proposition B was J. A. Smith, one of the owners of the San Diego Padres. Smith's Padres were a PCL team; the big league team of the same name did not come along until 1969. Smith very likely saw stopping the proposed new Dodger Stadium as a last-ditch effort to keep the National League from expanding to Los Angeles, a move that would have, and did, substantially cut into the Padres' fan base.

The proponents of Proposition B presented the new ballpark as essential to keeping the Dodgers in Los Angeles, and they built on the excitement that the Dodgers were generating in the first few weeks of their first season in Los Angeles. Proponents also mobilized celebrities and other famous baseball fans in support of the proposed new ballpark.

Today, the debate over whether or not to build Dodger Stadium at Chavez Ravine is primarily remembered as a struggle between the Dodgers and the Mexican American communities that had lived there for years. The powerful white people who cut the deal had either overlooked or ignored that the land where the Dodgers intended to build their ballpark was not empty park space or abandoned industrial space. Rather it was a neighborhood of lower-income people who had strong ties to the area and to each other.

These people were also largely Mexican American, and had fewer resources and less political influence than most other groups in Los Angeles in the 1950s. The effort to build Dodger Stadium was not the first time the community in Chavez Ravine had been embattled or even displaced. Residents of the area had been in the middle of a pitched battle around public housing in 1949 to 1952, when Los Angeles sought to build its first major public housing development in Chavez Ravine. This was a hotly debated project, primarily on ideological and planning grounds, rather than racial ones. However, most of the Mexican American residents of Chavez Ravine did not support the development because they wanted to keep their community the way it was and did not want to get pushed out of their homes. They resisted through protests, demonstrations, and the like, but were not able to prevent the initial displacement that was done in anticipation of the project being built. As John Laslett points out, "Once the formal purchase and demolition of Chavez Ravine began in earnest, the number of residents remaining there rapidly declined. By December 1952 more than two-thirds of the homeowners, believing further resistance to be futile, had packed up, sold their houses to the City Housing Authority, and left. Fewer than two hundred holdouts still remained."[29]

The proposed housing development in Chavez Ravine was defeated at the polls, ironically by a proposition that was also called Proposition B, but the damage to the communities at Chavez Ravine had already been done.

By 1958, when the more famous Proposition B was on the ballot, the Mexican American community in Chavez Ravine was smaller than it had been a decade earlier. However, the people were also toughened and more aware of the threat facing them, and city politics were beginning to change as well. Los Angeles was still a conservative city, certainly relative to New York, but Mexican Americans had more political representation and influence than they had earlier in the 1950s.

In the early 1950s, the only Latino member of the Los Angeles City Council, Edward Roybal, was a first-term council member, who was either unable or unwilling to vocally advocate for the people of Chavez Ravine. By 1958, Roybal, who later served 15 terms in the U.S. House of Representatives, was a more senior and more powerful member of the council and took a more visible role. Laslett contrasts how, in 1959, "Roybal would give helpful legal advice to the last holdouts when they were threatened with eviction. . . . Nevertheless, as the sole Mexican American on the City Council during these years, and a staunch liberal on many other issues, it is somewhat surprising not to find him speaking out on their behalf when they were faced with mass eviction in 1951–2."[30]

Proposition B passed by a narrow margin, with the "yes" side receiving just 51.9 percent of the more than 675,000 votes cast. The winning margin was only about 26,000 votes and came almost entirely from the eighth (South Central) and ninth (East Side) council districts. The "no" vote was strongest in districts 1, 2, and 3, which were all in the suburban San Fernando Valley.[31]

After the voters passed Proposition B in 1958, a second round of evictions began, aimed at those families who had remained in Chavez Ravine after the early 1950s. These evictions drew political opposition, again from Council-man Edward Roybal, but also largely because the evictions, including scenes of women and children being dragged from their homes by police so that the Dodgers could get their stadium built, were broadcast on television. The imagery and politics of what happened were hard to miss. Mexican American families of modest means were being forcibly removed from a community in which they had lived for decades so that the city could give a sweetheart deal to a millionaire from Brooklyn.

Of course, the story is not quite that simple. O'Malley wanted his ballpark, but there were other city interests and individuals who, perhaps for different reasons, saw replacing a lower-income Mexican American community with a shiny new ballpark as good for the city of Los Angeles. Podair points out that

> the loss of Chavez Ravine rippled through Latino Los Angeles leaving an anguished and bitter legacy. . . . This bitterness is misdirected. It would make nearly as much sense to refuse all dealings with the Los Angeles municipal government [as with the Dodgers] for its role in the destruction in the Chavez Ravine community. . . . But it has been the Dodgers . . . that have been most closely linked in historical memory with the Arechigas [the evicted family that drew the most media attention] and with the visual images of May 8, 1959.[32]

Walter O'Malley thus found himself in the unenviable position of being hated by at least a substantial minority of the people of two of the country's biggest cities. In Brooklyn, this animus lasted for decades. In Los Angeles, these feelings were not as widespread, but they persisted among many in that city's large Mexican American community until at least the early 1980s. Ironically, O'Malley had reached out early to Mexican Americans upon bringing Dodgers to Los Angeles, notably arranging for games to be broadcast in Spanish on the radio, beginning in 1958. Although he only joined the broadcast crew in 1959, Jaime Jarrin is still broadcasting Dodgers games today.

As the years went by, it is also likely that many people began to conflate the two rounds of evictions, the first one that had occurred in 1951 to 1952, due to the proposed housing project that was never built, and the second one in 1958, which preceded the successful construction of Dodger Stadium. While there is no housing project, Dodger Stadium remains as a very visible reminder, at least for some, of what had once been at Chavez Ravine.

The events and politics around the construction of Dodger Stadium was a blemish, perhaps unfairly, on the team, the city, and the ballpark that lasted for decades; however, the ballpark itself was almost immediately successful. Today, only one National League team, the Chicago Cubs, has played in their home longer than the Dodgers have been in Dodger Stadium. The expansion Angels also made Dodger Stadium home between 1962 and 1965. During the last 25 years or so, when many teams, including the Giants, have left ballparks built in the 1960s or 1970s for newer and more modern facilities, the Dodgers have remained in Dodger Stadium, making only occasional and modest improvements. A wealthy team like the Dodgers would only do that if they knew the ballpark was already excellent. The Dodgers led all of baseball in home attendance their first five years in Dodger Stadium and again in 1973–75 and 1977–86. In almost all other years, they have been at or near the top of attendance as well. That is not entirely due to Dodger Stadium, but it is evidence that the ballpark remains sufficient for the needs of a big market team.

Today Dodger Stadium is considered old, almost a throwback to a different era, but when it first opened, it was groundbreaking because it offered amenities and a general experience to fans that was different than other ballparks. Unlike most ballparks up to that time, Dodger Stadium was not just a place to see a baseball game. Dodger Stadium, from its beginning, was family-friendly, with restaurants and opportunities to buy souvenirs in a way that was unprecedented. Walter O'Malley also courted Hollywood personas, so that less famous families could add a celebrity spotting to the list of fun things that could happen at Dodger Stadium. Podair described this as "the first step toward transforming baseball into a commodity of mass leisure, a product comparable to a movie, television program, amusement park, or day at the beach."[33]

In the twenty-first century most major league ballparks offer many shopping, eating, and amusement opportunities in addition to baseball. This has allowed teams to increase the price of tickets and generate more revenue from each ticket holder, thus bringing more money into the game than ever before. This major development began with Dodger Stadium more than 50 years ago. This was part of Walter O'Malley's vision for the Dodgers in Los Angeles, one that was not quite shared by Horace Stoneham in San Francisco. Nonetheless, it is an example of how the move west facilitated more innovation in baseball, including beginning to reimagine the experience of attending a baseball game.

THE MOVE

Explanations of the Dodgers and Giants' move, their last years and months in New York, and the failed efforts to retain them can easily throw up a cast of villains, like O'Malley and Moses; dupes, like Horace Stoneham; victims, like the hard-working people of Brooklyn and, occasionally, New York Giants fans; and even would-be heroes, like the ambitious mayors Norris Poulson and George Christopher, who wanted to put a big league imprimatur on their respective cities.

There is some truth to these explanations and characterizations. Robert Moses never seemed to appreciate what the Dodgers meant to Brooklyn and was clearly not as cooperative with Walter O'Malley as he might have been. O'Malley, for his part, ultimately chose his team's, and his own, financial health over the emotional pull of Brooklyn. Horace Stoneham got stuck with a tougher market and an inferior ballpark when the two teams moved west. As Podair points out, part of the reason O'Malley was so roundly criticized in Brooklyn was "his application of business principles to the management of a baseball club that was perceived by its fans and by the media as constituting a public trust."[34] In this way, O'Malley was also a trailblazer, because within a decade or two of moving the Dodgers west, almost all owners were explicit that their perspective was that of a businessperson.

It is equally clear that there were other factors involved as well. There was almost an inevitability to these events, although most things look inevitable once they have already happened. Forces much bigger than a baseball team, even ones as storied as the Dodgers and the Giants, were behind these moves as well. Population shifts buoyed by improved transportation technology meant that MLB had little choice but to put teams on the West Coast, beginning at some point in the late 1950s or early 1960s. The period of roughly 30 years of decline, leading to loss of jobs, a declining tax base, and rising racial tension and crime, which was beginning in the late 1950s in New York meant that teams based in Harlem or central Brooklyn were not likely to remain workable economic projects. It is possible that New York could have found a way to build a ballpark for one of these teams, but the city had little ability or economic rationale to do that for both teams.

Demand for big league teams grew in both San Francisco and Los Angeles, particularly the latter, throughout the 1950s. As Mayor Poulson noted, by the late 1950s, it was absurd that Chicago had two teams, New York three, and Los Angeles none. Despite this, there was resistance to the Dodgers and Giants in Los Angeles and San Francisco on fiscal grounds as well as due to residual loyalty to the PCL. Additionally, the difficulty in finding space for and building appropriate stadiums for these two teams was significant. The events around the construction of Dodger Stadium created a rift between the team and the city's fastest growing demographic group, which lasted decades. The Giants had a much less tumultuous path to their new stadium, but ended up with a ballpark that was deeply flawed and that contributed to the Giants' subsequent struggles to compete, thrive, or even remain, in San Francisco. It was not until 2000 that the team finally got a ballpark that helped, rather than hindered, attendance and excitement around the team.

6

FIRST SEASONS IN CALIFORNIA

On April 15, 1958, more than 23,000 fans crowded into Seals Stadium, the onetime home of the Pacific Coast League Seals, which was the new home of the San Francisco Giants. The weather in the ballpark was pleasant and sunny. Those San Franciscans who were unable to make it to the game were still aware of the historical nature of the day, as the *San Francisco Chronicle*'s above-the-masthead headline blared, "Giants Open Up," in huge letters. Just below the masthead another headline stated, "S.F. Turns Out for the Giants," accompanied by a photo of a ticker-tape parade for the team on Montgomery Street, in the heart of the city's financial district.

The Giants' opponents that day were the equally new Los Angeles Dodgers. The Los Angeles media also enthused about the day and the game. The top of the sports section of the *Los Angeles Times* was a large headline proclaiming, "Dodgers, Giants Make History Today." The lead article, filed the previous day, opened by asserting the historic nature of that day's game:

> The Titans of the West, Los Angeles and San Francisco, come of baseball age tomorrow afternoon when the Dodgers and Giants play the first major league game in California's history. Tears will be shed in Brooklyn and the Bronx by die-hard diamond devotees as the momentous transcontinental trek of two National League teams from the world's greatest city becomes an accomplished fact.[1]

Los Angeles Times writer Frank Finch's excitement exceeded his knowledge of New York geography. While Brooklynites, and many in Manhattan, were distraught about losing their team, not too many in the Bronx were shedding tears. The Yankees were still there and beginning a season that would bring them their fourth consecutive pennant and a World Series victory.

This was the first big league game for either of these historic franchises in their new homes, and the first big league game ever on the West Coast. Giants starter Ruben Gomez began the match by striking out Dodgers left fielder and native San Franciscan Gino Cimoli, and baseball history had been made. The starting Dodgers pitcher that day was a 21-year-old Don Drysdale, who had won 17 games during his team's last year in Brooklyn in 1957 and was on his way to greater fame in Los Angeles. Gomez was 30 and coming off a 15-win season for the New York Giants. He would only win 17 more games in his career, but that day he outpitched Drysdale.

The Dodgers lineup that day featured Brooklyn stalwarts Pee Wee Reese, Duke Snider, Gil Hodges, and Carl Furillo. Other than Gomez, among Giants starters that day only Willie Mays and shortstop Daryl Spencer had been with the team in New York. Home runs by Daryl Spencer and Orlando Cepeda helped the Giants to an easy 8–0 win. The next day's *Chronicle* also had a huge above-the-masthead headline, "We Murder the Bums." The rivalry appeared to have survived the move west.

THE EARLY YEARS OF THE LOS ANGELES DODGERS AND SAN FRANCISCO GIANTS

When the Dodgers and Giants wrapped up the 1957 season, their last in New York, a part of baseball history concluded, and the final chapter in the history of two of New York's most important teams was written. However, baseball, and both the Giants and Dodgers, continued and ultimately thrived to a greater degree than before the move. Additionally, the first decade, actually the nine years from 1958 to 1966, after the teams moved west were, like most decades, important for understanding the development of big league baseball. The Giants and Dodgers were at the center of many of those developments both on and off the field.

Table 7 provides an overview of the Giants and Dodgers from 1958 to 1966. During these years, the two teams combined to win five of nine National League pennants and three World Series (marked on the table by an asterisk). This was during a period when there were still no divisions within the league. From 1962 to 1968, there were ten teams in the league; before 1962, only eight. There were also three good pennant races in 1962, 1965, and 1966 that were hard-fought battles between the two teams.

Award voting is a flawed way to understand baseball history, because voters do not always give the awards to the most deserving players. Sometimes these mistakes are understandable in the context of the year in question, but sometimes they are not. However, award voting gives a good sense of how players and teams were perceived at the time. For this reason, looking at how remarkably well these two teams did in winning awards helps demonstrate how influential and successful they were during these years. From 1958 to 1966, these two teams

Table 7. Overview of the First Nine Years in California

Season	Los Angeles Dodgers			San Francisco Giants		
	League Finish	Games Behind	Awards	League Finish	Games Behind	Awards
1958	7th	21	—	3rd	12	ROY (Orlando Cepeda)
1959	1st*	—	—	3rd	4	ROY (Willie McCovey)
1960	4th	13	ROY (Frank Howard)	5th	16	—
1961	2nd	4	—	3rd	8	—
1962	2nd	1	CY (Don Drysdale) MVP (Maury Wills)	1st	—	—
1963	1st*	—	CY (Sandy Koufax) MVP (Sandy Koufax)	3rd	11	—
1964	7th	13	—	4th	3	—
1965	1st*	—	ROY (Jim Lefebvre) CY (Sandy Koufax)	2nd	2	MVP (Willie Mays)
1966	1st	—	CY (Sandy Koufax)	2nd	1½	—

Asterisks indicate World Series champions. ROY = Rookie of the Year for the National League; MVP = Most Valuable Player for the National League; CY = Cy Young Award winner for both American and National Leagues.
Source: Baseball Reference (2018), https://www.baseball-reference.com/.

combined to win a total of 11 of the three major annual awards. Based on an average of nine teams in the league per year (because there were eight teams in the National League for four of these years and ten teams for the last five years), two average teams would have combined for six of these awards. This understates the success of the two teams in winning awards, because the Cy Young Award was given to the best pitcher in all of baseball during this period, rather than one per league. Again, not all of these picks were great ones. Maury Wills, for example, was almost certainly not the best player in the National League in 1962—Willie Mays was—but the voting shows that the baseball writers very much saw the two West Coast teams as the center of baseball gravity, particularly in the National League during these nine years.[2]

Although Wills may not have deserved that 1962 MVP award, he was one of the best and most important players on the Dodgers during their early years in Los Angeles. Wills was a shortstop who fielded his position well. He hit for little power, but was extremely fast. In 1962, he set a major league record for stolen bases with 104. That record lasted until Lou Brock broke it with 118 stolen bases in 1974. The record is now held by Rickey Henderson who stole 130 bases in 1982. Wills was also an intense competitor. "By 1962 his teammates viewed Wills as the Dodgers' fiercest competitor. He was their lineup's leadoff man, their offensive catalyst, their demanding on-field leader, and their hardworking, often tormented dynamo, capable of inspiring many of them even as he sometimes infuriated others."[3]

Wills's mark of 104 stolen bases has been eclipsed several times since 1962 and may seem less impressive to fans who remember Henderson, Brock, Vince Coleman, Tim Raines, and more recent speedsters; however, at the time, Wills was one of a small handful of players who were helping to bring the game out of the slow-moving form into which it had devolved during the 1950s. Some perspective on Wills's base stealing following the great era of New York baseball is helpful. Wills's 104 stolen bases in 1962 were more than each single team in the National League in 1947 and every year from 1950 to 1957. During the so-called golden age, the only times any National League team stole more bases than Wills did individually in 1962 was when the Brooklyn Dodgers exceeded that number in 1948 and 1949. The value of the stolen base as an offensive weapon can be debated, but it is an exciting play. In the early 1960s, Wills was not only helping the Dodgers win, but was bringing an energy back into the game that had not been seen in years.

The rivalry between the two teams remained strong during these first years, buoyed by several close races between them; however, the feel of the rivalry,

and of the two teams involved, began to change. First, the image of the Dodgers as "Dem Bums," a team that was never quite good enough to win it all, but
also of a lovable bunch from a less-than-glamorous outer borough, could not
endure in Los Angeles. The nickname is still employed from time to time, but
usually either ironically, or pejoratively by Giants fans.

Two things immediately changed the Dodgers. First, they won the World
Series in just their second year in Los Angeles, beating the White Sox in October 1959. They then went on to win the World Series again in 1963 and 1965,
although they lost to the Orioles in the 1966 series. It was the 1963 World Series
that demonstrated that the Los Angeles version of the Dodgers had a very different gestalt than that of their Flatbush antecedents. That World Series saw
the Yankees and the Dodgers play each other for the championship for the first
time since 1956, when the Yankees had won. Between 1941 and 1956, the two
teams had played each other seven times in the World Series, with the Yankees
winning six times.

The Yankees team that the Dodgers played in that World Series had dominated the American League in 1963, winning 104 games and finishing 10½
games ahead of the second-place White Sox. Although there were a lot of new
faces on that Yankees team, like Roger Maris, Tom Tresh, and Joe Pepitone,
who had not played in any of those Brooklyn Dodgers–Yankees World Series
of the 1940s and 1950s, some players remained. Yogi Berra was 38 years old
and in his last season as a Yankee. He appeared in the 1963 World Series only
as a pinch-hitter. However, the cleanup hitter on that 1963 team and their ace
pitcher had played similar roles in the 1950s—Mickey Mantle and Whitey
Ford were still great players in the midst of Hall of Fame careers when the
1963 World Series began.

Almost all of the stars from the old Brooklyn Dodgers were gone from the
team by 1963. Among position players, only Jim Gilliam and Don Zimmer remained from the 1956 team that lost to the Yankees in the World Series.[4] Among
pitchers, three remained. Two—Don Drysdale and Sandy Koufax—had been
young prospects during the Dodgers' last years in Brooklyn. The third, Johnny
Podres, had been the star of the 1955 World Series, throwing a shutout in Game
Seven to bring Brooklyn their only championship. It was those three pitchers who
started and won all four games of that series, as the Dodgers swept the Yankees.
Amazingly, Podres, Koufax, and Drysdale combined to pitch all but two-thirds
of an inning of that 1963 World Series for the Dodgers. With that World Series
sweep, the worst demons of the Brooklyn Dodgers years were totally exorcised.

Dodgers catcher John Roseboro explained the significance that victory had for longtime Dodgers: "Hell yeah, O'Malley liked it. After the Yankees kicked the Dodgers' asses all those times? I can see where beating them four straight might ease the pain. And man, we didn't just beat them. We gave them a pitching lesson. One time Koufax struck out Mantle on three pitches. Mantle never took his bat off his shoulder. The he turned around and said to me, 'How the hell are you supposed to hit that shit?'"[5]

During the first decade or so after the move, it was the Giants that would be increasingly seen as the hard-luck franchise. That perception remained in place until—in their fifty-third season in San Francisco—the Giants finally won the World Series, but it began in the 1960s, specifically in the 1962 World Series between the Yankees and the Giants. The Giants had won their third pennant in 12 years; with a nucleus of five Hall of Famers at the peak, or coming into their prime—Mays, Willie McCovey, Juan Marichal, Orlando Cepeda, and a still-unproven Gaylord Perry—the Giants were positioned to win a few more pennants before the decade was out.

The 1962 series came down to the bottom of the ninth inning of the seventh game with the Giants trailing 1–0. The inning began with a single by pinch-hitter Matty Alou. The next batter was the leadoff hitter, Felipe Alou. He failed to get a sacrifice bunt down and ended up striking out. Instead of a runner in scoring position with one out, Matty Alou was still stuck on first base. Second baseman Chuck Hiller then struck out for the second out. Things looked pretty bad for the Giants at that point, but the Yankees still had to get one more out. Fortunately for the Giants, the next batter was Willie Mays. Mays hit a double, but Matty Alou was held at third by coach Whitey Lockman, who had been on base 11 years earlier when Bobby Thomson had hit his famous home run. The tying run was now on third with the winning run on second. Alou was a fast runner and might have been able to score if Lockman had sent him. Yankees right fielder Roger Maris had a strong arm, so Lockman's decision was defensible, but Giants fans debated it for years.

The next batter was the Giants star first baseman, Willie McCovey. McCovey had slugged an impressive .293/.368/.590 that year playing mostly against right-handed pitchers. The Yankees pitcher, needing one more out for a complete game shutout, was the righty Ralph Terry. McCovey came up with runners on second and third; with the fast Willie Mays on second base, a hit would have won the game for the Giants. McCovey hit the third pitch from Terry hard, but right at second baseman Bobby Richardson, who caught it for the final out, securing the championship for the Yankees. Interestingly, Richardson was playing McCovey more or less straightaway. That was unusual, as most teams shifted, even back then, against the massive pull-hitting lefty Giants slugger. Had Richardson been playing McCovey to pull, the line drive might have gotten by him and been a game winning hit.

Charles Einstein described that bottom of the ninth inning, still probably the most agonizing in Giants history:

Then with two out, in the ninth inning of that last game, Mays got his double. It was a slicer to right. . . . And Candlestick Park, wet from unseasonal rains, now came to the Yankees' aid. Its rain-soddened turf slowed Mays' wrong-field shot just enough for [Yankees right fielder Roger] Maris to get in front of it and hold Matty [Alou] at third.

Why Yankees manager Ralph Houk now let Yankees pitcher Ralph Terry work to Willie McCovey is an abiding mystery. This was the one bat in the lineup that had hurt Terry the most—and most noticeably at Candlestick: a homer in that second series game, that triple last time up today. The winning run was on second. You could walk McCovey or you could bring in his proclaimed Achilles heel, a lefthanded pitcher. . . .

But Houk did neither. Terry pitched to McCovey. Stretch hit one a mile, but foul. He lined the next and second baseman Bobby Richardson was in its way. Two feet to left, right, down or up and it was through for the ball game and the Series. The hell with it.[6]

Charles M. Schulz expressed the feeling of many Giants fans, as well as Einstein's, exasperation, on December 22, 1962, when readers of Peanuts were greeted by a four-panel cartoon of Charlie Brown looking sad, sitting next to his friend Linus. The first three panels were the same wordless image, but in the last panel Charlie Brown stood up and cried, "Why couldn't McCovey have hit the ball just three feet higher?" A month later, Schulz published an almost identical strip, changing Charlie Brown's lament only slightly: "Or why couldn't McCovey have hit the ball even two feet higher?" Richardson might still have made the play if it had been hit two or even three feet higher, but Schulz had made his point. Even a Giants fan as pessimistic as Charlie Brown probably would have not anticipated that the Giants would not make it back to the World Series for 27 years.

The writers were not the only ones who had a difficult time processing that defeat. Felipe Alou remarked about his failure to get that bunt down, "That's something that's going to die with me. I didn't do my job . . . the lowest point of my life . . . the kind of thing that's engraved on your life, your mind and your heart." McCovey, who hit the ball very hard, just to the wrong place, expressed both sadness, "I cherish being up in that spot. I dreamed about it as a kid. But the results were different from what I dreamed about," and some bitterness, "I mostly blame Richardson for playing me out of position. No second baseman ever played me that close to second base."[7] These comments are not unusual for players on the losing side of a close and hard-fought game, but they were made in 2002, 40 years after the game. That is a measure of the impact of that ninth inning on the Giants.

The 1962 World Series marked the end of the Giants' first five seasons in San Francisco. Although their pennant-winning season had created great excitement in San Francisco, the team had not yet fully worked their way into the hearts of San Franciscans. Maybe if McCovey's line drive had not been caught it would have been different, but the legacy of the Seals, the continued feel that the Giants were not genuinely San Francisco lingered. Einstein's description of this disconnect between the team and its new city captured some of the challenges the Giants faced in their first five years: "The wedding of the nation's proudest city and proudest ball club was not without in-law trouble. To be accepted in San Francisco one had to be successful. Failing that, one should be native-born to the Bay area. . . . The Giants, when they moved west, possessed none of these . . . essential qualifications. They brought with them a sixth-place ball club [and] a roster whose personnel had been born and raised everywhere but San Francisco."[8]

The years 1963 to 1968 were when the Giants solidified their hard-luck identity. During those six years, competition for postseason spots was tougher than at any time in big league history. Expansion had begun to occur, but there were no playoffs, just the World Series, so only one in ten teams made the postseason. By contrast, today one in three teams get a postseason berth. During those years, the Giants finished third once, fourth once, and second four times. The only team in all of baseball with more wins during these years were the Cardinals, who won 547 games, two more than the Giants. The Cardinals won three pennants and two World Series during this six-year span.

Something else changed about the Dodgers in these years as well. During their last decade in Brooklyn, the team was viewed as one with plenty of offense, led by sluggers like Campanella, Snider, Hodges, and Furillo as well as other great hitters like Jackie Robinson, but they never seemed to have enough pitching. Their ace pitcher Don Newcombe was, unfairly and in part due to racial prejudice, viewed as not being able to pitch in the clutch. The rest of their pitchers during these years were never quite as good as their offense. When they finally won in 1955, it was because Johnny Podres, who up until then was a prospect who had yet to become a key member of the team, pitched two great games against the Yankees in the World Series.

This changed once the team got to Los Angeles. From 1959 to 1966, a period in which the team won four pennants and three World Series, the team was led by its pitching, particularly Don Drysdale and Sandy Koufax, but had a hard time scoring runs. During each of the three seasons, 1963, 1965, and 1966, when these two aces led the team to the pennant, the Dodgers gave up fewer runs than any other team in the National League. However, in these three seasons, respectively, they also finished sixth, eighth, and eighth in runs scored. If those Dodgers teams had league-average pitching, they would have been lucky to make it to fourth place.

The 1963 World Series, in which the Dodgers swept the Yankees, was a good demonstration of the Dodgers' new style. Three Dodgers starters, Drysdale, Koufax, and Podres, along with relief ace Ron Perranoski (who pitched two-thirds of an inning), combined to hold the Yankees to four runs and a meager .171/.207/.340 batting line over four games. The Dodgers, against much less formidable Yankees pitching, could only manage 12 runs and a .214/.279/.359 line.

Three years later the Dodgers were on the wrong end of a World Series sweep, but even then they held a powerful Orioles team, led by Boog Powell, Frank Robinson, and Brooks Robinson to only 13 runs and a .200/.267/.342 line. The Orioles had pretty good pitching too, but the Dodgers, who had finished eighth in the league in runs scored during the regular season, could manage two runs and a .142/.236/.192 line over those four games.

MAYS AND KOUFAX

On May 13 of their first season in California, the Giants again drubbed the Dodgers by a score of 16–9, jumping on former Brooklyn ace Don Newcombe for seven runs in 2⅓ innings. The win capped off an unusual four-game set between the two teams, the first two at Seals Stadium and the last two at the Los Angeles Memorial Coliseum. The Giants won all four and outscored the Dodgers by a total score of 32–17. When the game ended, the Giants were in first place, and the Dodgers in last. That day, the Giants offense had 26 hits, including nine for extra bases. Shortstop Darryl Spencer and Willie Mays were the hitting stars of that game. Mays was off to a great start that year, finishing the day hitting a torrid .427/.492/.816 up to that point in the season. Spencer had a double, triple, and two home runs in six times at the plate. Mays walked, singled, tripled twice, and homered twice on the day. First baseman Orlando Cepeda, catcher Bob Schmidt, and second baseman Danny O'Connell had four hits as well.

From a historical perspective, the most important of Mays's plate appearances that day was the walk he drew to load the bases with one out in the sixth. It was not the first time Mays had seen the Dodgers pitcher, a 22-year-old lefty who had been a fringe player on the 1955 championship Brooklyn team. Mays had already batted against him 13 times and had slugged .692/.750/1.125 against him. As Mays threw his bat aside, after his fourth walk in 14 career plate appearances against the erratic southpaw, Mays may have wondered how much longer the lanky Dodgers pitcher would last in the league.

By the time the Giants moved to San Francisco, Mays was already a superstar and baseball celebrity of the highest order. In his five full seasons with the Giants,[9] Mays had won one MVP award, finished fourth in the voting twice, won a Rookie of the Year award, appeared in four All-Star Games, and led his team to a World Series victory. He had won only one Gold Glove for his defense, but that is because the Gold Glove awards were only introduced in 1957.[10] From 1954, when he returned from the military, until 1957, Mays led all National Leaguers with 35.9 WAR, second in all of baseball only to Mickey Mantle, who had 39 WAR during those four years.

On that day in May 1958, the pitcher who walked Mays was not yet a baseball immortal, but he would become one. Moreover, that matchup between Mays and Sandy Koufax was the first on the West Coast between the two stars who would define the next, and in some respects most intense, chapter of the Dodgers–Giants rivalry, as well as baseball in much of the 1960s more broadly. During those years, Koufax and Mays achieved a level of fame that went beyond simply being great baseball players, and have successfully maintained that aura into their 80s. Koufax has not thrown a big league pitch in over half a century, while Mays has not played a game for the Giants since 1972, but each remains the most famous face of their respective franchises since moving to the West Coast. Between 1958 and 1966, Koufax's last year, the two faced each other 109 times. Mays was less successful against the West Coast version of Sandy Koufax, hitting .241/.394/.482. Those were excellent numbers for most batters against Koufax, as the whole league hit .202/269/.311 against Koufax for this period, but not quite up to Mays's overall numbers of .312/.388/.590 during those years. Call it a slight edge for Mays.

In their first few years in California, the Dodgers and the Giants were both fortunate to have star players who, for different reasons, were bigger than the game and became, and remain, national celebrities. In 1961, when Sandy Koufax finally became an impact pitcher, he was only 25 years old, but already in his seventh big league season; Mays was 30 years old and already an established star. For the six years from 1961 and 1966, which was Koufax's last year, Koufax was the best pitcher in baseball, and Mays was the best player in the game—but they both captured something that made them more than just great ballplayers.

To some extent, they both benefited from being at the right place and, more importantly, the right time. In 1961, the oldest baby boomers were in high school and, in what was the last year of the baby boom, the youngest were just being born. Thus, a huge proportion of the male population well into the late twentieth century had spent their formative years watching baseball, which was still broadly popular among boys and young men, when these two players were at the top of their game and playing for good teams in exciting cities. As these people aged, they naturally continued to build the memories and legends of Mays and Koufax.

These two superstars also benefited from the maturation of television during their careers. All of Koufax's big World Series games were televised nationally, as were the All-Star Games in which Mays appeared every year from 1954 to 1972. Additionally, the video from that time is relatively high quality and easily accessible today. Almost every fan has seen Mays's catch in the 1954 World Series, but almost none of us have seen similar video of earlier great center fielders like Tris Speaker or even Joe DiMaggio. Similarly, seeing video of even a few in-game pitches by pre–World War II greats like Walter Johnson or Christy Mathewson is very unusual; however, every left-handed little league pitcher in the twenty-first century has, or should have, studied Koufax's graceful and technically perfect delivery.

Mays is probably the second greatest player ever, behind only Babe Ruth. Competitors for that title include Barry Bonds, who put up better offensive numbers, but whose accomplishments are still tainted by widely believed rumors of his use of performance-enhancing drugs, and pitchers like Cy Young and Walter Johnson, who played around a century ago and whose numbers are hard to analyze in the context of baseball today. Beyond being a great player, Mays was almost the perfect player. He fielded a tough defensive position beautifully, was fast, got on base a lot, and had great power.

Minor league managers occasionally engage in hyperbole, but know they cannot oversell every prospect or they will lose their credibility. Mays's last minor league manager, Tommy Heath of the Minneapolis Millers, described Mays in 1951, shortly before he got called up to the Giants, saying that he was "as good, at this stage, as any young prospect I ever saw. In fact, I'll go out on a limb and say he's the best I ever had anything to do with. What do you look for in a player? You look for a good eye, speed, a good arm, baseball sense. He has 'em all."[11]

Today, Mays is most remembered for his speed and extraordinary and graceful defense, but he was also a great hitter. His 660 career home runs were good for third on the all-time list for 30 years. Henry Aaron only moved into second place ahead of Mays in 1972, the second to last year of Mays's career. Mays also played most of his career in a pitcher's era in a pitcher's park. Thus, while most data-oriented fans acknowledge that Koufax's numbers overstate how good he was, the numbers understate how good Mays was.

Mays made it to the majors during the 1951 season, but found himself hitless in his first 12 times at bat. His first hit came off Warren Spahn, one of the greatest pitchers of that, or any, era. It was not just a hit, but a home run that was lined ferociously out of the ballpark. Mays's manager was Leo Durocher, a man who had been in baseball for 25 years at that time, had played alongside Babe Ruth and Lou Gehrig, and played or managed with or against all of the great home run hitters since the mid-1920s. He summarized Mays's power after that home run eloquently, if profanely. "I never saw a fucking ball leave a fucking park so fucking fast in my fucking life."[12]

Koufax's route to stardom was less direct. He spent six years with the Dodgers from 1955 to 1960, appearing only occasionally and pitching erratically. When he finally put it together in 1961, he began a six-year streak of pitching brilliance that has had few parallels in baseball history. From 1961 to 1966, Koufax had a record of 129–47 including 35 shutouts with a 2.19 ERA and 46.6 WAR. During those six years, he struck out 1,713 and walked only 412. He was an All Star each of those six years, won three Cy Young awards, and finished third in the voting once. He also won one MVP award and had two second-place finishes. He led the league in wins three times, winning percentage twice, ERA five times, shutouts three times, innings twice, and strikeouts four times. And then, after the 1966 season, coming off of what may have been his best year, he retired because he could no longer throw without extreme pain.

It is impossible to understand the impact of Koufax and Mays outside of the context of the racial and ethnic politics of the era—indeed, to seek to separate these players from the broader currents of their era would be intellectually dishonest. Koufax is, along with Hank Greenberg, one of the two greatest Jewish players ever. Greenberg was a slugging first baseman who played from 1933 to 1947. He was a fantastic hitter who almost tied Babe Ruth's single-season home run record in 1938, missed three years of his career serving heroically in World War II, and used his size—he was 6'3" and 210 pounds—to make it clear to opposing players that he was not going to tolerate anti-Jewish bigotry. Greenberg spent 12 years with the Tigers; however, it was with the Pirates, in 1947, the last year of his career, where Greenberg offered words of support, based on his own experience as a minority, to Jackie Robinson during his rookie year.

Greenberg was a hero to American Jews in the 1930s and 1940s. His size, slugging ability, toughness, and service to his country were greatly admired by American Jews during what was the darkest period in our people's long history. However, Greenberg played in Detroit, not Los Angeles or New York, in an era before baseball, even the World Series, was televised.

Koufax was different. He was the first Jewish baseball star of the post–World War II era, the first Jewish star to have his big games televised nationally and to play in not one, but both of the two American cities with the largest Jewish populations. Koufax was born and raised in Brooklyn, played with the Dodgers during their last three years in Brooklyn, and came west with the team. Koufax had his best years as a transplanted New Yorker in Los Angeles, a city with tens of thousands of Jews who had similar personal stories.

As great a pitcher as Koufax was, and as important he is to the story of Jews in American sports, he is still best remembered for a game he didn't pitch. American Jews with little interest in, or even understanding of, baseball know the story of Game One of the 1965 World Series. Although they may not know the whole story, they know that Sandy Koufax, the best pitcher in the world, refused to play on Yom Kippur, the holiest day of the year for Jews.

In 1965, when Koufax made that decision, many American Jews were still changing their name or otherwise concealing their heritage. Outside of a few big cities, missing school or work on Yom Kippur or Rosh Hashanah was something that had to be negotiated, debated, and argued with teachers, employers, and administrators every year. It is not an overstatement to say that Koufax made it easier for every Jew in America to leave work or school on the High Holy Days.[13]

Jane Leavy's analysis of what Koufax's decision meant for American Jews is accurate. "On October 6, 1965, Koufax was inscribed forever in the Book of Life as the Jew who refused to pitch on Yom Kippur. . . . The Dodgers lost but Koufax won. In that moment, he became known as much for what he refused to do as for what he did on the mound. By refusing to pitch, Koufax defined himself as a man of principle who placed faith above craft. He became inextricably linked with the American Jewish experience."[14]

The rest of the story of the 1965 World Series only further burnished the Koufax legend. After the Dodgers lost Game One, Koufax pitched Game Two. In six innings, he struck out nine, but gave up two runs, only one of which was earned. That was a good start against a very good team, but the Dodgers offense and bullpen faltered and the Twins won that game. Koufax then came back to pitch complete game shutouts in Game Five and Game Seven, combining to give up seven hits and four walks, while striking out 20. Koufax's decision to not pitch on Yom Kippur did not stop the Dodgers from winning or stop him from winning the World Series MVP that year. As barriers for Jews began to break down in the 1960s, and as the generations of immigrants and their children began to give way to second- and third-generation American Jews, Koufax was a very visible symbol of what Jews could accomplish in America and that Jews could literally play America's game as well as anybody.

Willie Mays was, of course, African American and not Jewish. He began his career only four years after Jackie Robinson's name was first written in the Dodgers lineup. Unlike Koufax, Mays had a very long career that spanned much of baseball history. In his first season, the Giants won the pennant. In the World Series that year, the center fielder for the opposing Yankees was Joe DiMaggio. Mays also played in the World Series in his last season. The center fielder for his opponent in that World Series was, among others, Reggie Jackson.[15]

Jackie Robinson was born in Georgia, but grew up in Southern California. Many of the other African Americans who starred in those early years of the integrated big leagues were from the North. Larry Doby, the first African American player in the American League, and Monte Irvin, Mays's great teammate, were both from New Jersey. Robinson's teammates Roy Campanella and Don Newcombe were from Philadelphia and New Jersey, respectively. These players had all grown up with racism in the North and, through their experiences in the Negro Leagues, had encountered it in the South as well.

Mays was different. He had grown up in the Deep South, in Fairfield, Alabama, not far from Birmingham, when the apartheid system was still in place. He attended segregated schools his whole life and saw the ugliness and brutality of American apartheid from the time he was a very young boy. Beginning in the mid-1950s, other great African American players from the Deep South began to make their mark on baseball—Henry Aaron and Willie McCovey, for example, were also from Alabama. Mays was the first. Satchel Paige, who began his career in the big leagues in 1948, was also from the segregated South, but by then he was not a young man and never became a big star at the big league level.

Mays's roots in Alabama undoubtedly made a big impact on who he was. The stories of Mays living in Harlem and even playing stickball on the streets with children from the community during his first years with the Giants contributed to the legend of Willie Mays; it is also probably true that as a young African American man from the Deep South, like many similar people before him, Mays felt much more comfortable in Harlem, which was at that time very heavily African American, than in other parts of the city.

Mays was often criticized by other African American players and sports figures for not being outspoken or active enough on civil rights issues. In his excellent 2010 biography of Mays, James Hirsch described how in 1968 during spring training Jackie Robinson "characterized Mays, [and African American teammates] Willie McCovey and Jim Ray Hart as 'do-nothing' negroes.'" Later that year, noted sports sociologist Harry Edwards, who was also African American, referred to "black athletes making it to the top and then shutting up like Uncle Willie Mays."[16] These assertions probably come as a surprise to many, particularly if they have seen Mays discussing his reaction to Barack Obama's election as the first African American president in 2008. "I dreamed about this day ... dreamed about someone in my race being president. Not knowing that anyone would be. ... I cried for most of the [election] night in Chicago."[17] However, these were the views held by some during much of Mays's career.

Robinson is appropriately a national hero and among the most famous trailblazers of the civil rights era. Mays was the better baseball player; unlike Robinson, he became famous almost entirely because of his baseball skills, rather than because of the role he played in the fight for equality and civil rights. Robinson was a great ballplayer, but Mays was the first African American to be seen as an all-time great baseball player.

Mays was also probably baseball's first African American crossover star. He was nationally famous and beloved by both white and African American baseball fans. One interesting legacy of this is that beginning at some point in the 1950s or 1960s, when organized youth sports were increasingly common, children began emulating their favorite players by wanting to wear their uniform numbers. This continues today—so, for example, for much of the period from 1996 to 2014 or so, many kids in New York and elsewhere wanted to wear number 2 because of star Yankees shortstop Derek Jeter. Willie Mays retired in 1973, but if you watch youth baseball closely, you will notice even today that more than occasionally the best player, regardless of race or position, will be wearing number 24, the number Mays wore throughout most of his career. In many cases the player may not even know that was Mays's number, but Mays's fame and impact on American baseball culture was that profound. In many big league parks, before the game, particularly if it is a day game, John Fogerty's 1985 hit song "Centerfield" will be played over the public address system. Forgerty's lyrics remind fans of the pantheon of great center fielders, beginning with the greatest and most famous of all. "So Say Hey Willie, tell the Cobb and Joe DiMaggio. Don't say it ain't so, you know the time is now."[18]

During the 1960s, Mays was a great and extremely famous player, but he was never quite beloved in San Francisco. As late as the mid-1980s, Willie Mc-Covey was probably more popular among Giants fans. The great first baseman, unlike Mays, had never played for the New York Giants and was therefore considered to have a stronger tie to the San Francisco iteration of the franchise. Moreover, Mays was frequently, and unfairly, blamed for the Giants' failure to win another pennant after 1962. This is often the fate of the best player on an underachieving team. Jack Clark, a star-crossed Giants slugger in the late 1970s and early 1980s suffered a similar fate.

Charles Einstein explained: "On the one hand, San Franciscans resented Mays as the intruder from New York whose reputation was imposed upon the proud city upon the Bay, mother of so many baseball greats. On the other, they were warming toward Willie, gradually, for somewhere along the line they could not fail to sense that his reputation was deserved."[19]

MAYS, KOUFAX, AND THE JOHN ROSEBORO GAME

If the 1951 shot heard 'round the world game was the most famous and significant Giants–Dodgers game during the two teams' last decade in New York, the game that has come to occupy a similar historical space from the two teams' first few decades in California was not the third game of the 1962 playoff series, but a game played on August 22, 1965, in San Francisco. That Sunday was the final game of a four-game set between the two rivals in the thick of yet another pennant race. The Dodgers began the day in first place, a half game ahead of the Milwaukee Braves and 1½ games ahead of the third-place Giants. The game was the best pitching matchup of the series, and one of the best possible in baseball, as Koufax was set to square off against Giants ace Juan Marichal.

Marichal led off the bottom of the third inning for the Giants. Marichal and Dodgers catcher John Roseboro had a bad history; and after Roseboro returned a few of Koufax's pitches too close to Marichal's head, Marichal responded by clobbering the Dodgers catcher over the head with his bat.

The story of that incident is well known and has been retold and analyzed in numerous books, article, and even a theatrical production.[20] The incident changed Marichal's reputation for the rest of his career. It also almost certainly delayed Marichal's election into the Hall of Fame, although by only a year or two. He was elected in 1983, his third year on the ballot, but only after Roseboro had made it clear that he felt no ill will toward Marichal. Roseboro died in 2002, but the two men became friends long before that. Marichal is still alive and broadly respected as one of the greatest living pitchers and for his pioneering role as the first great Dominican star in the big leagues.

The Giants and Dodgers rivalry is now over a century old and has been marred by episodes of violence over the years. A few, like the beating of Giants fan Bryan Stow in the parking lot of Dodger Stadium in 2011, have become quite well known. There have been numerous on-the-field fights between the two teams as well. There have been many cases of violence between fans of the two teams, whether on the streets of New York before 1958 or all over the state of California since then, which were never reported or have simply been forgotten over time. Juan Marichal smacking John Roseboro in the head with a bat, however, was the worst and most memorable use of violence on the field in the long rivalry between these two teams.

Baseball may not be as explicitly violent as football, where hard hits occur on every play, but the possibility of violence is always present and is part of the primal struggle of the game, that between the batter and the pitcher. A batter who is unafraid and comfortable at the plate is at an advantage, but a pitcher can take away that advantage by occasionally brushing the batter back. The gradual rule changes in the last 30 years or so that limit the ability of the pitcher to throw too close to the batter may be as much responsible for the dramatic increase in home runs in the 1990s and early 2000s as performance-enhancing drugs. In the 1960s, several great pitchers, most notably Bob Gibson of the Cardinals and Koufax's teammate Don Drysdale, frequently brushed back batters who stood too close to the plate. Today, they would not be allowed to do that.

Violence, and the threat of violence in baseball, generally takes the form of chin music, a hard slide into a base, and the collisions at home plate that are now less frequent due to rule changes in those areas as well. They almost never, however, come from weaponizing a baseball bat. The reason for that is obvious—a baseball bat, when wielded like a weapon, can hurt somebody very badly. In the movies, and on the streets, people use bats as weapons, but on the ballfield it is verboten.

I have been around baseball as a fan, player, parent, and coach for more than 40 years and have only seen this happen once. A player on my bar league softball team tried to score from third on a fly ball to left. He was out by about 15 feet, but did not agree with the call. After arguing with the umpire for a while, he went back to our bench, grabbed a bat, and went for the umpire. My teammates, not a group of mild-mannered guys, looked in horror as our teammate, who was about 6'2" and very strong, violently threatened the umpire. Fortunately, the shortstop on the other team, an enormous man who had hit long home runs in each of his times at bat, flew across the field, disarmed our teammate, and restrained him until he calmed down.

Leonard Koppett, writing about the Marichal–Roseboro incident in the *New York Times* also noted the rarity and danger involved with using a bat as a weapon: "Fights that erupt under pennant pressure are not unusual, but they are always fist fights. Players, coaches and managers of both teams here could not recall ever seeing an attack with a bat."[21] Dodgers manager Walter Alston was livid about the incident and furious with Marichal. "It takes a lot of courage to hit a man on the head with a bat. . . . I'm sure the bat was flying before any fists were flying."[22]

Marichal's actions brought a level of violence and ugliness to the rivalry that had not previously been seen. It was also not completely out of nowhere. The two teams had been involved in several fights in the early 1960s. Marichal believed that Dodgers pitchers had been throwing at him and his teammates as well. However, Koufax was not one of the pitchers who had been accused of that. Koufax, like that other great fireballer Walter Johnson, was known to almost never deliberately throw at hitters. In his memoir when describing the event, Marichal affirms that Koufax rarely threw at hitters. "My peers, my teammates didn't like to bat against Drysdale. They would rather bat against Sandy. . . . Sandy wouldn't throw at batters." Marichal also indicated that Koufax's reluctance to throw at batters led Roseboro to buzz Marichal's ear.[23]

Catchers are often big, tough men. The better ones are respected by their teammates and are leaders on and off the field. It may be a coincidence that perhaps the greatest catcher of them all, Yogi Berra, was in the first wave of navy men sent ashore during D-Day, but it is nevertheless illustrative. Roseboro was no exception. Before he was through, he would play on four All Star teams and be respected as the regular catcher for one of the best pitching staffs ever assembled as well as a key player on four pennant-winning Dodgers teams. The muscular Roseboro had trained in martial arts and boxing. Predictably, the benches cleared, but there was more rancor and violence than in a typical baseball fight, and the two most famous and beloved players of their generation were in the middle of it—in Koufax's case, literally.

Both Sandy Koufax and Willie Mays handled themselves with grace and aplomb as the fight ensued, helping to solidify their image to millions of many Americans. Both sought to break up the fight, albeit in different ways. Photos from that game show Koufax shocked by the blood on his teammate's face, but also trying to disarm Marichal and stop greater violence from occurring. The incident also cemented Koufax's reputation for not throwing at batters. While this was, on the one hand, a flattering testament to his control and to how good his pitches were, it also has a tinge of profiling to it. It somehow suggests that the great Jewish pitcher was technically as good as anybody in the game, but was not as tough as some of the others, perhaps even lacking in the courage to defend his teammates.

Lou Johnson, who was the starting left fielder in that game, and went on to hit the winning home run in Game Seven of the 1965 World Series, had a different view of Koufax, and saw him as an extremely competitive player. "He was the best and kindest teammate you could have, but people didn't know everything. One thing you gotta know: you didn't fuck with Sandy on the field."[24] John Rosengren also pushes back against what he refers to as a "popular legend." "Koufax believed in the practice of intimidating opposing hitters and protecting his teammates. He didn't throw at their heads because he feared hurting them, but he was willing to deliver his own messages."[25]

The photos from that day also show Mays intervening to try to limit the violence of the fight, seeking to make peace and even helping to escort Roseboro to the safety of the Dodgers dugout. Mays behaved with honor and no small amount of bravery at a time when a lot more harm could have been done. The racial aspect of this was important as well. By August 1965, Mays was the dean of African American big leaguers, as he had been playing in the majors longer than any others. This helped make it possible for a Giant to reach out to a Dodger in this way. It is often overlooked that tensions between Latinos and African Americans, both within and between teams, were strong during these years. As an African American Giant, Mays, therefore, was uniquely positioned to reduce the tension that day, and that is precisely what he did.

Here is Hirsch's description of how Mays restrained Roseboro from continuing to pursue Marichal and brought some calm to a very fraught situation:

A photograph shows Mays . . . pulling Roseboro along surrounded by nine Dodgers. Blood from Roseboro's face had splattered his chest protector. . . . Flecks of
blood are scattered on Mays's uniform as well. . . . When the fight began, Mays
rushed onto the field and darted in and out of players, pulling them apart and
removing the bat from [Giants infielder Tito] Fuentes's hand. . . . Mays worried
that his friend [Roseboro] had lost an eye and knew that he needed treatment.
He also believed that as long as Roseboro was storming after Marichal, or was
close to any Giant, the fans would be tempted to jump the railing. Mays took
Roseboro to the dugout and sat down next to him, which defied all tradition
and logic—a player in the heat of a brawl, taking a seat on the enemy bench.[26]

Dodgers first baseman Wes Parker stated succinctly that "if it hadn't been for
Mays, there would've been a riot in the ballpark."[27] However, Mays was unable
to completely end the conflict, as a few seconds after bringing Roseboro safely
to the Dodgers bench, the Dodgers catcher "suddenly burst from the trainer,
tore past Mays, and rushed back for another shot at Marichal."[28] Fortunately,
he was restrained.

After Mays and others restored the peace, the game resumed. Koufax struck
out Bob Schroder who had pinch hit for Marichal; however, after retiring leadoff
hitter Tito Fuentes on a fly ball, he walked Jim Davenport and Willie McCovey,
bringing up Mays. The great Giants center fielder hit a home run to give the
Giants a 4–2 lead. They eventually held on to win by a score of 4–3.

The game was a fierce battle between two archrivals in the heat of yet another
pennant race. The Giants' win that day brought them to within half a game of
the Dodgers, but they ended up losing the pennant that year to the Dodgers by
only two games. It was also a demonstration of the complexity of racial politics
in America, and particularly California, in the 1960s. The game had occurred
less than a week after smoke had finally cleared in Watts, following several
days of some of the most large-scale rioting in urban American history. That
must have been on the minds of Roseboro, Mays, and other African American
players that day—like McCovey and Jim Ray Hart on the Giants and Maury
Wills, Jim Gilliam, and Willie Davis on the Dodgers. Marichal's homeland
was also in a period of strife as President Donald Reid Cabral's government in
the Dominican Republic was being destabilized by forces demanding, among
other things, fair elections.

MASHI

The Roseboro incident demonstrated that the Dodgers–Giants rivalry was every bit as impassioned in its first decade in California as it had been in New York. It also highlighted the increasing racial complexity of the rapidly diversifying major leagues and highlighted the peacemaking skills of one of the game's best and most respected players.

Juan Marichal was a workhorse, who completed 244 games in his career, but he got thrown out of that particular game after attacking John Roseboro. Ron Herbel picked up much of the slack, pitching 5⅓ solid innings of relief, but left the game in the ninth with two on and one out and the Giants leading by two. At that point, Giants manager Herman Franks turned to his most reliable left-hander out of the bullpen to get the final two outs. An unearned run scored on an error, but the Giants held on to win 4–3.

That reliever was not just another lefty, but one of the most notable pitchers in baseball history, particularly with regard to the ongoing story of baseball's globalization. When Franks called for the lefty, the pitcher who came in was a son of Kita Tsuru County, in Japan's Yamanashi Prefecture, in the Chubu region of the country's main island. Masanori Murakami was the first Japanese player to play in the major leagues. He was not a Japanese American, but a good young Japanese player, who spent two years with the Giants before returning to Japan, where he pitched from 1966 to 1982.

Murakami pitched for the Giants in 1964 and 1965, appearing in a total of 54 games. His numbers were excellent: 5–1 with a 3.43 ERA and nine saves. His peripheral numbers were even more impressive. In only 89⅓ innings, he struck out 100, while walking only 23 (five intentionally), with a WHIP[29] of 1.063—all before his twenty-second birthday. Today, a pitcher who put up numbers like that at such a young age would be seen as a future star and the kind of pitcher that championship teams need in their bullpens, but baseball strategy was understood differently back then.

Although Murakami did not enjoy a long career with the Giants or any other team in the big leagues, the fact that he could come to the United States, a relative unknown even in Japan (before he went to the Giants), and pitch very well was quite significant. To appreciate this, it is essential to remember that Murakami began his career with the Giants in 1964. This was less than 20 years after the end of World War II. Many of the most influential people in American politics, industry, media, and baseball were World War II veterans and had fought bloody battles against the Japanese at a time when anti-Japanese racism was an integral part of the American propaganda effort. That racism was exacerbated, and demonstrated, by domestic policies of internment for Japanese Americans.

By the 1960s, Japan was increasingly seen, certainly among the more politically astute, as a valuable Cold War ally, and baseball was understood to be central to rebuilding the relationship between the United States and Japan after the war. There had been a fair amount of goodwill barnstorming tours since the war, but these made headlines only in Japan; they received less media attention in the United States.

Murakami's tenure with the Giants was thus a risky one for everybody involved. The Giants weren't certain if Murakami would be good enough or if the fans would accept a Japanese player. Murakami had not traveled to the United States before and would have jeopardized his future in Japan by pitching badly in the United States. If Murakami had not done well with the Giants, it would have badly damaged the reputation of Japanese baseball in the United States. Moreover, in the mid-1960s there were many places in the United States where any Japanese person would still have been a subject of curiosity, perhaps even suspicion.

While it is therefore possible that Murakami could have played for any team, realistically the experiment had a much better chance of succeeding because he went to a team in California. By 1964 there were three such teams, as the Los Angeles Angels had joined the American League in 1961. Los Angeles and San Francisco both had sizable Japanese American communities, providing both a support network for a potentially homesick pitcher and an untapped reservoir of new and enthusiastic fans. Neither of these things would have been in place if Murakami had gone to the Cleveland Indians, Milwaukee Braves, Boston Red Sox, or many other teams.

When Murakami began his two-year stint with the Giants, few fans in the United States knew much about Japanese baseball. They probably knew that baseball was popular in Japan and that it was not quite up to the level of American baseball, but could not have named a single Japanese player or even Japanese team. Sadaharu Oh, the great Japanese slugger of that era, and the only pre-1995 Japanese player to become well known to American fans, was just beginning his career in the mid-1960s. By 1964, he had become one of the top sluggers in Japan, but was not known at all in the United States.

Murakami's experience with the Giants was a much bigger story in Japan than in the United States. In the United States, he was an oddity, a useful role player from a faraway country; however, for Japanese baseball fans, Murakami was playing for national pride. He did not let his fellow Japanese down, but quickly returned to Japan for the 1966 season because of contract disputes between the San Francisco Giants and his Nankai Hawks in Japan.

Because he played with the Giants, Murakami became well known and well liked in the Bay Area. Briefly, Mashi Mania bloomed in the Bay Area. Murakami's biographer Robert Fitts described how "Murakami mania swept through San Francisco in the weeks following his debut. For five straight days the *San Francisco Chronicle* ran articles on the young Japanese, most with accompanying photographs. Beat writer Bob Stevens covered his promotion [to the big leagues], debut and first day with the major league team, and sports editor Art Rosenbaum featured or mentioned him in each column."[30]

One of the most peculiar aspects of Murakami's time with the Giants was its brevity and its lack of an immediate impact. He played two years and then went back to Japan. By the mid-1970s, when I began to pay a lot of attention to baseball, and to the Giants, few fans under 20 years old even knew he was. This was partially because, despite holding his own on the field, Murakami did not immediately make American baseball accessible for his countrymen. After he went back to Japan, it would be 30 years before another Japanese player made it to the big leagues. Murakami is, in that sense, more of an aberration than a trailblazer, but his two years with the Giants were still an important moment in the continuing tale of baseball's globalization.

THE DODGERS, THE GIANTS, AND GLOBALIZATION

During Murakami's first year with the Giants, 33 men played for the team. Twenty-four of those players were born in the United States; the others were from Canada, Cuba, the Dominican Republic, Japan, Panama, and Puerto Rico. Ten years earlier, the Giants had used 38 players during the 1954 championship season, 36 of whom had been born in the United States. The Giants were one of the leaders in the increasing globalization of baseball and were well ahead of the Dodgers in this area. All 33 of the players who appeared for the Dodgers in 1964, by comparison, were American born.

During the 1958–66 period, the Giants began to scout and develop players from the Caribbean more than almost any other team. The Dodgers, despite playing in Los Angeles, lagged well behind the Giants, and several other teams, in this regard. It is additionally ironic that the Dodgers, who took the lead in bringing African American players into baseball, and continued in the early 1960s with stars like Maury Wills, John Roseboro, Willie Davis, and Tommy Davis, were so slow to bring in Latino players. This helped prolong the poor relations the Dodgers had with the large Mexican American community in Los Angeles.

The numbers here are striking. Between 1958 and 1966 only five foreign-born men played for the Dodgers, combining for a total of 186 games. However, 163 of those games were played by Tim Harkness (97), Elmer Valo (65), and Bill Harris (1). Harris and Harkness were Canadian. Valo was born in what was then Czechoslovakia in 1921, but immigrated to the United States as a young boy. Thus, in these years, only two non-U.S. born Latinos, Sandy Amoros from Cuba and Hector Vale from Puerto Rico, played for the Dodgers, for a total of 23 games.

The Giants, by contrast, had 18 foreign-born players during these years. Two, Georges Maranda and Ken MacKenzie, were Canadian. The rest were from seven different countries in the Caribbean, Central America, or Asia. Six of these players—Orlando Cepeda; Juan Marichal; Jose Pagan; and all three Alou brothers, Matty, Felipe, and Jesus—played more than 186 games each for the Giants, the total number of games played by all foreign-born Dodgers during this period. One way to understand the Giants' role in globalization in this period is that between 1958 and 1966, 119 men played in the big leagues who were not born in the United States, Canada, or Europe. The European-born players tended to be older players like Valo or Bobby Thomson, who had immigrated to the United States years before they started playing baseball. Of those 119, 15 (13 percent) started their career with the Giants. Of the 100 who started their careers during this period, 12 were Giants.

The Giants did not just have more Latino players than the Dodgers, or anybody else, during these years, but they had good Latino players. From 1958 to 1966, there were five Latino players who stood out from their peers as the best in the game. One was the Pirates' star right fielder Roberto Clemente. Clemente was the game's first great Puerto Rican star. He died tragically on New Year's Eve of 1972 while trying to bring assistance to victims of an earthquake in Nicaragua. Clemente was a great player during this period, hitting .320/.361/.474, while leading his Pirates to a World Championship, winning one MVP award, and being selected to the All-Star team seven times.

Another great Latino star of that era, who is not quite as well remembered, is the Venezuelan Luis Aparicio, a wonderful fielder and very fast shortstop. From 1958 to 1966, he won seven Gold Gloves, helped the White Sox win the 1959 pennant, led the league in stolen bases every year from 1957 to 1964, and was an All Star every year from 1958 to 1964. Camilo Pascual is also somewhat forgotten now, but the Cuban pitcher was one of the best in the American

League during this period. A five-time All Star, he won 20 games in both 1962 and 1963, while leading the league in strikeouts from 1961 to 1963.

These were great Latino players, but the two best during this period played primarily for the Giants. Juan Marichal did not really get started until 1962; however, between 1962 and 1966, he averaged 21 wins, 21 complete games, 214 strikeouts, and a 2.14 ERA per season. He made the All-Star team every year during this period. Marichal was the first great Dominican star.

Today, Orlando Cepeda is remembered as somebody whose career was derailed by injuries. In the first part of his career, however, he was an extraordinary hitter, good enough to keep a future first-ballot Hall of Famer, Willie McCovey, in a part-time role for several years. While Cepeda was never the defensive player that Clemente was, he was at least as good and probably a better hitter from 1958 to 1966. Cepeda hit .307/.353/.528, slightly better than Clemente over these same years, while playing on five All-Star teams. Cepeda's OPS+ of 139 during this period is, among people with 4,500 or more plate appearances, tied for eighth with Eddie Mathews and Al Kaline and exceeded only by Mickey Mantle, Mays, Henry Aaron, Frank Robinson, McCovey, Harmon Killebrew, and Norm Cash. Clemente lagged behind with an OPS+ of 128.

Thus, in these early years of globalization, two of the very biggest stars, both appropriately memorialized today with plaques in Cooperstown and with statues at the Giants new ballpark, played for San Francisco. Additionally, Cepeda, Marichal, and Felipe Alou combined to play in 11 All-Star Games; other first-wave Latino stars in this period combined to play in a total of 42. During these years, when an All-Star manager wrote a Latino name in, more than 20 percent of the time that player was a Giant.

By the time Murakami came to the Giants, they were one of the few teams with African American, white, and Latino stars. The presence of Murakami made them the most diverse team in big league history until that time. This diversity strained racial relations and forced baseball to begin to recognize the complexity and racism and multiculturalism in America. These strains were not made any easier by Alvin Dark, who managed the Giants from 1961 to 1964. Dark was a former standout Giants infielder and a devout Christian; hailing originally from Oklahoma, he was not deeply familiar with Latinos, Latino cultures, or the Spanish language.

Dark told a *Newsday* reporter in 1964, "We have trouble because we have so many Negro and Spanish-speaking players on this team. They are just not able to perform up to the white players when it comes to mental alertness."[31] This is the kind of racist remark that can, and probably should, destroy a manager's career. It is possible that Dark did not really believe this or that his words were taken out of context, although it is hard to imagine a context in which these words would not be racist. Nonetheless, he said them while managing a team whose biggest stars—four future Hall of Famers—were all African American or Latino.

Dark made these comments during his fourth year at the helm of the Giants. For several of those years, players had complained about Dark and some of his racist policies, such as forbidding Spanish in the clubhouse or noting his disapproval of nonwhite players dating white women. That Dark was able to stay on as the manager speaks to the power of the old-boy network and a residual racism in baseball, but also to how woefully unequipped baseball was in the early 1960s to respond to an increasingly diverse set of players.[32]

Before Dark became manager, and before Marichal became the Giants ace, the Giants had a disappointing 1960 season, finishing in fifth place, 16 games behind the pennant-winning Pirates. They did this despite the presence of Mays, McCovey, and Cepeda in their lineup. This, in the words of Willie Mays's biographer James Hirsch,

> brought into focus the racial tensions on the club, though the tensions may have involved the white reporters who covered the team as much as the players themselves. The relatively high number of black and Latin Giants always made race and ethnicity a subtext. While most San Franciscans welcomed the nonwhite players, others wrote hate mail to the Giants complaining about "Rig's Jigs" and then "Sheehan's shines." . . . After the season J. G. Taylor Spink, visited San Francisco to conduct an autopsy on what happened to the squad. . . . [H]is story enumerated the problems, which included "too many negroes."[33]

It is not surprising that, in the early 1960s, a team whose best players were nonwhite and who frequently came up just a little bit short in the pennant race found themselves the target of racism from writers and fans. Nor is it a big surprise that a white baseball lifer like Alvin Dark had less-than-enlightened views on racial equality. However, the racial tensions between African Americans and Latinos on the Giants was something new to baseball and that has remained one of the more rarely discussed elements in the game ever since.

The Marichal–Roseboro game led some to comment on this tension, both among the Giants themselves and between the Dodgers and the Giants. Dick Young, who at the time was an influential and respected baseball writer, argued in his column that "the true problem is that the American Negroes and the Latin Negroes do not like each other—not even a little bit."[34] Young's language may have been a bit heavy-handed, but there was at least some truth to it.

The second great Dominican player on the Giants was a solid-hitting outfielder named Felipe Alou. Alou was overshadowed by the more famous hitters on his team and often had to fight for time in left or right field. Center field was already occupied. Alou competed for playing time with whoever of the McCovey/Cepeda duo was not playing first base as well as players like Harvey Kuenn and Willie Kirkland who were on some of those Giants teams. Two of the players with whom Alou sometimes had to struggle for playing time were his own brothers, Matty and Jesus. The three Alou brothers all started their careers with the Giants and were teammates in 1963.

All of the Alou brothers had good careers with flashes of greatness, but Felipe was the best, hitting a solid .286/.318/.433, with 42.2 WAR, over a 17-year career. He also spent the longest time in the game of any of his brothers, as he went on to manage the Expos for ten years and the Giants for four. Alou was also one of the first Latinos to draw attention to the challenges that Latinos uniquely faced in the big leagues. In 1963, he coauthored an article in *Sport Magazine* with legendary sportswriter Arnold Hano called "Latin-American Players Need a Bill of Rights." In that article, Alou wrote about the discrimination many Latin American ballplayers encountered based on race and language, the lack of cultural sensitivity by many in baseball, the vulnerability to mockery because of their insufficient English-language skills, and other difficulties unique to dark-skinned players from Cuba, the Dominican Republic, Venezuela, and Puerto Rico. Alou argued that "far worse than the language barrier are the insults thrown in the faces of Latin ballplayers. It is said that Latin players 'don't care.' That Latin players 'don't hustle.' Latin players 'are lazy.' Or—and this is the worst—Latin players have no guts."[35]

The issues raised by Alou, the challenges of a multiracial clubhouse, and the possibility of conflicts between players on different teams to take an ugly racial undertone continue today. Racism on big league ballfields began, in some respects, when Jackie Robinson first began playing for the Dodgers, but the challenges that the Giants confronted in the 1960s have been very durable and did not yet exist during Robinson's era.

KOUFAX AND DRYSDALE

The greatest star of the Dodgers during those first years in Los Angeles was Sandy Koufax, but the Dodgers' identity was not forged around Koufax alone. Instead, the Dodgers in those years were defined by the tandem of superstar pitchers who led their team. Both were tall men who threw hard and were intense competitors. Both began their careers as Dodgers in Brooklyn. Both enjoyed spending time with beautiful women (although Drysdale got married in 1958, so wasn't actually single). There were differences, too. Don Drysdale was known for pitching inside and was never afraid to use a little chin music against an opposing pitcher hitter. Koufax rarely did that. Drysdale was a great right-handed pitcher. Koufax was even better, but was left-handed.

The two also came from different backgrounds. Drysdale was a gentile from the San Fernando Valley in Los Angeles who had blond hair and conventional good looks. Koufax was Jewish and from Brooklyn, also handsome, but in the way that might appeal to a thoughtful grad student, rather than somebody hanging out at the beach in Southern California. Both Drysdale and Koufax appeared in small roles in movies and television shows during the Dodgers' first years in Los Angeles. At the time, their friendship, despite their different backgrounds, with an emphasis on their different religious background, received a great deal of attention in the media.

Jane Leavy, one of Koufax's biographers, described the relationship between the two pitching stars: "[In] the words of Drysdale's second wife, Anne Meyers Drysdale, 'they shared an unbelievable moment in time.' With Drysdale what you saw was what you got: Big D, California large and California handsome. Koufax was 3D—his essence elusive. . . . They were perfect foils if not perfect friends. 'They were so different,' she said. 'That's why they were so good together.'"[36]

In the early and mid-1960s, the Dodgers won three pennants with mediocre offenses in years where these two players were dominant. In 1963, the two aces combined to start 82, or more than half, of the Dodgers regular-season games and two of the team's four World Series games. In 1965, they combined to start an amazing 85 of the Dodgers regular-season games and five of seven World Series games. In 1966, the duo fell to only half of the Dodgers' regular-season games and three of their four World Series games.

In addition to being great pitchers and part of the celebrity scene in Southern California in the early 1960s, Koufax and Drysdale also played a very important role in the history of baseball's labor–management relations and participated in one of the earliest cases of collective action by ballplayers in the modern era. In the mid-1960s, there was no free agency, no arbitration, and the reserve clause was in full force. This meant that once a player signed with a team, unless he was traded or released, the team had complete control over his contract. In this environment, contract negotiations were relatively one-sided; the players had little leverage they could use to get more money from the owners.

The one significant tool the players had in this setting was the holdout. A player could simply refuse to come to spring training in the beginning of the season. This ploy, however, could only be used by valuable and well-known players; if a backup infielder or even a starter coming off a bad year held out during spring training, the team could simply ignore the holdout, leaving the player no choice but to sign the contract offered to him or stop playing professional baseball. It is not, therefore, surprising that most holdouts were brief and that this tactic was rarely used by players who were not stars.

As spring training of 1966 approached, Sandy Koufax and Don Drysdale were very much stars. The Dodgers offered $100,000 to Koufax and $85,000 to Drysdale. This was good money at the time and consistent with what most of the best players in the game were making. Willie Mays would make $105,000 in 1966, and Mickey Mantle $100,000. It was a lot more than other top National League pitchers, who happened not to be white, like Bob Gibson ($50,000) and Juan Marichal ($72,000), would make in 1966.[37]

These salaries had not been arrived at through collective bargaining or even an honest negotiation, but simply by the owners deciding on a number and the players eventually accepting it, in some cases after what amounted to some very minor haggling. Drysdale and Koufax had a new idea and—because of the extraordinary value they brought to the team and their unique circumstances, being two high-profile stars who also happened to be good friends on the same team—were able to implement their strategy.

The Dodgers were the defending World Champions when spring training of 1966 began. Koufax and Drysdale were the best players on the team. Without their two pitching aces, the Dodgers were not only a middle-of-the-pack team, but they would have no stars as marketable as their top two pitchers. They had other good players, but speedster shortstop Maury Wills, their only other recognizable star, was not as well known or marketable as either Drysdale or Koufax.

Koufax and Drysdale realized that their value to the Dodgers was greater together than individually. This is a pretty fundamental notion for workers when they negotiate, but Koufax and Drysdale were in an unusual industry—and in an unusual position within that industry—so their decision to hold out together was groundbreaking for baseball. The two pitchers asked for a total of one million dollars over the course of a three-year contract. The money was to be divided evenly between the two pitchers.

In 1966, these were stark demands. It would have meant almost doubling both Koufax and Drysdale's salaries as well as guaranteeing them three more years. Multiyear contracts were unusual in that era. The two pitchers proposed sharing the money equally, so they would have both been the highest-paid player in the game, at $167,000 per year. This would have been an enormous boon for Drysdale who, as good as he was, was not equal to Koufax.

The reactions to the holdout varied. Baseball management was outraged. The owners had spent decades working to ensure the reserve clause stayed in place and that any hint of collective bargaining was quickly squashed. The owners' sentiments were best expressed in an article penned by Buzzie Bavasi, who was the Dodgers general manager at the time of the holdout.

> To tell the truth, I wasn't too successful in the famous Koufax-Drysdale double holdout in 1966. I mean, when the smoke had cleared they stood together on the battlefield with $235,000 between them, and I stood there with a blood-stained cashbox. Well, they had a gimmick and it worked; I'm not denying it. They said that one wouldn't sign unless the other signed. Since one of the two was the greatest pitcher I've ever seen (and possibly the greatest anybody has ever seen), the gimmick worked. But be sure to stick around for the fun the next time somebody tries that gimmick. I don't care if the whole infield comes in as a package; the next year the whole infield will be wondering what it is doing playing for the Nankai Hawks.[38]

Leavy put the holdout in a broader perspective and argues that Koufax and Drysdale had a very valid and important point to make. "In challenging Walter O'Malley, the power behind the commissioner's throne, they were taking on not just the Dodgers but the Institution of Baseball. No one else could have done it; no one else had their standing or the irrefutable attendance figures to assert their value. The Dodgers acknowledged they drew an additional ten thousand fans every time Koufax started and three thousand when Drysdale pitched."[39]

The holdout lasted most of spring training. During the holdout, Koufax and Drysdale both announced plans to star in a Hollywood movie, presciently called *The Warning Shot*. The holdout ended March 30, just before the start of the season, when Koufax signed for $130,000, and Drysdale for $110,000. *The Warning Shot* was made in 1967, but neither Koufax nor Drysdale was in it.

Among the stars that appeared in that film were Joan Collins, Steve Allen, and Carroll O'Connor, who became famous in the 1970s as television's Archie Bunker.

The holdout was only possible because of the unusual role Drysdale and Koufax played on the Dodgers, but it would not have been hard for other players on other teams to replicate it. Mays and McCovey or Harmon Killebrew and Tony Oliva on the Minnesota Twins were also duos of great players without whom their teams would not be very good. No other players ended up following the Koufax and Drysdale template, but it was an early salvo in the labor strife that was a big part of MLB in the next 15 years, resulting in massive changes to player–owner relations. The holdout may, in fact, be unrelated to the decision of the players to form the Major League Baseball Players Association and hire noted labor lawyer Marvin Miller as their representative during that spring training, but it is likely that the lesson from the Koufax-Drysdale holdout helped make it clear to the players that they needed to work together and hire a tough negotiator like Miller.

WHAT ABOUT THE YANKEES, AGAIN?

For most of the time they were in New York, and particularly during the last decade or so, the fates of both the Giants and Dodgers were deeply tied to the third New York team. During those years, the Yankees were the best team in New York and therefore in all of baseball. They drew more fans, won more championships, and were more often than not the World Series opponent waiting for whichever of the other two New York teams won the National League pennant. The Yankees continued to play a part in the story of the Giants and Dodgers in the 1960s as both teams played the Yankees in the World Series shortly after moving west. The Dodgers, in the middle of the most successful era in their history, swept the Yankees in 1963, while the Giants, beginning the most disappointing era in their history, lost a heartbreaking Game Seven to the Yankees in 1962.

During the first seven years the Dodgers and Giants were in California, the Yankees won six pennants, including five in a row from 1960 to 1964, but then their fortunes changed. The Yankees finished in sixth place in 1965 and then in last place, for the first time since 1912, a year later. From 1921 to 1964, a period of 44 years, dominance by the Yankees had been a central dynamic of the sport. During these 44 years, the Bronx Bombers won 29 pennants and 20 World Series. They also never went more than three years without a World Series appearance. After 1965, for many reasons, including expansion, free agency, revenue sharing in various forms, and the amateur draft, baseball would never be dominated like that again—by the Yankees or anybody else.

As the 1960s went on, it became very apparent that the age of the Yankees' dominance was over and that other teams, including the Giants and Dodgers, might occasionally have a good five-year run, but winning four or five championships in a row or sustaining excellence across decades was not going to be possible anymore. This meant that while the Yankees, particularly once they got good again in the mid-1970s and again in the 1996–2009 period, could remain the highest profile and most polarizing team, baseball's talent and its winning teams were now more dispersed than in the past. The Giants, through their early movement in scouting the Caribbean, and the Dodgers, with their strong record of scouting, drafting, and player development, were both a big part of that.

CONCLUSION

As the Giants and Dodgers settled into their new homes in California, they also began to take on new personas. The Dodgers had moved not only across the country, but their previous home had been a borough that had always been secondary to Manhattan in the eyes of the world. Their new home, however, was a global center of film and glamor—the place where not just dreams, but images and fantasies for many Americans were made. Los Angeles was a city to which people still migrated, not just hoping to make it big in the entertainment business, but in the postwar Southern California boom more generally. This made the Dodgers a different kind of high-profile team. Ballplayers from the Dodgers, and less frequently the Los Angeles Angels as well, appeared in nightclubs with Hollywood stars and other well-known entertainment figures, and even occasionally could be seen as extras or in bit parts in television shows.

The Dodgers almost immediately after arriving in Los Angeles became part of the fabric of celebrity culture in Los Angeles. Milton Berle was one of the many Hollywood personalities who became fans of the newly arrived Dodgers. "My wife and I had season tickets. We had eight box seats between home plate and first. And we would take other performers. Walther Matthau, Jack Lemmon, Neil Simon. Everyone wanted to go and see the Dodgers. That was the great place to be in Los Angeles."[40]

In Los Angeles, by building links between Hollywood and baseball beginning in the early 1960s, the Dodgers helped forge a new kind of sports celebrity. This helped baseball become a bigger industry and a greater presence in the media and the culture. Michael Leahy writes: "The Dodgers represented the model of the superstar athlete to come, one with a wryer sense of sports as showbiz and quick to see the benefits in moving back and forth between baseball and the entertainment world. . . . Koufax popped up on other TV shows, playing a cop on a flashy detective series . . . and a civil war veteran in a western. . . . The biggest names in Hollywood wanted the players for their show."[41]

After the move west, another change experienced by the Dodgers related to racial diversity and integration. In the 1950s the Dodgers had been leaders in the effort to integrate baseball. Indeed, a big reason for their success was that they had great African American players like Robinson, Campanella, and Don Newcombe. By the 1960s, that had changed. On most teams in the 1960s, the most visible duo of stars—for example, the Giants (Mays and Marichal), Cardinals (Bob Gibson and Ken Boyer), Cubs (Banks and either Billy Williams or Ron Santo), and Twins (Tony Oliva and Harmon Killebrew) usually included at least one nonwhite player. Even the Yankees, with Elston Howard, may have fit this description. However, the two biggest stars on the Dodgers were white. The Dodgers had several good nonwhite players, but they would not soon again have an African American, Asian, or Latino player as the face of the team in the way Jackie Robinson had been, Willie Mays still was, and Reggie Jackson, Willie Stargell, or Ozzie Smith would be for several championship teams in the following decades.

If the Los Angeles Dodgers were gradually rebranding themselves as a whiter, more glamorous, and more winning version of what they had been during their last few years in Brooklyn, by the end of their first decade in San Francisco, the Giants were moving toward a very different image. As the 1970s approached, the Giants were now the hard-luck team. It was becoming clear that the collection of talent the team produced in the late 1950s and early 1960s and added to a team that already included Willie Mays—a group that included future Hall of Famers McCovey, Marichal, Cepeda, and Gaylord Perry as well as Jim Ray Hart, Jim Davenport, the Alou brothers, and more—had led the team to a period not of multiple championships, but of much frustration.

Candlestick Park was proving to be a problem. After drawing more than 1.5 million fans in six of the first seven years the Giants played there, attendance fell to 1,242,480 in 1967 and below one million in 1968. The Giants would not draw 1.2 million again until 1978, when they drew more than 1.7 million fans, their highest attendance since their first year at the 'Stick. The Dodgers fit in well into their new home, becoming part of the culture of their new city generally and of Hollywood specifically, but San Francisco was different.

By the late 1960s, both the greater Los Angeles area and the Bay Area each had two big league teams. Southern California was both bigger and more populated than the Bay Area, so it was able to adjust to having two teams reasonably easily. The Angels were never a strong team in the 1960s, other than in their second year, when they finished a surprisingly strong third. They also never challenged the Dodgers' attendance figures, but managed to survive the decade as a second-tier franchise with regard to attendance and their play on the field. By the 1970s, they began to draw better. Unlike the A's and Giants, there have been no rumors of the Angels moving since they began play.

The same was not true in the Bay Area. During the Giants' first decade in San Francisco, they had the entire Bay Area to themselves. It turned out they needed that to be a successful franchise. The A's, while hardly an attendance juggernaut themselves, began to draw fans away from the Giants almost immediately. Robert Garratt writes that within a few years it was clear that "sharing the Bay Area market with another major league ball club was proving disastrous for the Giants' ability to maintain financial health."[42] This dynamic never really improved over the next four decades. For the rest of the twentieth century, the Giants and A's both struggled to draw fans, sometimes at the same time. They have each also had periods of great success, but rarely at the same time.

The Bay Area has consistently struggled to support two teams (see Table 8). Only eight times in 50 years have both teams drawn two million fans. The two Southern California teams have met that threshold 23 times, albeit in seven more total seasons.

The 1960s were also the time when San Francisco permanently changed from being a more or less typical American city, albeit more beautiful and with better food than most, to being a center of counterculture and progressive politics. It would take the Giants a very long time to figure out how they fit into that city. Thus, by the 1960s, the Giants, while still fielding good teams, were on the periphery of San Francisco's life and culture. There are a huge number of books about San Francisco in the 1960s, but even those that seek to look at the bigger picture, rather than just focusing on music, drugs, and Haight-Ashbury, almost never mention that there was a pretty good baseball team in San Francisco in the late 1960s, or that one of the very best baseball players ever was still patrolling center field for the home team in those years.

After the Orioles swept the Dodgers in the 1966 World Series, Sandy Koufax retired. The pain in his arm had gotten to be too much for the star pitcher, who was coming off another extraordinary season, going 27–9 while leading the league in wins, ERA (1.73), starts (41), complete games (27), shutouts (5)

Table 8. Attendance in Southern California and the Bay Area

Attendance for Each Team	Seasons in Southern California (Dodgers and Angels)	Seasons in Bay Area (Giants and A's)
1–2 million	(Total: 13) 1962, 1967, 1968, 1970, 1973, 1975–78, 1994–97	(Total: 27) 1982–84, 1986–88, 1990–92, 1994–2000, 2006–13, 2015–17
2–3 million	(Total: 11) 1979–80, 1982–93, 1998–2002, 2011, 2012	(Total: 8) 1989, 1993, 2001–5, 2014
3+ million	(Total: 13) 2003–10, 2013–17	

Source: "MLB Ballpark Attendance," Ballparks of Baseball (2017), http://www.ballparksofbaseball.com/baseball-ballpark-attendance/.

innings (323), and strikeouts (317). He was a unanimous choice for the Cy Young Award and came in a very close second to Roberto Clemente in the MVP ballot. Without their dominant lefty, the Dodgers fell out of contention in 1967 and 1968. The Giants finished second in both those years, but an era for those two teams had come to an end when Koufax retired.

The two teams would remain in their homes, but the feeling of newness had gone. Attendance fell for both teams, as the Dodgers dropped to second in the league in 1967 and third in 1968, and the Giants fell to sixth in attendance in 1967 and seventh and 1968. For the Dodgers this decline was brief, but for the Giants it was a harbinger of a tough few decades. With Koufax retired and Mays and Drysdale both on their way out, the Dodgers and Giants were losing any direct connection to their old homes in New York and becoming more deeply rooted in California.

7

AFTER MAYS AND KOUFAX

By the late 1960s, other baseball cities had supplanted Los Angeles and San Francisco. Koufax had retired; Drysdale's career was winding down; Mays and Marichal were getting older. McCovey, however, as seems vaguely appropriate for the strangely overlooked slugger, was finally getting healthy and entering a three-year period, from 1968 to 1970, when he was the best hitter in the game. For that period, he hit .325/.425/.603 for an OPS+ of 188, the best in all of baseball, while accumulating 21.6 WAR, second only to Carl Yastrzemski's 25.5. McCovey led the Giants to the NL West division title in 1971. That was the last gasp of the great Mays-Marichal-McCovey teams, but they were eliminated by the Pirates in the National League Championship Series.

In 1969, New York was back on top of the baseball world as the Mets won an unlikely World Series, bringing the championship back to that city for the first time since 1962. That was the longest New York had gone without a World Series winner since 1921. It had only been five years since the Yankees had appeared in the World Series, but for many New Yorkers, given the changes on and off the field in those years, it felt like a lot longer. The biggest star on the Mets team was a hard-throwing righty named Tom Seaver. Seaver was a dominant pitcher who was good-looking and media-friendly. He was the first great Mets star and quickly became the biggest baseball name in New York after Mickey Mantle retired at the conclusion of the 1968 season.[1]

When the 1969 season began, there was a new expansion team in San Diego, while the A's were starting their second season in Oakland. Major League Baseball on the West Coast was no longer new, as more than 20 percent of all big league teams called California home between 1969 and 1976. In 1969, with the Seattle Pilots playing their only season, six of the 24 major league 24 teams were located on the West Coast, in cities spanning San Diego to Seattle.[2]

In the early 1970s, the best of the California teams was not the Dodgers or the Giants, but the Oakland A's. From 1971 to 1975, the A's, led by future Hall of Famers Rollie Fingers, Catfish Hunter, and Reggie Jackson as well as several other very good players, like Vida Blue, Ken Holtzman, Gene Tenace, Joe Rudi, Bert Campaneris, and Sal Bando, won five straight division titles, including three consecutive World Series, from 1972 to 1974.[3]

The Giants and Dodgers were not the most visible teams in baseball during these years, but by the mid-1970s, the Dodgers would again be one of the most important and high profile teams in the game. However, the Giants waited a long time to regain that status. Nonetheless, the 1970s and 1980s were an important time for these teams as they sought to find their place and identity in the rapidly changing baseball world.

LABOR STRIFE, MONEY, AND FREE AGENCY

Andy Messersmith is not one of the best-remembered Dodgers of the last 50 years, despite being one of only a handful of players to star for both Los Angeles teams. Messersmith and Bill Singer, the man for whom he was traded in November 1972 in a multiplayer trade that also sent Frank Robinson and Bobby Valentine to the Angels, are the only two pitchers to make the All-Star team playing for both the Dodgers and Angels. The same two pitchers are also the only men who have won 20 games in a season for both teams.

Messersmith began his career with the Angels, where he enjoyed his best season in 1971 at age 25, going 20–13 with a 2.99 ERA on an otherwise undistinguished Angels team. Messersmith came into his own after being sent to the Dodgers following the 1972 season. There he joined a pitching rotation that included future Hall of Famer Don Sutton and lefty Tommy John. The Dodgers were recovering from their late 1960s funk and beginning to put a team together that would go on to win four division crowns and four pennants, but only one World Series, between 1974 and 1981. Messersmith pitched very well in his three years with the Dodgers, going a combined 53–30 with a very impressive 2.51 ERA, good enough to finish in the top five in Cy Young voting in both 1973 and 1974.

Messersmith was also at the center of one of the first successful challenges to the reserve clause, the regulation that had kept players tied to their teams for their entire careers and that effectively limited player movement and salaries. Many fans have heard the story of Curt Flood, the star center fielder for the

Cardinals in the late 1960s, who refused to go to the Phillies following a trade after the 1969 season, and went on to sue MLB before being forced out of the game by the owners. More famous still is the great Oakland A's pitcher Catfish Hunter, who was liberated from his contract on a technicality following the 1974 season and signed an agreement for five years and roughly $3 million with the Yankees, where he won three more pennants and two more championships before arm injuries forced him into retirement when he was only 33.

The role played by Messersmith, whose fortunes were linked to those of Dave McNally, a top left-handed pitcher for the Orioles teams of the late 1960s and early 1970s, may have been more important in changing labor arrangements in MLB than Hunter or Flood. Rather than achieve free agency through a technicality, as Hunter did when A's owner Charlie O. Finley did not honor an agreement to pay Hunter's insurance premium, or object to an unwanted trade, Messersmith and McNally took the reserve clause on directly.

The two pitchers played the 1975 season for the Dodgers and Expos, respectively, without contracts, earning only the major league minimum wage. They then argued that, because of this, they should be free to go to the highest bidder for the following seasons. The owners did not see it this way and argued that the reserve cause should still apply. The two sides went to arbitration, where the arbitrator, Peter Seitz, ruled in favor of McNally and Messersmith.

This made Messersmith and McNally the first real free agents after the 1975 season. McNally had already announced his retirement, leaving Messersmith alone in the free-agent pool. Messersmith signed a three-year deal with the Braves that paid him a total of about $1.4 million. This was not quite as much as Catfish Hunter, but Messersmith was also not quite as good a pitcher as Hunter. It was still very good money for the time. Messersmith did well financially; however, after a decent 1976 season, when he went 11–11 with a 3.04 ERA, he encountered arm trouble and struggled over the remaining two years of the contract, playing with the Braves and Yankees. He then ended his career pitching in 11 games with the Dodgers in 1979.

Following the 1977 season, the free-agent floodgates opened. A huge group of players, many from the A's, were available on the open market. Reggie Jackson, coming off his only season with the Orioles; Rollie Fingers; Sal Bando; Gene Tenace; Don Baylor; and Bert Campaneris, all from the A's; and Bobby Grich, Jackson's teammate in Baltimore, were in this first full free-agent class. Free agency has changed a lot since the late 1970s. The size of contracts has grown exponentially, with overall values over $100 million not unusual for a top star, but there have been other evolutions as well. Teams are now smarter about signing young stars to generous but below-market contracts that keep them from reaching free agency in their prime, and are also more aware of the perils of signing older free agents. In recent years, compensation in the form of draft picks for some top free agents has kept spending down somewhat.

Additionally, for most of the last 20 to 30 years, it was assumed that the big-market teams would get the best free agents. This was not entirely the case in the 1970s. The Yankees were very active in the early years of free agency, signing Hunter, Jackson, and Goose Gossage to generous contracts in the 1970s. The Angels, who signed Baylor and Grich following the 1976 season, were another big-market team that played heavily in early free agency; however, some of the other teams that spent a lot of money like the Padres (Fingers and Tenace) or the Brewers (Bando) played in much smaller markets. Additionally, the Montreal Expos actually offered Reggie Jackson more money, but the slugger was strongly drawn to the idea of becoming a star in New York.

The Dodgers, who played in a big market, as well at the Giants, who played in a much smaller market by the late 1970s, both resisted jumping into the free agency process. The Dodgers added free agents Willie Crawford and Terry Forster in the 1977–78 offseason. These were both useful, even very good players, but they were not big stars signing bigger contracts. The Giants got into the act by bringing Willie McCovey back for the 1977 season, but that was more a nice gesture to an aging star, than a major player move. That nice gesture worked out well for the Giants, as the great slugger won the 1977 Comeback Player of the Year award. San Francisco's first major free agent, other than McCovey, was Billy North, a speedy leadoff hitter and center fielder, whom they signed from the Dodgers before the 1979 season.

The Yankees, helped by Jackson and free-agent pitcher Don Gullett, late of the Cincinnati Reds, won the World Series in 1977. The next winter the Yankees added yet another future Hall of Famer, reliever Goose Gossage, and won the World Series again.[4] The Yankees opponents in both those World Series were the Dodgers. When the Dodgers and Yankees met in the 1977 World Series, for the first time in 14 years, it reignited what had once been a major New York baseball rivalry, while solidifying it as a national one.

There were many contrasts between those two teams. The Yankees constantly squabbled with each other, while the Dodgers appeared much more cohesive. The Yankees were led by stars who were outspoken like Reggie Jackson, perpetually angry like Thurman Munson, or quirky and funny like Graig Nettles and Sparky Lyle. The Dodgers projected a much more wholesome image, with stars like Steve Garvey, Don Sutton, and Tommy John. Another major difference was that the Yankees built their team largely through trades and free agency, while many key players on the Dodgers, like Garvey, Sutton, Davey Lopes, Bill Russell, and Ron Cey, were products of the Dodgers farm system. Nonetheless, the Yankees proved to be the better team, beating them in six games in 1977 and again in 1978.

When the two teams met in the World Series three years later, it was under different circumstances. The nadir of labor relations in baseball would be 1994, when a players' strike forced MLB to cancel almost the entire last third of the season and the postseason. The World Series had been played every year from 1905 to 1993, but what two world wars, the Great Depression, and periodic civil unrest could not disrupt was undone by stubborn owners, who ended up conceding on most points anyway. The strike and subsequent cancellation of the World Series in 1994 has come to overshadow previous baseball labor disputes, but 13 years earlier baseball had encountered its first major labor crisis of the free-agent era.

Major League Baseball did not cancel the World Series or any of the postseason in 1981, because the strike began in June, which meant that, while one-third of the season still was lost, it was the middle third. This allowed MLB to split the season into two parts. For the first part, the teams in first place when the strike began were declared winners. For the second part, which began following the strike, all teams started anew. Major League Baseball then added a mini-series as a first round of the playoffs between the winners of the two parts. The Dodgers and Yankees had both been in first place before the strike. The Dodgers then made it to the World Series by winning two tough series against the Astros and the Expos, each of which went the maximum five games.

By 1981, the Dodgers had recaptured some of their old Brooklyn magic and had lost the World Series the last four times they had made it there. At the tail end of the Koufax-Drysdale years, they were swept by Baltimore. In 1974, they lost to the A's in five games. In both 1977 and 1978, they fell to the Yankees in six games. When the Yankees and Dodgers met in 1981, it was their third World Series against each other in five years. The core of both teams was aging. For the Dodgers, holdovers from the late 1970s were still a key part of the team, but they were no longer young. Garvey, Lopes, Russell, Cey, Dusty Baker, Rick Monday, Steve Yeager, Reggie Smith, and Burt Hooton were all over 30 years old, with Lopes, Smith, and Monday all at least 35. There were of course some good younger players on that team, including slugger Pedro Guerrero and their star left-handed pitcher, Fernando Valenzuela. The Yankees too relied on older players. Holdovers from the late 1970s included Nettles, Lou Piniella, and

Jackson, who were all over 35, as well as Oscar Gamble, Jim Spencer, and Ron Guidry, who were over 30. The oldest player on those Yankees was standout pitcher Tommy John, who was 38 and had won 52 regular-season games for New York since leaving the Dodgers for the Bronx as a free agent following the 1978 season.

By 1981, the Dodgers had gone 16 years without a World Series championship. The Dodgers quickly dropped the first two games of the 1981 World Series, including a 3–0 loss in the second game, when Tommy John held his old teammates to only three baserunners in seven innings. Another World Series defeat at the hands of the Yankees seemed almost inevitable and would have placed the Dodgers of 1974 to 1981 among the great underachieving teams of all time. However, there was some reason for hope. Only three years earlier, the Dodgers had won the first two games of the World Series in Los Angeles, only to lose the next four and the championship. Perhaps the Dodgers thought they could do the same thing to a Yankees team that had won two games, but was also aging and a little beat-up.

The first thing the Dodgers had to do was get by the Yankees' 22-year-old, left-handed pitching phenom Dave Righetti. Righetti—who went on to a strange career as the best left-handed closer of his era and then became one of the most respected pitching coaches in baseball history with the San Francisco Giants—was coming off a season where he had gone 8–4 with a 2.05 ERA. He was a hard-throwing lefty and was viewed as the natural successor to the Yankees ace Ron Guidry.[5] However, Righetti was the second-best rookie lefty in that Game Three matchup. In what was one of the best pitching matchups between rookies in World Series history, the Dodgers countered with their own rookie, who would not only be the NL Rookie of the Year in 1981, but also the Cy Young Award winner and finish fifth in MVP voting. Fernando Valenzuela was a 20-year-old pitching star who had been the story in baseball in 1981. If anybody could save the Dodgers' season it had to be young Valenzuela.

That is precisely what Valenzuela did. He was not at his best, but managed to throw a complete game, allowing 16 Yankees to reach base, but only four to score. The powerful bats of the Dodgers knocked Righetti out after two innings, and went ahead 5–4 in the bottom of the fifth. That was the final score, meaning that the Dodgers were still alive. They won the next two games in Los Angeles, both by one run, and went back to New York for Game Six.

Game Six in New York was not close. The Dodgers won 9–2, in part because of Yankees manager Bob Lemon's very questionable decision to lift Tommy John, who was handcuffing his former teammates as he had done in Game Two, for a pinch-hitter in the bottom of the fourth.[6] With John out of the game, the Yankees quickly let the game get out of reach. The Dodgers brought in their closer, Steve Howe, for the last 11 outs, including a fly ball by Bob Watson that late-inning defensive replacement Ken Landreaux easily caught for the third out in the ninth inning.

The Dodgers victory in that World Series was their first in 16 years, but it remains one of the most unusual championships in baseball history. The World Series capped off a postseason that included three rounds for the first time ever. That seemed extraordinary at the time, but only 14 years later MLB would adapt a three-tiered playoff system. Unlike what would happen in 1994, the 1981 strike did not cancel the World Series, but it nonetheless played havoc with it. Roughly a third of the season was canceled, leading to unbalanced schedules and a playoff system that created unique incentives and outcomes. The team with the best record in both NL West and NL East, the Reds and Cardinals, did not make the playoffs at all because both teams finished a close second in both halves of the season. The Dodgers had won the first half by half a game and played only one game over .500 during the second half. The Dodgers' World Series opponents, the Yankees, won the first half, a title for which they were not even aware they were playing at the time, by 3½ games. However, in the second half they were one game under .500 and finished in sixth place in the AL East. Overall, they had the fourth best record in their division.

Despite this, the Dodgers' victory in the 1981 World Series was sweet because it vanquished the defeats in 1977 and 1978. It also finally brought a championship to an aging core of players like Garvey, Lopes, Russell, Cey, Hooton, and Steve Yeager. The Dodgers therefore bookended the first phase of labor disputes around free agency. The first real free agent, by many measures, was a Dodger, Andy Messersmith, while the team that won the World Series in the first real strike season was also the Dodgers.

THAT INFIELD AND THAT FIRST BASEMAN

In the final game of the 1981 World Series, the first four batters in the Dodgers lineup were Davey Lopes, Bill Russell, Steve Garvey, and Ron Cey. They were also the four starting infielders that day, with Garvey at first, Lopes at second, Cey at third, and Russell at short. That was the last game they would ever play together. Lopes was traded to the A's during the offseason. After the 1982 season, Cey was traded to the Cubs and Garvey signed with the Padres as a free agent. Bill Russell finished his career with the Dodgers, remaining on the team as their shortstop and later utility player through the 1986 season.

These four Dodgers had come up through the Dodgers system together, had been teammates on the big league club since 1972, and were the Dodgers starting infield from 1974 to 1981. No other infield unit in big league history stayed together as many as eight years. At least two of these infielders represented the Dodgers on the National League All-Star team in each of these years. This is a remarkable tribute both to the skills of these players, who were among the best at their position during these years, and the stability of the Dodgers franchise.

Despite being together so long, the Dodgers infield was not the best in baseball during those years. Not all four players were stars: Russell was a solid, but unspectacular player. More pertinently, the Dodgers were in the same division as the Cincinnati Reds, who were known in the 1970s as the Big Red Machine. In 1975 to 1976, the Reds fielded one of the greatest infields ever, with Tony Perez at first, Joe Morgan at second, Davey Concepcion at short, and Pete Rose at third. This quartet was better than the Dodgers infield. Even in 1974, when Rose was in left and Dan Driessen was at third, and in 1977, when Rose was at third, but Driessen had replaced Perez at first, the Reds were still probably stronger. The Phillies infield that included Mike Schmidt at third, Larry Bowa at short, Dave Cash at second, and various first baseman during these years, such as Dick Allen and Rose, was also probably just as good as the Dodgers. At various times during these years, the Milwaukee Brewers and California Angels also had starting infields that were probably better than the Dodgers.

The Dodgers infield was, nonetheless, very good. Good enough to help win four division titles in this eight-year period. By the late 1970s, these players had come to symbolize the Dodgers franchise. At a time when free agency was leading to a perceived increase in player movement, salaries were skyrocketing, and there was a sense of general tumult throughout the game, the Dodgers infield was stable year in and year out. The Dodgers benefited from this and were seen as a well-run, steady team, in stark contrast to the Yankees, whom they frequently ended up playing in the World Series. Similarly, the Dodgers' 1974 World Series opponent, the Oakland A's, was decimated by free agency and other financial issues between 1975 and 1978.

Advanced metrics suggest that the best player in that infield was third baseman Ron Cey, with a career total of 53.5 WAR. Cey was an odd-looking ballplayer. He was 5'10" and 185 pounds, but looked shorter than that because his torso was long, but his legs were not. He was known throughout baseball as

"The Penguin" because of his body type. Cey's career overlapped almost entirely with that of Mike Schmidt, who was the greatest third baseman in National League history, so Cey was never quite a nationally recognized star. Moreover, for some of Cey's best years, Pete Rose was also playing third base for the Reds, making Cey, at most, the third best known at his position in his league.

Cey was, however, an excellent player. He was a dependable defender at third, although not quite as good as Schmidt, Graig Nettles, Aurelio Rodriguez, or other great defenders of the era; however, Cey could hit. He was a consistent right-handed slugger, hitting 20 or more home runs every year from 1975 to 1985, other than the strike-shortened 1981 season. His lifetime .261 batting average doesn't show quite how good a hitter he was. His ability to draw walks and hit for power made his career slash numbers .261/.354/.445 for an OPS+ of 121. Cey also was able to stay healthy most of his career, appearing in 150 or more games nine times between 1973 and 1983, and he continued to be a useful player until he retired at age 39, following the 1987 season.

Among the players in that infield, second baseman Davey Lopes was second only to Cey, with a career 42.2 WAR. Lopes's career trajectory was unusual. He did not play his first big league game until he was 27, as a loaded Dodgers farm system and some poor player evaluation led to him being overlooked for many years. Like Cey, Lopes made his biggest contributions on offense. He was the leadoff hitter on those excellent Dodgers teams. Lopes stole over 557 bases in his career, an impressive figure, good enough for 26th place all time; however, his stolen base percentage was a spectacular 83 percent, making him very valuable at the top of the order, particularly given his career on-base percentage of .349. Only eight men in baseball history have stolen 200 or more bases with a higher percentage of success; among them, only Tim Raines and Willie Wilson stole more bases than Lopes. Lopes might have had an even better career had he gotten a chance to play in the big leagues at a younger age, but he played through age 42, spending his post-Dodgers years as a utility man and pinch-hitter.

According to his career 37.7 WAR, the third best player in that infield was Steve Garvey; however, in the 1970s almost all baseball fans considered Garvey to be the best player on the Dodgers, and one of the best in baseball. Garvey was a huge star in the 1970s, but there are few players in baseball history for whom the discrepancy between how they were appreciated during their playing years and how they were evaluated after retiring is as dramatic as it is for Garvey. The overrating of Steve Garvey began in 1974. That year he won the National League MVP after a good year, when he hit .312 with 21 home runs, while winning a Gold Glove for his play at first base. Garvey's .312/.342/.469

season was excellent and helped his Dodgers win the pennant, but he was very clearly not the best player in the league.

Wins Above Replacement is not a perfect indicator of value, but it is a good heuristic. Garvey's 4.4 WAR in 1974 suggests the kind of season that Garvey enjoyed—a good one, but not great or historic—the kind of season that pennant-winning teams need, but not good enough to carry a pennant winner. In fact, three of Garvey's teammates, center fielder Jim Wynn (7.7), Messersmith (6.6), and Cey (4.8), all had more WAR than Garvey. Wynn, for example, had a higher on-base percentage and slugging percentage with more home runs and stolen bases, while playing a more-demanding position than Garvey. The best player in the National League in 1974, and not by a particularly close margin, was Mike Schmidt, who accumulated 9.7 WAR by hitting .282/.395/.546 for the Phillies. His OPS was .130 higher than Garvey's, but Schmidt also had 15 more home runs, 18 more stolen bases, and was a much better defender at a more demanding position.

Garvey was a consistently overrated player because he did a few things well that sportswriters and other analysts at the time considered very important. He drove in a lot of runs, got a lot of hits, and hit for a high batting average. Between 1973 and 1980, he hit .300 or better every year but 1977, when he hit .297. This was a time when a .300 batting average was still understood to be the preeminent indicator of excellence for a player. He also drove in 100 or more runs—another widely recognized indicator of excellence at the time—five times between 1974 and 1980. During that seven-year period, he had 200 or more hits every year, a legitimately significant accomplishment. Garvey was also a solid defender, but righties who are good defensive first basemen are usually there because they can't do what is needed to play another position. Garvey, for example, had a notoriously weak arm. During the heart of his career, Garvey was also known for a consecutive game streak. Between 1975 and 1983, he played in 1,207 consecutive games, still a National League record, and had an outside chance of breaking Lou Gehrig's record, since broken by Cal Ripken Jr., of 2,130.[7]

Garvey fell short of being a truly great player because of the things he could not do. He rarely walked, never drawing more than 50 in a season. For a first baseman, he had decent but not great power, hitting 30 or more home runs only once, and finishing among the top ten in home runs only three times in his career. He also grounded into a lot of double plays, leading the league in that category twice. He was not fast, stealing only 83 bases in his career. That would not have been a problem, but he also managed to get caught stealing 62 times, meaning that he was hurting his team on the basepaths.

In the late 1970s, particularly in Southern California, Garvey was much more than a baseball player. During the 1970s and early 1980s, he was the most visible Dodgers player and their biggest star since Koufax and Drysdale. Garvey also cultivated a squeaky-clean image. He was the kind of player who was always telling kids to stay in school and follow the rules, but who also had a vaguely, and sometimes not so vague, right-wing feel about him. Garvey was the conservative face of baseball. Accordingly, he was very popular in the more conservative areas of Southern California, but did nothing to make the Dodgers more appealing among nonwhite Angelenos.

Michael Fallon's book about the Dodgers of the late 1970s captures the image Garvey and the Dodgers sought to present to the public:

> Steve Garvey was, in many ways, the heart and soul of the Dodgers in 1977. Or, more precisely, he was the player that the public saw as the team's heart and soul. Easily the team's most popular player among its fan base, Garvey cultivated a clean, wholesome, and friendly image. He was known for always taking extra time to talk to sportswriters, to stop and sign autographs or acknowledge fans, and to participate in a number of highly visible public charities around Los Angeles. Garvey, with his thick, dark hair parted across his forehead and his square All-American jaw, was nearly as telegenic as a Hollywood star. It helped too that his wife, Cyndy, was tall and blonde and as put together as a shampoo model. . . . The Garveys, as they built their presumed dream life together, were featured often in the media as the "Ken and Barbie" of baseball. Mostly this was said with admiration, but not always. At least outwardly, the Garveys were made for Los Angeles and the Dodgers, and the Dodgers and Los Angeles were made for the Garveys.[8]

Because of his clean-cut image and conservative politics, Garvey was frequently mentioned as a possible future political candidate. In a 1983 *Sports Illustrated* article about Garvey's first game in Los Angeles after signing with the San Diego Padres as a free agent, Steve Wulf wrote without irony, "But then Steven Patrick Garvey, past superstar, present franchise and future senator from California, has always been too good to be true."[9]

Garvey's image, and the self-righteousness that often accompanied his image, did not always lead to great relations with his teammates. He clashed with several of them over the years. The most famous of these was a pregame fight with Dodgers ace Don Sutton early in the 1978 season. In May 1981, a few months after Sutton had left the Dodgers to sign a free-agent contract with the division rival Houston Astros, Garvey reflected on that fight. Garvey's words demonstrate his high regard for himself and the difficulty Garvey had imagining that some people might have grown tired of what they viewed as an act: "It was tough coming to work knowing that some people resented you. They resented you for your way of life, for your image, for signing autographs. I don't want to say anything about Don Sutton, but my locker was next to his and I felt the tension every day. . . . I know all the reasons for the jealousy. . . . I can understand why some guys resented me."[10]

Garvey's longtime teammate Davey Lopes expressed the attitude of Dodgers who had run out of patience with Garvey. According to Lopes, "Steve had his own agenda. He wanted to be Mr. Dodger. And there was some bullshit involved. . . . There was a lot of favoritism from the Dodgers. Special favors were given to Steve. . . . Just stupid little shit when you look back on it. But I think you get caught up in the atmosphere. You're in Hollywood, you forget who you are, what you do, and you get carried away with the whole scene."[11]

While Garvey was a beloved role model for some Dodgers fans, particularly white ones, these same traits made him widely disliked by fans who were less conservative, nonwhite, or simply did not like the Dodgers, contributing to Garvey being one of the most hated visiting players in San Francisco history. He was regularly booed and insulted when he played at Candlestick Park with either the Dodgers or the Padres.

This was, on one hand, natural, as he was the best, or at least generally perceived as the best, player on the Giants' archrival, but there was more to it than that. In the middle to late 1970s and early 1980s, when Garvey was at the height of his stardom, California was a very different place demographically and politically than it is today. Table 9 provides a very brief overview of demographic changes in California between 1980 and 2010. The major finding in the table is that between the time Steve Garvey was at his most popular and the present, as reflected in the 2010 census, the white population of California has dropped dramatically. This was slightly less true in Los Angeles and San Francisco Counties, where there was already some diversity by 1980. Thus, when Garvey was playing, the market in Southern California for a white star with a white conservative image was much greater than it would be today.

There is another reason Garvey was so hated in San Francisco. By the late 1970s, San Francisco and Los Angeles looked very different from each other politically. Today, California has become a bulwark of progressive politics and Democratic Party dominance. The state has cast its electoral votes for every Democratic candidate for president since Bill Clinton in 1992, usually

Table 9. Demographic Shifts in California, 1980–2010

Region	White Population, 1980	White Population, 2010
Statewide	67%	40%
Los Angeles County	58%	50%
San Francisco County	59%	49%

Sources: "2010 Census: California," CensusScope (2011), http://censusscope.org; "SOCDS Census Data: Output for Los Angeles City, CA," State of the Cities Data Systems, https://socds.huduser.gov; "Population of Los Angeles County, California," CensusViewer (2012), http://censusviewer.com; "San Francisco City and County," Bay Area Census (2011), http://www.bayareacensus.ca.gov; "Quick Facts: San Francisco County, California," U.S. Census Bureau (2016), https://www.census.gov/quickfacts.

with a large proportion of the popular vote. There has not been a Republican U.S. senator from California since the easily forgettable John Seymour lost to Dianne Feinstein in 1992. The congressional delegation from California is heavily Democratic, and people like Maxine Waters, Adam Schiff, Ted Lieu, and Barbara Lee are among the most high-profile progressives in Washington.

In the late 1970s, however, things were different. San Francisco was the most progressive city in the United States, leading the way on a range of issues, most visibly LGBT rights. Los Angeles, however, was Reagan country. Today, the major political divisions in California are east–west, with the areas closer to the Pacific Ocean being more to the left of those inland, but back then there was still a north–south division; at times, the greater metropolitan Bay Area was on one side, and the rest of the state on the other.

There are many ways to measure this, but data from two statewide elections, the 1978 governor's race and the 1980 presidential election, provide some straightforward evidence. Table 10 shows the percentage of the vote for the Democrat in each of those races statewide, as well as in Los Angeles and San Francisco Counties. In all these cases, as well as in census data for those areas, countywide data is an imperfect measure, but one that still reflects the broader trends. San Francisco County is contiguous with the city, while Los Angeles County includes many suburban communities. Additionally, the Los Angeles area includes some more conservative (at least back then) counties like Orange and Riverside. The Bay Area also includes counties like Alameda and Marin that are progressive. Nonetheless, the data provides a useful heuristic for understanding the differences between these regions in the late 1970s.

In 1978, Jerry Brown was a 40-year-old boy-wonder governor running for his second term. In some respects Brown presented himself as the future hope

Table 10. Percentage of Democratic Vote in California Governor's Races, 1978 and 1980

Region	Democratic Percentage, 1978	Democratic Percentage, 1980
Statewide	56%	41%
Los Angeles County	57%	40%
San Francisco County	70%	52%

Sources: "1980 Presidential General Election Data Graphs—California" and "1978 Gubernatorial General Election Data Graphs—California," Dave Leip's Atlas of U.S. Presidential Elections (2012), http://uselectionatlas.org.

of the party, but he was also a strange California character, whom the rest of the country thought was too far out. Brown's career in politics has been sui generis in American history. He left the office of governor in 1983 and was elected to the position again in 2010. He thus has been the youngest and oldest governor in California history. In 1978 he was popular enough to drub challenger Evelle Younger, California's Republican attorney general, and get reelected easily by a margin of 56–36. In Los Angeles, Brown got the same margin he won statewide, but in San Francisco he won 70 percent of the vote. These two urban centers voted very differently in that election, reflecting in electoral terms what was already obvious to any observer.

Brown was a San Franciscan, so that contributed to his appeal there. Two years later there was a presidential election in which embattled Democratic incumbent Jimmy Carter lost to former California governor Ronald Reagan. Reagan had stronger roots in Southern California than in the north of the state, but had eight years as governor to win over voters in the more liberal parts of the state before he was ever president. He failed in that endeavor, preferring to use the Bay Area as a foil for his conservative politics and quips. In the 1980 election, as shown in Table 10, Reagan carried the state handily; however, Carter, like Brown two years earlier, ran 12–13 points better in San Francisco than he did in the rest of the state.

Being a right-wing Dodger was about the worst thing you could be at Candlestick Park in the late 1970s and early 1980s. Garvey felt the consequences of that every time he came to bat at the 'Stick. It was only after Garvey retired, however, that his story became truly strange. In the mid-1980s, as his career was winding down, Garvey's marriage collapsed, and his numerous extramarital affairs became public knowledge. For a man who had built such an all-American image, even having a middle school in Southern California named after him, this was devastating. Garvey's reputation never recovered. That, combined with a better understanding of what makes players valuable, caused him to be seen very differently even by the mid-1990s than during the prime of his career.

It turns out, however, that Garvey's personal life was just a bit more complicated than his mid-1970s image, or even his divorce, suggested. He and Cyndy, the woman whom he met when they were both students at Michigan State and married when he was 23 years old, were divorced in 1983. The marriage was beginning to fall apart by the early 1980s. In an extraordinary article in *Inside Sports* in 1980, Pat Jordan interviewed Cyndy Garvey, discussing the trouble in their marriage. The piece reads like a John Cheever short story, but as nonfiction it is also very much a product of the cultural moment and a stark chronicle of a marriage that would make anybody but the most hardened Giants fan, like my 12-year-old self when I first read it, empathize with the star first baseman and his wife. In the piece, Cindy Garvey describes how

we don't talk baseball or my show, anymore. . . . Just the children. We're not good in certain areas. I'm not as affectionate as I used to be and he, he's so jumbled up in his career and his outside interests. . . . When I say, "Let's talk about it," he says, "Whoa! Is this gonna be the same old stuff? How unhappy you are?" I say, "Oh, forget it, then!" Maybe relationships are just bound to deteriorate gradually, I don't know. Don't get me wrong, we're not serving papers, or anything. It's just . . . I wonder, are marriages ideal anymore? I mean, I'm out here in the land of fantasy and I see relationships come and go and I don't know whether or not it's worth it to cash in on something stable in order to find something more fulfilling. That's why I want to try everything to make this thing work. During the off-season we're going to Europe. I really hope in the next year my husband can develop to keep my interest. I want to see if what I fell in love with is still there.

Sometimes, though, I feel I'm banging my head against the wall. I'm trying to get him to see other possibilities, that the way he sees things is not the only way. But he's so satisfied with the way he is. He's stayed the same all these years. He does everything the way people wish they could do them. He can't break that mold. It's really him. He's a nice guy. He gives and all, but . . . ah, I want electricity, a spark, some idiosyncrasy. . . . Now catch this act. It was so stupid. A few days ago we had three hours to ourselves. We're driving in the car. He says to me, "Where do you want to go to eat?" I mean, I'd love my man to say, "I'm taking you here and then back home to make love." Now, I could have said that, but it wouldn't be the same. I want him to be smart enough to arrange his meetings around me. I don't want him to have to be told. I don't want to teach him anymore. Oh, he tries, but he can't be something he's not. He has no interests other than baseball. He doesn't understand music, or art. Those LeRoy Neiman prints? They all look alike to me. And he's not a sexual guy.[12]

Many baseball players get divorced, so other than the alarmingly public nature of the Garveys' divorce, it was not very significant or damaging to Garvey. However, in the late 1980s it was learned that Garvey had gotten numerous women pregnant and was facing several paternity suits. This more or less destroyed his reputation. A 1989 *Sports Illustrated* article sought to summarize the numerous scandals related to these paternity suits.

Well, boys and girls, stick this in your lunchboxes: Garvey currently is on one side or the other of four lawsuits, having settled two others since Oct. 6. He keeps at least five lawyers in suspenders. In the space of eight months, he had affairs with three women at once, impregnated two and married a fourth. . . . He's up to his chiseled chin in debt, into the scary seven figures. Two former business associates have sued him. Other than that, it has been all apple pie and porch swings.[13]

Garvey's changing fortunes gave millions of baseball fans, including many in the Bay Area, who had long thought that the Dodger's all-American image was a bit much, a feeling of vindication. In his 2015 book, Greg Proops, a social critic with an abiding interest in the role of sports in society, listed Garvey as the backup first baseman on the all-time controversial team, noting that "Garvey had a junior high school named after him while he was active. No other player has enjoyed that honor. . . . Later turned out he had babies with more than eight women, most of whom he was not married to. So the junior high came in handy."[14]

Despite the revelations about Garvey that became known after he retired, following the 1987 season, he was an important person in Dodgers history and was instrumental in repositioning the Dodgers as having a very different image than their Brooklyn antecedents. Garvey, and the teams he led to the playoffs, were All-American and wholesome in a way the Boys of Summer had never been. In this regard, Garvey's Dodgers seemed more like the Yankees of the Ford and Mantle era than any Brooklyn Dodgers team.

TOMMY, GLENN, AND FERNANDO

While Steve Garvey may have been the most famous player on his team while he was playing, three of his teammates played a bigger role in changing big league baseball in the following decades. It is now relatively common for pitchers to have Tommy John surgery. Hearing that one of the game's best young pitcher's will be out for a year or two for the surgery and recovery period has become one of the more depressing spring training rituals. Even school-age kids who pitch too much sometimes find themselves needing this surgery, known more formally as ulnar collateral ligament reconstruction. The surgery involves taking a tendon from another part of the body, usually the leg, and putting it in the elbow to replace the damaged one. The surgery requires a long recovery time, but is often very successful. The surgery itself is so well known that it is easy to forget that Tommy John was a real pitcher, and a very good one. John was a Dodger from 1972 to 1978, missing about half of 1974 and all of 1975 with an injury that led to the surgery that now bears his name. When John had this surgery it was highly experimental, but it worked. John's post-surgery record made him a borderline Hall of Famer and a very good pitcher for many years. On the 1977 and 1978 pennant-winning Dodgers teams, he won 20 and 17 games as part of an excellent pitching rotation that also included Don Sutton and Burt Hooton. After being on the losing side of the 1978 World Series, John signed with the Yankees at age 35 and pitched in the big leagues for 11 more years, during which he won 117 games before retiring at age 47.

As the years pass, it is possible that the most famous and influential member of those 1970s Dodgers was not Garvey, John, Sutton (who ended up in the Hall of Fame), Mike Marshall (who pitched in over 100 games in 1974), or any of the other great players on those pennant-winning teams. The most influential Dodger of the 1970s may be a backup outfielder who only came to bat 245 times for the Dodgers between 1976 and 1978, playing in a total of 124 games.

Glenn Burke's story is one of the most intriguing, tragic, and important of any fringe player in baseball history. Burke was the first big league ballplayer who was an out gay man, except he was never quite out when he played. His teammates probably knew he was gay. At least two of the big league managers for whom he either played or tried to play, Tommy Lasorda and Billy Martin, ether knew Burke was gay or had a good enough idea of his sexual orientation to make Burke the target of homophobia. Lasorda made it clear that he wanted Burke traded from the Dodgers, not least because Burke had befriended Lasorda's gay son. Burke's views of his trade from the Dodgers capture the homophobia at the time as well as the clash between Burke and the conservative Dodgers culture. As he told the story: "In the seventies, the Dodgers were drawing three million fans a year. They had a pristine, clean image. Management was afraid of my sexual orientation, even though I never flaunted it. To this day, the Dodgers deny trading me because I was gay. But it was painfully obvious."[15] Martin, who was Burke's manager on the Oakland A's in 1980, introduced Burke to his new teammates by saying, "Oh, by the way, this is Glenn Burke and he's a f—t."[16] Burke was cut from that A's squad before the season began.

Burke played in the big leagues at a time when the gay liberation movement was just beginning to become a major civil rights issue. However, baseball, like much of society, was still rife with bigotry and homophobia. This made life in baseball very difficult for Burke. He encountered homophobia from managers and front offices, found himself lonely and isolated on the road, and was likely never given a real chance to make it in the big leagues. Looking back on his career a few years after he retired, Burke commented: "Straight people cannot know what it's like to feel one way and pretend to be another. To watch what you say, how you act, who you're checking out. . . . I could have been a superstar but I was too worried about protecting everybody from knowing. If I thought I could be accepted, I'd be there [in the big leagues] now. . . . No, I'm not disappointed in myself. I'm disappointed in the system. Your sex should be private and I always kept it that way."[17]

Burke was also a player of moderate ability. Had he been a star, he might still have been pushed out of baseball, but he might also have had a more significant impact on the gay liberation movement. Baseball's first African American player in the modern era, Jackie Robinson, was a great player; Burke, who was also an important civil rights figure, was not. That makes Burke's story more complex. Some players can build 15-year careers as fourth outfielders or backup catchers, but to do that they have to be respected by teammates and viewed by management as low maintenance. By most accounts, Burke achieved the former, but was never able to win over the conservative baseball establishment of the time.

Many of the descriptions of Burke written since his retirement note that he was frequently compared to Willie Mays.[18] In 1976, for example, the year in which Burke made his debut with the Dodgers, longtime Dodgers player and coach Jim Gilliam said of Burke, "Once we get him cooled down a little bit, frankly we think he's going to be another Willie Mays."[19] These reports often overlook an important piece of context. Burke was African American; in the 1970s, almost all African American and dark-skinned Latino outfielders with speed and power, like Bobby Bonds, George Foster, Cesar Cedeno, Rupert Jones, and many who were much less well known and who never made it in the big leagues, were compared to Willie Mays. Burke, however, was never going to be the next Willie Mays. He was an excellent defensive center fielder, ran extremely well, and had some power, but he never hit well in professional baseball. He was the kind of player who could bring a lot of value to a contending team, but simply didn't hit enough to be a consistent everyday player. His .230/.270/.291 career slash line is what one might expect from a slick-fielding middle infielder, not a strong-hitting outfielder. Burke hit better in the minors, but he only started showing real power when he was 24 in AAA. This is an age when most good big leaguers are already out of the minors and contributing at the big league level. Burke was an important and heroic player, but overstating how good he was and suggesting it was only bigotry that held him back oversimplifies his career and the challenges he faced.

Burke did not hit in Oakland after coming over in a midseason 1978 trade from the Dodgers or in 1979.[20] He was out of big league baseball by his twenty-seventh birthday. Then Burke, an Oakland native, came out and moved to San Francisco. He was an active member of San Francisco's large gay community and its most famous athlete. Burke died in 1995 of AIDS-related complications. His last few years were painful, both emotionally and physically, as he struggled with health and financial difficulties. In the two decades since then, he has become an important figure in baseball history, a trailblazer decades before his time.

Burke's book *Out at Home* is an honest portrayal of his experiences. It is striking, and encouraging, how many teammates Burkes writes were supportive of him when he was playing, including Davey Lopes, Don Sutton, and even Steve Garvey. There was also one Dodgers teammate who had a special role in Burke's life and career. If Burke had not been gay, but just another straight ballplayer who never quite made it, he would have been remembered by some for being the inventor of the high five. The person on the other end of that high five was slugging Dodgers left fielder Dusty Baker, who had just hit a home run for the Dodgers. When they were teammates, early in Burke's career, Baker was an established veteran. He was also a friend and mentor to Burke.

Baker remained a part of Burke's life until the end. When Burke was dying of AIDS, Baker, uniquely among baseball people, stayed in contact and visited him.[21] Baker is a baseball lifer who was a very good player for a long time before becoming a respected manager. He is still known for his ability to motivate veterans and young players and for genuinely caring for the players with whom he works. He may end up in the Hall of Fame someday.

Baker's relationship with Burke is rooted more deeply in baseball history. Baker began his career in 1968 as a 19-year-old part-time player on the Atlanta Braves. The best and most respected player on that team was another African American outfielder, Henry Aaron. Aaron, during his playing days, always tried to help and mentor young African American players. Baker was a beneficiary of that. Therefore, some of Baker's motivation for watching out for Burke was paying forward something he learned from one of baseball's greatest players.

About two years after Burke was traded to the A's, the Dodgers, stuck in a tight race for the NL West title with the Houston Astros, brought up a 19-year-old rookie left-handed pitcher named Fernando Valenzuela. Valenzuela was a valuable addition to that Dodgers team pitching 17 2/3 innings over ten games in 1980. During that time he allowed 13 runners to reach base, while striking out 16 and allowing no runs. The Dodgers finished that season tied with the Astros for first place and lost a one-game playoff 7–1, as starter Dave Goltz pitched poorly. Valenzuela got in two innings of scoreless relief in that game.

Valenzuela was the Opening Day pitcher for the Dodgers in 1981, throwing a complete game shutout against the Astros. He would go to pitch an extraordinary four shutouts in his first five starts. Valenzuela was the biggest and best on-the-field baseball story of 1981, a year otherwise remembered for a major strike. Fernando, as he was widely known, won 13 games in that shortened year, including eight shutouts. He won the Rookie of the Year and Cy Young Awards and shut down the Yankees in the pivotal game of the World Series.

Valenzuela would go on to pitch until 1997, winning 173 games and throwing just short of 3,000 innings. From 1981 to 1986 he was a perennial All Star and Cy Young contender, ranking among the best pitchers in baseball every year while averaging 16 wins, 200 strikeouts, and an ERA+ of 118.[22] During those years, he led all National League pitchers with 27.1 WAR.

Valenzuela's electric pitching beginning early in the 1981 season made him a nationally known figure in two countries. He was boyish looking, good with the media, particularly given that English was not his first language, and, because he had been discovered as a teenager in rural Mexico, had a backstory that only added to his growing legend. Fernando threw hard and had excellent control, but also caught the imagination of the public because he was on the chubby side and did not exactly look like an athlete. He had a very distinctive windup with a high leg kick, although not as high as Juan Marichal's. He took his eye off the catcher and looked toward the sky just before releasing the ball. His mechanics looked a little bit like a slightly less graceful, but more consistent Orlando Hernandez. The role in helping the Dodgers win made Fernando part of the process for baseball fans seeking to move on from the strike. Jeff Katz chronicled the rise of Fernandomania in his book about the 1981 season.

Fernandomania was still cresting like the waves at Redondo Beach when the Phillies came to town on May 18. The groupie scene around him was growing. It wasn't uncommon to see young women waiting for him after a game. He was a big-time celebrity, entering the domain of Cheryl Tiegs and Erik Estrada, when he signed a poster deal for $50,000 over two years, not bad for a rookie making $42,000. Offers were pouring in from Coca-Cola and 7UP; the William Morris Agency called. The luxury life of a big leaguer was easy to get used to—the planes, the fancy hotels, the food. Oh, yes, the food. Strip steak was at the top of his list these days. He'd ring up room service for a meal as he watched cartoons. The *Pink Panther* was his favorite; it had no dialogue. There was a lot of excited talk before the game. [Pete] Rose had his picture taken with Valenzuela.[23]

Valenzuela was of additional import to the Dodgers, and to baseball in general, because, although there had been good Mexican players in the big leagues in the past, he was the first Mexican ballplayer to become a nationally known star in the United States. He was also the first Latino star on the Dodgers. By 1980 numerous Latinos had played for the Dodgers, including Manny Mota, Elias Sosa, and Vic Davalillo, but none of these men were Fernando.

For the Dodgers, having a great Mexican player like Fernando was instrumental in broadening their support to Los Angeles's growing Mexican American population. Some Mexican Americans, still smarting from the events around the construction of Dodger Stadium, had previously been hesitant to embrace the Dodgers. Fernando changed that, making the Dodgers the favorite team of many Mexican Americans, even those who lived far from Los Angeles. He has helped maintain that fan base by being part of the Dodgers' Spanish-language broadcast team since 2003.

Jamie Jarrin, the longtime Spanish-language announcer of Dodgers games, who served as Valenzuela's interpreter in 1981, reflected of Fernando:

He was popular in every city. And, of course, he was very popular with Latins. In the early sixties, the Hispanics coming to Dodger Stadium were probably eight percent of the crowd. When Fernando came on that eight percent went up to about 28 percent.

Now it's 38 percent Hispanics who come to our park. Same thing in Chicago, in New York, in Miami. And that's because of Fernando Valenzuela. In my honest opinion, he created more baseball fans than anyone in the game.[24]

On the tenth anniversary of the beginning of Valenzueala's extraordinary 1981 season, George Vecsey wrote of the great lefty's impact on Los Angeles during his rookie year:

There are men and women who look like Fernando Valenzuela standing on busy street corners all over southern California, wearing straw hats and selling oranges and grapes off trucks for low prices. There are women who work hard to clean motel rooms and smile when thanked in their own language. And of course, in southern California, there are lawyers and doctors and teachers of Mexican ancestry.

Every one of them now had a hero in the burly, quiet, polite youth. When he pitched at the palace the O'Malley family had built in Chavez Ravine, the attendance rose by an average of 9,000 tickets.[25]

Adrian Burgos placed Valenzuela in the broader context of Latinos in baseball:

Winning his first eight decisions and the hearts of Dodgers fans, a new cultural phenomenon, "Fernandomania," was born. Mexican and Mexican American fans poured into Dodger Stadium whenever the stocky left-hander took the mound. Fernandomania spread through the entire circuit, as Latino fans came out to celebrate the Mexican pitching sensation who was helping vault the Dodgers to the top of the National League West.

Valenzuela's ascent made international headlines. In addition to his success on the ball field, his physical appearance strengthened his appeal. The prominence of his brownness and his indigenousness made him a cultural hero to Mexicans and many Latinos. He was not racially ambiguous and was therefore quite distinct from those Latino (and Mexican) big leaguers in pre-integration days who had claimed Spanish blood, stressed their European (often Castilian) ethnic roots, or kept tight-lipped about their Mexican ancestry.[26]

Fernando was a key figure in Dodgers history because he brought the team out of their longtime Los Angeles profile as the white bread, conservative, All-

American team, where the white players like Garvey looked good and flirted with careers in politics, and where the African American players like Baker and Reggie Smith didn't say much. While there is no concrete evidence that the Dodgers were any more racist than other teams during this era, they were not progressives during this period either. Their shoddy treatment of Glenn Burke may have been what any team would have done in the 1970s, but Burke played for the Dodgers.

Most good teams during these years were led by white, African American, and Latino players. The Reds had Johnny Bench and Pete Rose, but also Joe Morgan and George Foster. The Yankees had African American stars like Reggie Jackson and Mickey Rivers, as well as white stars like Thurman Munson and Graig Nettles. Tony Perez was a great Latino player for the Reds, while Ed Figueroa, a Puerto Rican, was a very reliable starting pitcher for the Yankees in the late 1970s. The Dodgers were notable because, despite having African American stars, the white players were so unequivocally the face of the team. Reggie actually displaced Munson as the face of the Yankees in 1977. Morgan, by virtue of his extraordinary play, was as big a star as any other member of the Big Red Machine. Things were different on the Dodgers. Reggie Smith and Dusty Baker were as good as or better than Garvey during the years from 1977 to 1981, when the Dodgers were winning three pennants, but they never got the press that Garvey did. The faces of that team were always Garvey and Sutton, rather than the two African American outfielders.[27]

Again, the question of whether or not this made the Dodgers any more or less racist than most big league teams of the era is subjective. For those who were inclined to believe this, or who simply didn't like the Dodgers, an interview that Al Campanis, a longtime Dodgers official, gave in April 1987 provided even more fodder for this view. Campanis was a Dodgers lifer, who had continuous ties with the franchise going back to the early 1940s. He had been a player, scout, and executive. He had been friends with Jackie Robinson and close to the Dodgers of Robinson's era. All of this made the comments he made on *Nightline* with Ted Koppel on April 6, 1987, a show that had been intended as a commemoration of the fortieth anniversary of Robinson's debut, even more bizarre.

These comments were, rightly, viewed as racist—particularly since every time Koppel gave Campanis an opportunity to apologize or restate his views, Campanis just made things worse. While the interview reflected very badly on Campanis and the Dodgers, it was also a sad reflection of just how pervasive racism remained in the late 1980s, even among Americans who viewed themselves as liberals. Campanis was asked why there were so few African

American managers and executives in the game. His response was extraordinary, meandering through several offensive racist stereotypes. Some of the interchange is quoted here:

> Campanis: No, I don't believe it's prejudice. I truly believe that they may not have some of the necessities to be, let's say, a field manager, or perhaps a general manager.
> Koppel: Do you really believe that?
> Campanis: Well, I don't say that all of them, but they certainly are short. How many quarterbacks do you have? How many pitchers do you have that are black?
> Koppel: Yeah, but I mean, I gotta tell you. . . . That really sounds like garbage, if—if you'll forgive me for saying so.
> Campanis: No, it's not—it's not garbage, Mr. Koppel, because I played on a college team, and the center fielder was black, and the backfield at NYU, with a fullback who was black, never knew the difference, whether he was black or white, we were teammates. So, it just might just be—why are black men, or black people, not good swimmers? Because they don't have the buoyancy.[28]

Campanis made these remarks in 1987. By that time, the Dodgers team of the late 1970s was no longer around. Instead, the Dodgers had become a diverse bunch, led by stars like Pedro Guerrero and Orel Hershiser. It was also Fernando's last big year with the Dodgers. Despite Campanis's remarks, Valenzuela had finally made the Dodgers something of a global team in the way the Giants had been for decades, making baseball, and the Dodgers, more popular than ever among Southern California's huge Mexican American population, thus reshaping baseball's oldest rivalry.

YES, THE GIANTS WERE STILL IN THE LEAGUE

Between 1974 and 1983, the Dodgers won five divisions, four pennants, and one World Series. During this same ten-year period, the Giants never appeared in the postseason or finished higher than third place in the NL West. They found a way to play better than .500 ball in three of these seasons, one of which was the strike-shortened 1981 campaign. After winning the NL West in 1971, the Giants fans had to wait another 16 years before their team made it back to the playoffs. In 1987, as in 1971, the Giants then went on to lose the

National League Championship Series. They finally won the pennant, their first in 27 years, in 1989.

The mid-1970s through the mid-1980s was a difficult time for the Giants, probably the worst in their long history. The rivalry between the Giants and Dodgers had become one-sided. The Dodgers were always in contention, played in a beautiful ballpark in front of sold-out crowds, and had well-known stars like Garvey and Valenzuela. The Giants were not good, played in a cold and mostly empty ballpark, and (other than an aging Willie McCovey) had few players who were known outside of San Francisco. Their best players in this period, players like Darrell Evans, Chili Davis, and Jack Clark, never received the national recognition they deserved. By the time Vida Blue came over from the A's in 1978, he no longer was quite the national figure he had once been, although he could still be an excellent pitcher and remained wildly popular in the Bay Area.

In some respects, at least in San Francisco, the feel of rivalry was as intense as ever. If you grew up in San Francisco in that era, even though the Giants were often bad, and the Reds, not the Giants, were usually vying for NL West supremacy with the Dodgers, you were taught to hate the Dodgers. Evidence of this rancor is that during these years, the two biggest moments for the Giants were not pennant-winning home runs or great pitching performances in late September by Vida Blue or Bob Knepper, but two big home runs against the Dodgers. This was a time when Giants fans rarely were rewarded by a winning team, but they still reveled in beating the Dodgers.

The last day of the 1982 season fell on, what else, October 3. The Dodgers began the day with a record of 88–73, while the first-place Braves were 89–73. If Los Angeles won and Atlanta lost, the Dodgers could force a one-game playoff. Both teams were playing on the West Coast that day, the Dodgers in San Francisco and the Braves in San Diego. The Braves lost 5–1 and were behind by that score late in the game by the time the seventh inning of the Dodgers–Giants game began, a few hundred miles up the coast. The Dodgers had eliminated the Giants from the race the previous day, and most of the 47,000 fans at Candlestick Park badly wanted the Giants to do the same to the Dodgers.

The Dodgers had their ace, Fernando Valenzuela, going for them, while the Giants countered with a workmanlike starting pitcher named Bill Laskey. Laskey and Fernando both pitched ably, but not spectacularly. Fernando left the game after six innings with the two teams tied at two. The game would be decided by which of the two strong bullpens faltered first. It didn't take long. In the bottom of the seventh, a single from catcher Bob Brenly, followed by pinch-hitter Champ Summers doing the same, started a Giants rally, but pitcher Greg Minton and outfielder Jim Wohlford made two quick outs without driving in a run, bringing up veteran superstar Joe Morgan. Morgan had been part of every non-Dodgers team to win the NL West since 1972, and was one of the most complete players in baseball history. Morgan could do it all—run, draw walks, play splendid defense, hit, and show surprising power for a man who stood only 5'7". That last trait was efficiently demonstrated that afternoon, as Morgan promptly hit a huge three-run home run off ace Dodgers reliever Terry Forster. The Giants, on their way to a third-place finish, had knocked the Dodgers out of the race. We celebrated, but were also aware of the sadly unequal nature of the rivalry of that time.

Morgan's home run was given a prominent role in the highlight reels used by the Giants, until the team's fortunes changed decisively in 2010. It was a clutch home run that was a reminder both of how bad things were for the Giants in the 1972–86 period and how good it always feels for the Giants to beat the Dodgers. Morgan's blast became more famous as time went by, but it was not definitively the biggest Giants hit of the era.

The hit that might claim this title had come almost four years earlier in a game in May at the 'Stick. It is hard to imagine why the forty-third game of the season would be so important, but 1978 was a strange year in San Francisco, both on and off the ballfield. It was the year that changed San Francisco forever. Members of the Peoples Temple, a San Francisco–based cult, were part of the biggest murder–suicide in history in the jungles of Guyana in November. A few days later, a disgruntled and bigoted former member of the city's board of supervisors named Dan White murdered San Francisco's mayor George Moscone and the first out gay elected official, Harvey Milk, the tireless human rights advocate. It was the year the culture shifted in San Francisco, as the 1960s ended and the 1980s began. The Grateful Dead closed out the year with the last concert ever at the legendary music venue Winterland, but also that year the Dead Kennedys, the seminal San Francisco punk band, played their first concert.

The Giants, in the midst of that memorable, murderous, and significant San Francisco year, had a renaissance of sorts, leading the NL West for most of the summer before falling back into third place and drawing 1.7 million fans to Candlestick Park. The high point of that season was the game against the Dodgers on May 28. The Giants started the day half a game ahead of the Reds and 2½ games in front of the Dodgers. A loss in what was the final game of a three-game series, in which the two teams had split the first games, would have brought the Dodgers to within 1½ games of first place.

That is what seemed to be happening after the Dodgers jumped ahead by three runs against John "The Count" Montefusco, a colorful Giants pitcher who was erratic but sometimes very effective, while their ace Don Sutton was throwing a shutout. The Giants strung together three singles and a double to load the bases with one run already in and two outs in the bottom of the sixth inning, bringing up Vic Harris, a weak-hitting shortstop. Manager Joe Altobelli made a somewhat unorthodox move, sending up a right-handed pinch-hitter against the right-handed Sutton. Mike Ivie was a good hitter who no longer had a natural position in the field and was enjoying a very good year in a career that was later sidetracked by his battles with nerves and the stress of being a big leaguer. In 1978, however, Ivie was a legitimate power threat on his way to a .308/.363/.475 season, while sharing first base with the legendary Willie McCovey. Ivie made manager Altobelli look brilliant by hitting a grand slam, putting the Giants ahead 5–3. The Giants held on to win 6–5, extending their lead to 1½ games over the Reds and 3½ over the Dodgers.

Because that game occurred early in a season in which the Giants ended in third place, six games behind the Dodgers, it has been forgotten over the decades, but at the time it was a joyous and important moment for Giants fans. The ballpark that day was packed with more than 56,000 people on a beautiful Sunday. I was at both the Mike Ivie game and the Joe Morgan game. The crowd at the former was louder, larger, and more enthusiastic. Well into the late 1980s, the Ivie home run, even more than Morgan's, was a where-were-you moment for Giants fans.

The late 1970s and most of the 1980s were indeed a tough time for the Giants. As the Dodgers built on a strong first decade or so in Los Angeles to become a team that reflected the sunny, but still conservative disposition of their home-town, the Giants struggled to find a place in a rapidly changing city, one where the place of baseball was growing more complex. In the two decades between 1964 and 1984, San Francisco changed dramatically. In 1964 San Francisco shared essential characteristics with most American cities. Manufacturing was an important part of the economy. It was a union town, while not being radical in any significant way. It had slightly different demographics than most cities, including a large Chinese American population, and had been a place where many soldiers had stopped on their way to or from the Pacific theater of World War II. That summer the city hosted the Republican Convention, where Barry Goldwater, in the context of that time a very conservative candidate, was nominated. Goldwater went on to lose badly to Lyndon Johnson in November.

Twenty years later, in 1984, when the Giants were on their way to a 66–96 season, a last-place finish, and their worst winning percentage since 1946, it would have been unthinkable for the Republicans to hold their convention in San Francisco. That year Republican president Ronald Reagan was reelected with 59 percent of the national vote, 57 percent in California as a whole, and 31 percent in San Francisco.[29] The Democrats, however, held their 1984 convention in San Francisco, nominating former vice president Walter Mondale, only to see him lose 49 states in November. For some reason, no major party has held their national convention in San Francisco since.

Between 1964 and 1984, San Francisco transitioned from being, politically speaking, an ordinary, if slightly more liberal than most, American city to being the progressive capital of America. The Summer of Love in 1967 rooted the city to the 1960s counterculture. The 1970s saw the entrenchment of progressive politics, the birth of the gay liberation movement in San Francisco, and a rapidly changing city. During those years, San Francisco was increasingly a city where a mediocre baseball team had no obvious place. The novelty of having big league baseball had worn off by the mid-1960s. The great Willie Mays was traded in 1972. It would be more than 20 years before the Giants would again have such a genuinely nationally known player in their lineup.

The Giants missed the postseason every year from 1972 to 1986. During that 15-year stretch, they finished below .500 ten times and ended the season in fourth place or worse—in a six-team division—ten times. From 1972 to 1977, their attendance was terrible, falling below 700,000 four times and never exceeding 850,000. They were dead last in the big leagues in attendance every year from 1974 to 1976, and last in the National League in 1977. The Giants were also in the bottom quadrant of attendance for big league teams every year of this period except 1978, 1979, and 1986. The combination of generally poor teams and a dreadful ballpark drove attendance and, in many respects the franchise itself, into the ground.

The worst years of this period were 1974 to 1977, when the Giants had the lowest attendance in the National League for four consecutive years. This was a rough time for baseball attendance generally, as most years saw many teams drawing fewer than one million fans; however, even in that context, the Giants' attendance numbers were pretty terrible. The Dodgers were a good team during this period, winning two pennants and finishing second in the NL West twice. In these years, the rivalry with the Dodgers was one of the few things bringing fans to the ballpark. The rivalry was not what it once was—the Giants were pretty bad, and crowds of 10,000 or fewer for a Giants–Dodgers game at the 'Stick were not unheard of—but in general these games had an appeal. Table 11 shows the proportion of the Giants' annual attendance that came from

Table 11. Home Attendance at Giants Games Versus the Dodgers

Season	Attendance for Giants–Dodgers Games	Percentage of Overall Attendance	Expected Attendance	Highest One-Game Attendance
1974	155,341	29.87%	60,778	22,526
1975	134,395	25.7%	61,120	35,517
1976	141,706	22.61%	65,129	37,261
1977	191,730	27.39%	81,824	48,771

The percentage of overall attendance is based on an estimated 77 home dates a year, because at that time teams still played doubleheaders. The expected attendance shows what the total attendance would have been for those games if they were only an average draw.
Source: Baseball Reference (2018), https://www.baseball-reference.com/.

games with the Dodgers for each of these years. In these years, the Dodgers' eight or nine days, or evenings, in San Francisco generally accounted for a quarter or more of the fans who came to a Giants game in any given year. The rivalry was pretty one-sided in the mid-1970s, but it was still very important to a struggling Giants franchise and to their fans.

The mid-1970s were a period when former Giants prospects like George Foster and Dave Kingman were slugging home runs and helping other teams, while the Giants had nothing to show for trading them away. The Giants also made unwise free-agent decisions during these years, spending money on mediocre players like Rennie Stennett, an oft-injured second baseman who could no longer hit. The veterans they brought in to help the team, players like Al Oliver or Manny Trillo, were often well past their productive years.

In these years, mediocre Giants teams struggled to find an identity in a city that was wrestling with liberation struggles, mass killings, and assassinations and was then overwhelmed by the early days of the AIDS crisis. The Giants sought ways to remain relevant as a bad team in a city that was at the epicenter of a moment that seemed to reject everything about establishment America, including baseball. These were days when, even in San Francisco, it was rare to see an adult anywhere but the ballpark discussing the team, radios were rarely tuned to the ballgame, and many saw the once-famous franchise as some strange thing that happened in a cold and forgotten southeastern corner of the city.

During the late 1970s the Oakland A's had fallen on bad times as well. The advent of free agency had helped rapidly to dismantle the team that had won five straight divisions from 1971 to 1975 and three straight World Series from 1972 to 1974. By 1977, almost all of the A's top stars, except for Vida Blue, were gone and the team looked like a poorly run expansion team. This was reflected in their record, as they finished in last place in 1977 and 1979 and in sixth in 1978. Their attendance for these three years was a dismal 495,599, 526,999, and 306,763. The notion that the Bay Area could provide enough support for two teams seemed implausible during these years.

As both Bay Area teams were playing poorly and drawing few fans, rumors swirled around them. In 1976, the A's were thought to be heading for Denver. The A's ended up staying in Oakland, but in early 1976 the Giants were seen as Toronto-bound, following perhaps one last season in San Francisco. On January 10, 1976, the front-page headline of the *San Francisco Chronicle* was "Giants Approve Sale—Would Go to Toronto." The lead was very straightforward: "The San Francisco Giants announced yesterday they had reached an agreement in principle to see the team to Canadian interests who would move the Giants to Toronto this season."[30] The article went on to describe the need to get league approval and the potential obstacles there, while another front-page article that day quoted San Francisco's new mayor, George Moscone, pledging, "The Giants will remain the San Francisco Giants if I have anything to say about it."[31]

However, that changed in spring of 1976, when Bud Herseth and Bob Lurie bought out Horace Stoneham and pledged to keep the team in San Francisco. Following the season, Toronto got an expansion team, the Blue Jays, while the Giants remained in San Francisco. Almost 20 years after the move west, the state of the Dodgers and Giants could not have seemed more disparate. The Dodgers were playing and drawing well and about to win two consecutive pennants. The Giants were barely holding in San Francisco with no identity, few recognizable players, and no clear path forward.

A QUARTER-CENTURY LATER

Joe Morgan's home run that knocked the Dodgers out of the 1982 pennant race in the NL West also brought the first quarter-century of baseball in California to a close. Evaluations of the move up to that point would have been mixed. The Dodgers were among the most successful franchises in professional sports, both on and off the field. The Giants were among the least successful and were about to enter a period in which things would get worse before they got better. The Giants were not a good team, had almost no national profile, and played in a ballpark that was cold, unfriendly, and far away from most of San Francisco. While the Dodgers had become an institution in Southern California, the post–Willie Mays Giants were increasingly out of step with the gestalt of an unusual and rapidly changing American city.

It didn't help the Giants that in January 1982 the 49ers won the Super Bowl, bringing San Francisco a major sports championship for the first time ever. The 49ers would go on to win three more Super Bowls over the following ten years. These excellent 49ers teams and the generally mediocre Giants meant that in the 1980s San Francisco became a football town. By the late 1980s, the future of the Giants was again very much in doubt. It remained unclear whether San Francisco would be their long-term home and, if so, where in the city that home would be. In a more pedestrian sense, many Giants fans wondered whether the team would ever be good again.

Calls to build a downtown ballpark grew louder during these years, but the voters consistently voted down measures to fund that project. In 1987, 53.2 percent voted against an initiative to build a downtown ballpark. Two years later, a similar initiative lost by a margin of only 1.1 percent. It is likely that if the Loma Prieta earthquake had not occurred in the World Series just a few weeks earlier, or if the Giants had managed to upset the A's in that World Series, the initiative would have passed.

GLOBALIZATION, PEDS, AND
THE RIVALRY SINCE 1990

As the 1980s wound down, the Giants, at least on the field, had begun to turn their fortunes around. The Dodgers had remained a good team throughout the decade, highlighted by a 1988 World Series win. The most famous moment of that World Series was the dramatic pinch-hit walk-off home run, which injured slugger Kirk Gibson and was hit off of dominant A's closer Dennis Eckersley in the first game. Gibson's home run with two outs and one man on in the bottom of the ninth won that game for the Dodgers. The Dodgers built on that victory to upset the heavily favored A's in five games.

In 1986, led by rookie first baseman Will Clark, the Giants won 83 games and finished in third place. Clark stayed with the Giants through the 1993 season and, more than any other player, helped them slough off the poor performance and image of the post–Willie Mays years. The Giants managed to win the NL West in 1987 for their first trip back to the postseason since 1971. They dropped that 1987 National League Championship Series (NLCS) to the Cardinals in seven games, but two years later won the division again and this time beat the Cubs in five games to earn a trip to the World Series. The Giants were drubbed in four games by a far superior A's team.

That 1989 World Series is now largely remembered as the earthquake World Series. The Loma Prieta earthquake, the largest in the Bay Area since 1906, hit just minutes before Game Three was supposed to start. Although nobody in Candlestick Park, where the game was being played that evening, was hurt, there was a lot of damage to some neighborhoods in San Francisco, Oakland, and the surrounding areas. Because that game was nationally televised, people outside of California got to see an earthquake occur on live television. Most of the fans there, whether they were rooting for Oakland or San Francisco, had experienced earthquakes in the Bay Area before, but (unless they were at least 83 years old) none that big.

Despite the Dodgers and Giants winning pennants in successive years for the first time since 1962 to 1963, neither season featured a close race between the two teams. In 1988, the Giants finished a distant fourth in the NL West. In 1989 the Dodgers did the same. During these years, the rivalry was still strong among the fans, but the two teams rarely competed for a division crown.

The Dodgers and Giants have now been on the West Coast for roughly 60 years. Those years can be divided into two periods using 1990, a nice round number, as a dividing line. During this second period, baseball has changed dramatically primarily in four areas: technology, economic structures, globalization, and the struggle to control the use of performance-enhancing drugs (PEDs). The Giants and Dodgers have continued to play an important role in globalization. Additionally, and less fortunately, they have also been deeply involved in PED-related questions.

THIRTY YEARS AFTER MASHI

One of the most intriguing questions surrounding Masanori Murukami's two years with the Giants is why, after he returned to Japan, it took 30 years for another Japanese player to make it back to the big leagues. There are several possible reasons for this. First, for many years, there was a perception that Japanese play was not as good as MLB. This was probably true, but that truth did not preclude the likelihood that the best Japanese players were good enough to succeed in the United States. During the 30 years following Murukami's stint with the Giants, many big league players went to Japan. Some were castoffs, but some were good players like Warren Cromartie or Cecil Fielder, who could have continued to hit in the big leagues. While as a rule these players did well, few dominated and some failed altogether. This suggests that the United States probably had a higher level of play, but the difference wasn't that great.

There were other reasons as well. The relationship between Nippon Professional Baseball (NPB) and MLB during these years was complex. Following the controversy around Murukami's contract status that led to his departure from the Giants, MLB and NPB crafted a working agreement that made it very difficult for players from Japan to come to the United States. During these years, there was little cross-fertilization of players between the two countries. Player movement was limited and unidirectional, going only from the Americas to Japan, but not the other way. One exception to this was Cecil Fielder, who after a few years not quite breaking through in the big leagues went to Japan, where he slugged 38 home runs for the Hanshin Tigers, and then came back to the United States and became a top slugger for the Detroit Tigers and the New York Yankees.

Baseball in the 30 years following Murukami's tenure with the Giants was also much less global than it is today. While the number of Latinos in the big leagues continued to grow, few American baseball fans paid attention to baseball in Japan, and almost none to baseball in Korea or Taiwan. Teams continued to periodically travel to Japan in the offseason, but there were no official games played overseas, the World Baseball Classic was still decades away, and baseball made almost no effort to market itself internationally. By the early 1990s, there were two big league teams playing in Canada, but the future of one of them, the Montreal Expos, was beginning to be in doubt. The Expos would remain in Montreal through the 2004 season and survive talk about possible contraction, but in 2005 the team moved to Washington, D.C., and became the Nationals.

It now seems natural, even inevitable, that MLB would begin to draw players from Japan, but in 1995 it was not widely expected. This was the environment in which Hideo Nomo, a 26-year-old right-handed pitcher with the Kintetsu Osaka Buffalos, temporarily retired, making himself a free agent able to sign anywhere. Nomo had been a top pitcher for five years with the Buffalos, winning between eight and 18 games every year, while striking out well over a batter an inning.

Nomo did not disappoint when he got to the Dodgers. During the first half of his rookie season in 1995, Nomo started 13 games; won six, including two shutouts; and lost one. His ERA was 1.99, a particularly good number given the offensive explosion in baseball that was underway by the mid-1990s. He was also averaging 11.9 strikeouts for every nine innings. These numbers were good enough for Nomo to be named the starting pitcher in that year's All-Star Game, where he pitched two shutout innings while striking out three. Nomo finished the season at 13–6 with a 2.54 ERA, winning the NL Rookie of the Year Award and coming in fourth in the Cy Young Award voting. The next year, he was a very solid 16–11 with a 3.19 ERA and again finished fourth in the Cy Young Award voting. Other than a good 2003 season at age 34, Nomo was never a great player after his first two seasons with the Dodgers. His last season was 2005, although he had a brief three-game comeback attempt in 2008. On balance, his career numbers, 123–109, an ERA+ of 97, and 21.8 WAR, suggest that he was a good pitcher who sprinkled three very strong seasons into an otherwise unspectacular career.

Nomo was one of the top pitchers in the game in 1995, but he also had a profound impact on baseball globally. As the first Japanese player to make it in the United States in 30 years, he would have been a story in Japan regardless of the caliber of his performance on the field; however, because he pitched so well, he became a huge phenomenon in both the United States and Japan. Nomomania was one of the most exciting things about the 1995 season. Writing in the *Los Angeles Times* on July 4, 1995, a few days before the All-Star Game, Bob Nightingale described how "in just a few weeks, he [Nomo] has emerged as a hero in Japan, a celebrity in Los Angeles, and baseball's greatest public relations coup since Bo Jackson."[1]

That summer, whenever Nomo pitched, more fans came out to the park. According to Acey Kohrogi, who served as the Dodgers director of Asian operations for much of the time Nomo played for Los Angeles: "When Hideo Nomo [pitched], we averaged about 8,000 increase in attendance in every ballpark. Not just Dodger Stadium, but every ballpark in the nation and even more than that. . . . That's not all Japanese people that came. These are regular American baseball fans that came to see Hideo Nomo, a Japanese man perform on the mound, so it's exciting."[2]

Nomo's journey to the Dodgers was different than that of later Japanese stars like Ichiro Suzuki or Yu Darvish coming to the big leagues. Nomo's decision to sign with the Dodgers was not a major news item, so when he started throwing shutouts, striking out more than a batter an inning, demonstrating his unusual windup that earned him the nickname "The Tornado," and showing American baseball fans that the Japanese could play ball, too, Nomo was still an unknown. This only added to Nomomania.

The similarities between Nomomania and Fernandomania 14 years previous are easy to see. Both pitched for the Dodgers, had distinctive windups, were the first big star from their respective countries to make it in MLB, and benefited from very fast starts to their careers. On the day of the All-Star Game in 1995, *San Francisco Chronicle* writer Joan Ryan made this point explicitly: "There has not been anyone like Nomo since former Dodgers pitcher Fernando Valenzuela burst into baseball in 1981."[3]

Like Valenzuela, Nomo became a sensation the year following a strike that had been very damaging to baseball. The 1994 strike was worse than the one in 1981. In 1994, the last third of the season was canceled, as was the entire postseason. This outraged baseball fans, who felt angry at both players and management. Many vowed not to return to baseball again. Major League Baseball was very concerned about this possibility as the 1995 season began. Nomomania could not have been predicted by MLB, but a star from a new country with a large baseball-loving population, pitching for one of the game's marquee franchises, was more than interim commissioner Bud Selig could have hoped. Nomo did not single-handedly lead baseball back into fans' hearts in 1995, but he was one of the more important players who helped make that possible.

Fernandomania was bigger than Nomomania. Fernando had a better year in 1981 than Nomo did in 1995. Nomo got off to a very hot start in 1995, but Fernando got off to a hotter one in 1981. Moreover, the 1981 Dodgers ended up winning the World Series with Fernando playing a big part. The 1995 Dodgers won their division; however, in the first year of the three-tiered playoff system with three divisions and a wild card, the Dodgers got swept in the first round by the Reds. Nomo did not pitch well in his one postseason start, lasting five innings while giving up five runs in the final game of that series. Los Angeles lost that game 10–1.

The value Nomo brought to the Dodgers and to baseball, with regard to both his pitching ability and his appeal to fans in two countries, made it impossible for MLB to ignore Asia anymore. Major League Baseball learned through Nomo not only that the best players in Asia could play, even star, in the big leagues, but that there was a lot of money to be made by expanding MLB's brand to Japan, and potentially elsewhere in Asia. It was equally clear that the best way to do that was by opening MLB to players from Japan, Taiwan, and Korea.

Major League Baseball then sought out more Japanese players, eventually creating a posting system that made it easier for Japanese players to come to the United States, and thus embarked on the second major phase of the globalization of MLB. By the end of the 1990s, seven more Japanese players had come to the big leagues. By early in the following decade, Japanese were relatively common on big league rosters. Players like Ichiro Suzuki, Hideki Mastui, Yu Darvish, and Masahiro Tanaka have been among the most exciting ballplayers of the twenty-first century, but dozens of less well-known Japanese players have also contributed to baseball's globalization. In the 2017–18 offseason, several teams sought to sign Shohei Otani, a pitcher and outfielder with the Hokkaido Nippon-Ham Fighters. Otani ended up signing with a California team, but neither the Dodgers nor the Giants, opting instead for the Angels.

Nomo had been preceded on the Dodgers by Chan Ho Park, a Korean pitcher who pitched four innings in 1994. Park would put together a good 17-year career in the big leagues, but was more of a curiosity in 1994. He did not become a valuable pitcher until 1997. Korean fans always were aware of Park, but he was not an international story the way Nomo was. Following 1995, Korean players, and to a lesser degree Taiwanese players, began to have an impact on baseball. The presence of more Asian players in MLB has brought more international revenue into the game, and made events like the World Baseball Classic possible. The Classic, for example, now includes players from Japan and Korea who are well known in the United States, making those games more interesting for American audiences.

THE GIANTS FINALLY GET THE NEXT WILLIE MAYS

The Dodgers, because of Nomomania, played a central role in the second phase of MLB's globalization, just as the Giants, because of players like Ozzie Virgil, Orlando Cepeda, Juan Marichal, and the Alou brothers, were probably the most important franchise in MLB's first phase of globalization. Globalization may have been the most positive theme of MLB's immediate post-strike years, but during these years another much less positive dynamic also began to have a significant impact on MLB—PED abuse.

The PED scandals that began in the 1990s continue today, most visibly in discussions of Hall of Fame candidates. From 1994 to 2006, no franchise was unscathed by PEDs. The Cardinals and Cubs were dupes in the feel-good story of 1998—the battle for the single-season home run record between Mark McGwire and Sammy Sosa. This was later revealed to be a competition between two PED users. The Red Sox finally won a World Series in 2004, their first since 1918, with one star player, Manny Ramirez, who eventually came to be known as a PED abuser and another, David Ortiz, about whom rumors of PED use periodically surfaced through much of his career. Several Yankees, including Roger Clemens, Jason Giambi, and Alex Rodriguez, were linked to PED abuse. Fans of the Houston Astros had to wait years to see Jeff Bagwell elected to the Hall of Fame because of unsubstantiated rumors that he had used PEDs.

Although there were many players, including many great ones, who were accused of using PEDs or who tested positive for PED use between about 1994 and 2015, a good case could be made that the most important player of the PED scandal and the era around it was Barry Bonds. Bonds began his career with the Pittsburgh Pirates, but was a Giant from 1993 to 2007, the heart of the PED era.

Bonds signed a free-agent contract with the Giants in December 1992. At that time, the franchise was not in great shape. Candlestick Park was still dreadful. The city had twice consistently failed to cooperate with the Giants and build them a new ballpark. Voters had rejected a ballot initiative calling for a new ballpark as recently as 1989. Accordingly, an agreement had been made to sell the team to a group of investors from Tampa, who would move the team to that city. This was not well past the rumor stage. In August 1992, the *New York Times* reported:

> Thirty-five years after they left New York and helped open the West Coast to big-time baseball, the San Francisco Giants put themselves in position yesterday to move back east and help open Florida to the major leagues. A group of investors from the Tampa Bay area of Florida announced that they had signed a memorandum of agreement to buy the Giants and move them from San Francisco to St. Petersburg in time for the 1993 season.[4]

Most Giants fans spent the fall of 1992 coming to terms with what we thought was reality. Then the Giants' sojourn in San Francisco was extended at the last minute by Peter Magowan, who had made his money in the Safeway grocery-store chain. Magowan led a group of investors who were prepared to buy the team from longtime owner Bob Lurie and pledge to keep them in San Francisco. Magowan's interest in the team prevented Lurie from getting the ten votes he needed from fellow owners to approve the sale that would have sent the Giants to Tampa. Many owners wanted to keep the team in San Francisco for scheduling and other reasons.

Magowan's first move, once he got control of the team, was to sign Barry Bonds, the best player in the game, to a record contract of more than $43 million. However, Magowan moved a little too quickly, offering Bonds the big contract before actually taking control of the team. This concerned Lurie, who did not want to end up having to pay Bonds if the sale fell through, but the problem was resolved relatively quickly.

Bonds's first season with the Giants in 1993 would have been a great season for many fans simply because the team was still in San Francisco. The pre-steroid Bonds helped make it even better, leading the league in home runs, RBIs, slugging percentage, on-base perecentage, OPS, total bases, and, in a harbinger of his later career, intentional walks. For good measure he stole 29 bases and won a Gold Glove. For his efforts, he was handily elected the league's MVP. It was a strange year for the Giants. Bonds led an offense that included Will Clark, Robby Thompson, Matt Williams, and Willie McGee, complemented by starting pitchers Bill Swift and John Burkett and closer Rod Beck, to a 103-win season. No Giants team had won more games than that since 1905. Those 103 wins gave them the highest winning percentage ever for a San Francisco Giants team. The 1962 Giants won 103 games as well, but they did that in 165 games, because the playoff series against the Dodgers at the end of the year counted as part of the regular season for statistical purposes.

Despite their great year, the Giants missed the postseason in 1993. That was the last season before the wild card was introduced. The Giants lost a very close divisional race to the Braves, who won 104 games. In every year since then, 103 wins would have been enough to secure either a division or a wild card, but that was the kind of break that the Giants, even with Barry Bonds, were getting in those years. Bonds's play in 1993, which is linked in the minds of older Giants fans to narrowly escaping losing the team to Florida, is one of the reasons he has remained so popular in San Francisco.

Despite his enduring popularity among Giants fans, Barry Bonds is one of the most controversial players in baseball history. During the height of the PED era, he put up numbers that were freakishly, even implausibly, good. He was reputed to be a difficult teammate and unfriendly with the media. In his 2005 book about the PED era, Howard Bryant describes Bonds as "sullen and mercurial," adding that "to Barry Bonds there were those who actually had the ability to play the game, and those who were privileged to watch them. He did not play for the public, which once it had hurt him could never be given another opportunity for reconciliation. It could watch or it could not. As one teammate said, 'When Barry Bonds says, fuck you, he actually means it.'"[5]

Bonds's father had been a very good player who had never quite achieved the great stardom predicted for him. This contributed to the younger Bonds frequently seeming a little bitter and very suspicion of an industry that he knew did not treat people fairly. Bonds was also African American at a time when the number of African American players was dwindling, and had heard about his father's experiences of racism in baseball in the late 1960s and early 1970s. Barry Bonds was also baseball royalty. His father had been a three-time All Star, hitting .268/.353/.471 over a 14-year career. Barry Bonds's father had been a very good player, but Barry's godfather had been an even better one.

Bonds's career, particularly his time with the Giants, can be better understood by probing his connection not just with his father, but with his father's teammate and Barry's godfather, Willie Mays. Bonds, who was born in 1964, probably never really saw Mays at his very best, but he was always aware of Mays as the greatest player of his era and the greatest Giant ever. Bonds was raised in San Mateo County, just south of San Francisco and not far from where the great Giants center fielder lived in retirement. After briefly wearing number 7, Bonds switched to 24, Mays's old number, during his time with the Pirates. When Bonds signed as a free agent with the Giants after the 1992 season, Mays told the Giants they could take his number out of retirement so his godson could wear it. Due to his respect for Mays, Bonds declined and selected number 25, his father's old number, instead. He wore that number during his entire tenure with the Giants.

Like Glenn Burke, both Bobby and later Barry Bonds were frequently compared to the legendary Giants center fielder, but unlike Burke, Bonds *père* and *fils* hit well enough for the comparison to be reasonable. Bobby Bonds was a rare player because he shared Mays's power and speed. Like Mays he was also a standout defender, although not quite as good, and possessed a strong throwing arm. Additionally, Bobby Bonds was a product of the Giants farm system. He and Willie Mays were teammates for four and a half years, and generally got along well.

Bobby Bonds was a very good player. Five times between 1968 and 1978, he stole 30 bases and hit 30 home runs—a 30/30 season. He was a unique offensive weapon, but one that few managers could figure out how to deploy. He stole a lot of bases and was fast, but had too much power to be a true leadoff hitter. However, Bobby Bonds struck out too much, reaching over 100 strikeouts in 11 different seasons, in an era when strikeouts were less common than they are today, to reliably be the big bat on a contending team. As a result, Bonds got traded a lot, often hit well, but never became the next Willie Mays. His later struggles with alcohol abuse did not help his career either. Nonetheless, he retired with a career OPS+ of 129, 461 stolen bases, four Gold Gloves, and 57.7 WAR. There are Hall of Famers with less formidable statistical credentials.

While Bobby Bonds struggled with living up to being the first of what turned out to be many who were proclaimed as the next Willie Mays, his son Barry came the closest of any to actually achieving that unrealistic goal. Barry became a player who had the same dazzling combination of power and speed as his father, but also had better strike zone judgment and was an even better fielder, although his arm was not as good as his father's had been. The first thing to understand about Barry Bonds and the PED era is that from 1986 to 1998, when there was no rumor or whiff of PED use around him, the younger Bonds established himself as one of the greatest players ever. However, there was more to Bonds than that. The pre-PED Barry Bonds was not just a great player, but, like Willie Mays, an extraordinarily complete one. The Bonds of that era was fast enough to steal 445 bases, an average of 34 a year. He was also powerful enough to hit 411 home runs, averaging 32 a year. Over a 13-year period, Bonds averaged a 30/30 season. He managed to reach that milestone in five of those seasons. Bonds also established himself as an elite defender, winning eight Gold Gloves during that period. Demonstrating what was one of his greatest skills, Bonds walked over 1,300 times during these years. In these 13 seasons, Bonds led the league in home runs once, walks five times, slugging three times, on-base percentage four times, and OPS five times. He won three MVP awards and was an All Star eight times.

From a more analytical, quantitative perspective, through 1998, when he was 33, Bonds had an OPS+ of 164 and 99.6 WAR. Had he retired after the 1998 season, he would have been twentieth in all-time WAR, between Jimmie Foxx and Joe Morgan on the career list. Looking at Bonds through age 33 suggests that he was better than that. Bonds is tied with Mickey Mantle for eighth in WAR by age 33, behind only Rogers Hornsby, Babe Ruth, Ty Cobb, Willie Mays, Alex Rodriguez, Henry Aaron, and Lou Gehrig. Similarly, only 15 players in baseball history had OPS+ higher than Bonds's 164 before their thirty-third birthday.

Bonds signed a six-year contract with the Giants for a total of $43.75 million when he was a free agent after the 1992 season. That contract was the biggest ever for a Giant up to that time and was considered a bold move by the Giants new ownership group, led by Peter Magowan. That signing, along with the commitment by the new owners to keep the Giants in San Francisco was welcome news for Giants fans. For the Giants, signing Bonds was both a very valuable addition to the team and a statement that the team, already buoyed by two division titles in the previous six seasons, was going to continue to contend. That 1993 team narrowly missed the playoffs, despite winning 103 games, but Bonds did not disappoint, having his best year yet and easily winning his third MVP. Bonds's initial contract continued through the 1998 season.

After that contract expired, Bonds played nine more years with the Giants on a series of short-term contracts. Those nine years were wrought with rumors, accusations, and stories about PED use. These began in earnest around 2003, but included the years beginning in 1999. Despite the assumptions and conventional wisdom regarding PEDs, there is no conclusive evidence that PED use makes people better baseball players. Joe Sheehan, one of the smartest and most compelling baseball writers of his generation, has spent years arguing that the impact of PED use on players has been vastly overstated. In 2016, Sheehan wrote, "You don't find greatness in a pill, or a syringe or a cream."[6] Three years earlier, in an article presenting data on home run rates from 1993 to 2013, Sheehan wrote, "The big lie is this: Steroids caused home runs and testing stopped home runs."[7] There are also many other variables that contributed to increased offense beginning in the mid-1990s. This includes several teams moving to smaller ballparks and more teams seeking power hitters, accepting high strikeout rates, and being willing to sacrifice defense at some positions to get another power-hitting bat in the lineup. Nonetheless, the anecdotal evidence that indicates a relationship between PED use and improved baseball skills is too strong to ignore altogether. Bryant notes that when Padres slugging infielder Ken Caminiti's steroid use become public in 2001, it "changed the conventional wisdom. It [steroids] worked well enough, in fact, that both Caminiti and [José] Canseco had been crowned the best players in their league thanks to steroids. Suspicion transformed itself into reasonable doubt. Now, virtually every home that cleared the fence would have trouble passing the smell test. The secret was out."[8]

During the PED era, Mark McGwire transformed from a slugger to a record-setting home run hitter, Rafael Palmeiro from a solid player to a superstar, and Sammy Sosa from a toolsy but flawed player to a great slugger. Many other players also took PEDs and saw their numbers improve. Pitchers also took steroids during these years, so PED-era sluggers were often hitting home runs against pitchers who used PEDs to give their fastball a little something extra. Barry Bonds did something of an entirely different order: He went from being the best player of his generation—a title that some claim belonged to Ken Griffey Jr., but the numbers from 1989 to 1998 demonstrated pretty clearly that Bonds was better—to being a better hitter than anybody in history.[9]

Although almost all of Bonds's many critics recognize that he was clean through the 1998 season, there is no consensus for when his PED use began. It is most likely that he began using sometime in 1999. Nonetheless, his 1999 season, when he hit .262/.389/.617, was, by his standards, not a great year.

From 2000 onward, however, Bonds was a very different player than he had been. He was no longer a lithe, quick player who could do anything on the field. He only stole 69 bases from 1999 through the end of his career. During those years, he was no longer a valuable defender. He was much bigger and more muscular than he had been earlier in his career. His shaved head even appeared bigger than it had been when he was younger. He was also an even better hitter than he had been earlier in his career—for a few years, the best baseball has ever seen.

Bonds's numbers in these years were not just historically excellent, but in some respects unprecedented. For example, in the history of baseball, there have been only 25 seasons in which a player had an OPS+ of 210 or better. Eight players have combined for these 25 seasons. From 1999 to 2007, Bonds averaged a 214 OPS+, including the three highest single-season figures ever:

268, 263, and 259 in 2002, 2004, and 2001, respectively. In 2001, Bonds set the all-time single-season home run record with 73; in 2007, he broke Henry Aaron's all-time home run mark. From 2001 to 2004, he won an unprecedented four consecutive MVP awards.

Bonds was such a great power hitter during these years that his walk totals were inflated and record setting. He walked 150 or more times every year from 2001 to 2004, leading the league in that category every year from 2000 to 2007, except for 2005 when injuries limited him to 52 games. His 2004, 2002, and 2001 seasons are the three highest single-season walk totals in baseball history. Bonds became the all-time leader in walks during this period, retiring with 368 more than runner-up Rickey Henderson.

Bonds was issued 399 intentional walks during these years, including 120 in 2004. That means that he was given a free pass to first base in just under one out of every five times of the 617 times he came to the plate that year. Overall, he walked in 38 percent of his plate appearances. Many hitters would be happy with that on-base percentage, but that was Bonds's walk percentage. Bonds's career total of 688 intentional walks is more than twice as many as anybody else in baseball history.

All of this made Bonds the most visible player suspected of PED use, as the problem began to dominate baseball. McGwire and Sosa, both PED users, had battled each other to break Roger Maris's single season record in 1998, but that record was quickly broken by Bonds only three years later. Even Bonds's assault on Henry Aaron's all-time record presented a conundrum for baseball, as few in the leadership, including Commissioner Bud Selig, wanted to see the most visible of all baseball records broken by a steroid user who was widely disliked by the media.[10] When Bonds finally broke the record in 2007, there was relatively little fanfare on the part of MLB.

Bonds remained extremely popular in San Francisco, but was greeted by boos and chants of "steroids" in every other city where the Giants played. Bonds was so widely disliked that after the 2007 season, when at 42 he led the league in on-base percentage and hit 28 home runs, no team wanted to sign him. A player who would have been an upgrade at designated hitter for almost every American League team was forced into retirement.

Because of Bonds, the Giants were squarely in the middle of the PED controversy, but their location in San Francisco contributed to this as well. Across the Bay, the A's were the team at the epicenter of the early years of the PED scandal. Mark McGwire had been a slugging first baseman there, where he apparently began his PED use before being traded to the Cardinals. In the early 2000s, while

Bonds was setting records in San Francisco, the star player on the A's was Jason Giambi, who later tested positive. The ur-PED abuser was longtime A's slugger José Canseco. Additionally, the Bay Area Laboratory Co-Operative (BALCO) at the center of later PED investigations was located a few miles south of San Francisco in San Mateo Country, where Barry Bonds had grown up.

After no team offered him a contract, following his strong 2007 season, Bonds retired. Since then, MLB has sought to put the PED era behind it, but problems remain. Players, often in the minor leagues, continue to test positive for PED use. Occasionally a player, including some who are well known, like now-retired Yankees slugger Alex Rodriguez, gets suspended for PED use. The Hall of Fame voting every year is MLB's way of asking the baseball writers to pass judgment on the stars of the PED era. Thus far, no known PED-using star has been elected. Among players linked to PED use whose career numbers reach Hall of Fame level—including Roger Clemens, Manny Ramirez, Sammy Sosa, Mark McGwire, and Rafael Palmeiro—none were better or more controversial than Bonds.

THE STEROID WORLD SERIES

In 2002, the second of Bonds's four consecutive MVP seasons, in which he hit an astounding .328/.515/.863, the Giants won the National League pennant, their first since 1989 and only their third since moving to the West Coast. The Dodgers, by comparison, had won their third pennant on the West Coast in 1965. The Giants won that year mostly by slugging, rather than finesse. Bonds led the way with 46 home runs. Additionally, Jeff Kent, David Bell, Benito Santiago, and Reggie Sanders slugged 37, 20, 15, and 23 home runs, respectively, giving the team a powerful middle of the order. The starting pitching, led by Kirk Reuter (14–8, 3.23 ERA) and Jason Schmidt (13–8, 3.45 ERA), was pretty ordinary. Robb Nen, with 43 saves, led a strong bullpen.

The Giants' opponents that year were the California Angels, making the World Series an all-California event for the fourth time.[11] The Angels were determined not to let Bonds beat them, but he almost did anyway. In the seven-game series, he came to bat 30 times and drew 13 walks. Seven of those were intentional, and several of the remaining six walks were semi-intentional. In his 17 official at-bats, Bonds hit two singles, two doubles, and four home runs. His numbers for the series were a sensational .471/.700/1.294.

Bonds almost single-handedly carried the Giants to the World Championship, but it didn't quite work out that way. As the bottom of the seventh inning of Game Six began, the Giants were leading 5–0—with help from Bonds, who had already homered and walked—and were six outs away from their first World Series championship since 1954, and their first ever on the West Coast. In that seventh inning, with one out, after back-to-back singles by Troy Glaus and Brad Fullmer, Giants manager Dusty Baker, Glenn Burke's onetime teammate, removed starter Russ Ortiz from the game. Set-up man Felix Rodriguez then surrendered a three-run home run to Angels first baseman Scott Spiezio. The Giants lead was cut to 5–3, and victory seemed much less certain; however Rodriguez made it out of the inning with no further damage. The Giants went out quickly in the eighth, setting up a half inning that, along with the bottom of the ninth of Game Seven in 1962, was among the most agonizing in Giants history.

Tim Worrell, the Giants second best reliever, was now in the game. The Giants still had a two-run lead and only needed six more outs. Center fielder Darrin Erstad greeted Worrell with a home run to lead off the eighth, and the game was suddenly very close. Worrell was unable to get a single out, giving up singles to Tim Salmon and Garrett Anderson before Giants manager, and former Dodgers slugger, Dusty Baker pulled Worrell in favor of closer Robb Nen. The first batter Nen faced was star third baseman Troy Glaus, who hit a double that scored both runners and gave the Angels the lead. They held that 6–5 lead to win Game Six. Shawon Dunston, a 39-year-old reserve infielder on that team, who had hit a two-run home run earlier in the game to give the Giants a 2–0 game, remarked after the defeat, "I'm not heartbroken. We've got a game tomorrow. Hopefully we can keep them quiet and cage that monkey [referring to the Angels mascot the rally monkey]."[12] The next day the Giants could not accomplish that, losing to the Angels 4–1, as Los Angeles's second team finally got their first championship.

The bottom of the eighth inning of Game Six meant that Giants fans, already 48 years and 3,000 miles removed from their last championship, would have to keep waiting. It turned out that wait would only be another eight years, but nobody knew that then. On the one hand, that defeat was devastating for fans of the team, but when the team finally won in 2010, we began to look at it differently. As Bonds's PED use became more difficult to ignore—and the idea that he had not been using PEDs in 2002 more absurd—many Giants fans were glad that when their team finally won, in 2010, it did so without any suspicion of PED use. The success the Giants enjoyed from 2010 to 2014 has justifiably overshadowed that Bonds-led team in 2002, but that team came the closest to winning a World Series of any Giants team in the almost fifty years between 1963 to 2009.

THE NEW BALLPARK

On September 30, 1999, the Giants and Dodgers played their final game of the season at the 'Stick. That day, more than 61,000 fans came to the old ballpark to see the two rivals, neither of whom were headed to the postseason. That enormous crowd, of which I was part, did not see a pitching matchup like Koufax against Marichal or even Sutton against Montefusco. Instead the Dodgers started journeyman Jeff Williams, while the Giants countered with lefty Shawn Estes. Estes was a mainstay of the Giants' rotation from 1997 to 2001, but, other than 1997, was rarely anything special.

Neither starter pitched particularly well that day. The Dodgers took a 9–4 lead into the bottom of the ninth, with closer Jeff Shaw, their fourth pitcher of the day, on the mound. With two out and two on, longtime Giants center fielder Marvin Benard hit a ground ball to Dodgers first sacker Eric Karros. Karros fielded the ball cleanly, tagged first base, and the game—and an era in San Francisco Giants history—was over. That was the last baseball game ever played at Candlestick Park.

The following year, the Giants opened the season on the road, but came back to San Francisco to host the Dodgers on April 11. The Dodgers won that game 6–5, behind three solo home runs from light-hitting shortstop Kevin Elster. That game was played at the Giants beautiful new ballpark, known as Pacific Bell Park then, but now AT&T Park. The Giants were able to build the ballpark in the late 1990s because they did it with private money, rather than city funds. The 1996 initiative that green-lighted the new ballpark was, in an interesting echo of Chavez Ravine, also called Proposition B. It was not a funding bill, but one that only sought to change land-use codes.

It is difficult to overstate the significance the new ballpark had on the Giants and their place in the city of San Francisco. One quick indicator is that the 18 highest attendance years in the two-city history of the franchise have been the 18 years they have played in their new ballpark. This is true despite the new park having less seating capacity than Candlestick or the Polo Grounds during the last decades the Giants played there. In their worst year for attendance at AT&T Park, 2009, the team still drew 250,000 more fans than their best year at Candlestick Park, 1993.

The new ballpark is in a much better location, in a corner of the city once considered part of the large South of Market area, but rebranded for the twenty-first century as South Beach. The neighborhood's climate was a huge improvement over Candlestick Point. Day games at the new ballpark are still warm, but night games, while chilly, are not nearly as cold as they were at the 'Stick. The new ballpark is extremely well served by public transportation and part of a neighborhood favored by newer affluent San Franciscans, particularly if they have to commute to Silicon Valley. There is even free valet parking for bicycles at the ballpark, demonstrating the team's commitment both to reducing traffic around the ballpark as well as its sensitivity to the growing popularity of cycling in the Bay Area.

For years the Giants had been unable to resonate with the culture of one of America's most intriguing and visited cities. The Giants descent into mediocrity and decreasing relevance can also be attributed to erratic marketing and poor management—trading George Foster for Frank Duffy and Vern Geishert in 1971 or dropping three million dollars in 1980 on a 29-year-old second base-man named Rennie Stennett, who had hit .242/.282/.301 over the previous two seasons, is not how champions are built. However, the stadium was a big part of the problem. Candlestick Park was out of the way, almost hidden, in a low-income African American neighborhood that was increasingly separate, physi-cally, economically, and socially from the rest of the city. By 1999 it was also one of the oldest continually used stadiums in the National League, second only to Wrigley Field. Candlestick Park had become old and a bit rundown, but lacked the charm of prewar ballparks such as Wrigley Field and Fenway Park.

During the last 20 years or so the Giants played at the 'Stick, it was not only unusual to see tourists or visitors to San Francisco at the ballpark, it was strange even to see them within a mile or so of the ballpark, unless they had family in the neighborhood. The new ballpark has played a very different role in the city. It has become a destination for tourists and a place for affluent young tech workers to be seen. Additionally, unlike a lot of new ballparks, in San Francisco, Pac Bell Park, as it was first called, was built with almost no public money. San Francisco was able to meet the Giants' needs, in those days of the first tech boom, without having to resort to the socialism for the rich so disliked by San Francisco's left-of-center electorate.

This dynamic between the team and the city began to change when the Gi-ants moved to their new home. Within a few games it was apparent that after more than 40 years the Giants were building a new relationship with their city. The ballpark was not only accessible by public transportation and featured all the usual amenities of contemporary ballparks, such as luxury boxes, good food, and activities for children, but it also had a real San Francisco feel. Fans could watch boats sail by just over the outfield fence. Home runs from powerful left-handed hitters, most frequently Barry Bonds, sometimes landed in the San Francisco Bay and were known as "splash hits." That part of the bay was renamed McCovey Cove. Local specialties like crab sandwiches and wine from Napa and Sonoma were part of the food and drink selections. Outside of the ballpark, there are statues of Juan Marichal, Orlando Cepeda, and Willie Mc-Covey. The biggest and most visible statue is of Willie Mays. A few hundred meters from the Willie Mays statue is a small bridge that the team named for Lefty O'Doul to recognize the team's PCL antecedent in San Francisco. AT&T Park, as it is now called, remains one of the best ballparks in the big leagues and has helped make the Giants one of the game's marquee franchises.

THE GIANTS FINALLY WIN

The Dodgers and Giants both won three World Series in a short span of time after moving to their new homes. The Dodgers won three times in a seven-year period, while the Giants did even better, winning three times in five years. The difference is that Dodgers' winning ways began during their second year in California, while it took the Giants more than half a century in San Francisco before winning the first of those three championships.

The Giants won three World Series with a group of players developed by their farm system, including Madison Bumgarner (known to Giants fans as MadBum), Matt Cain, Sergio Romo, Tim Lincecum, Buster Posey, Brandon Belt, Joe Panik, Brandon Crawford, and Pablo Sandoval. Only Posey, Romo, Sandoval, and Bumgarner were significant contributors on all three teams, but the others were big parts of two of the championship teams. The winning rosters were filled out with valuable veteran players, some of whom were major contributors, like Aubrey Huff in 2010, Hunter Pence in 2012 and 2014, or Marco Scutaro in 2012, as well as role players like Ryan Theriot or Cody Ross, who got a few big hits.

Those teams had many great moments in the three-tiered postseason. Tim Lincecum culminated a very strong postseason with eight innings of one-run ball in the fifth and deciding game of the 2010 World Series. The three-run home run by Edgar Renteria in that game, which came two batters after a surprise bunt by Huff, might be the second biggest hit in Giants history, after only Bobby

Thomson's 1951 shot heard 'round the world. Sergio Romo struck out the side in the bottom of the ninth inning of Game Four of the 2012 World Series to help the Giants sweep the Tigers that year. Cody Ross, Juan Uribe, and Travis Ishikawa hit big postseason home runs. Pablo Sandoval hit three in Game One of the 2012 World Series against a Tigers team that was considered the favorite. Joe Panik and Brandon Crawford made numerous spectacular plays, including a game-saving double play in Game Seven of the 2014 World Series.

Two players drafted by the Giants in the first round, Posey in 2008 and Bumgarner in 2007, proved to be the most valuable members of those three Giants championships and the face of the twenty-first-century Giants mini-dynasty. Posey, a fifth overall pick, was expected by the Giants to be their star catcher and help a team already fortunate enough to have a pitching staff anchored by Lincecum and Cain. Posey did not disappoint. Posey played in a few games for the Giants at the end of 2009, but started 2010 in the minor leagues. He was called up in late May and made his first start of the season on May 29 at first base. The Giants already had a veteran catcher, Bengie Molina, whom they believed was a valuable player. Posey remained at first base until early July, but gradually it became clear that the team was stronger with Posey behind the plate. Molina was released, as Posey became the full-time catcher. He went on to hit .305/.357/.505 and win the Rookie of the Year award.

Posey helped that 2010 team win the World Series with both his hitting and his ability to work with a young but very good pitching staff. His 2011 season was cut short by a broken leg, suffered during a collision at home plate. The accident led to a rule change prohibiting catchers from blocking the plate until they have the ball. Posey came back at full strength in 2012 to hit .336/.408/.549, win the MVP and Comeback Player of the Year awards, help his team to another World Series, and take his place among the great players of the game. Since then, he has continued on a pace that will likely end with him getting elected to the Hall of Fame. Posey is the first nonpitcher to be developed and reach stardom for the Giants since Matt Williams, and has helped set the tone for this Giants era.

MadBum was originally the youngest member of a trio of Giants starting pitchers, all of whom were products of the farm system, who helped the Giants win in 2010. Bumgarner's major contribution that postseason was eight innings of shutout ball to help the Giants win Game Four of the World Series. At that time, Bumgarner was a 21-year-old coming off a season where he had pitched 111 innings with an ERA+ of 131 after a midseason promotion from the minors. He had pitched a great game against a very powerful Rangers lineup in the World Series. Giants fans expected Bumgarner to be a left-handed complement to Lincecum and Cain, but few expected him to emerge as the best pitcher on the team, and one of the best in postseason history.

MadBum has become a very good pitcher, but few would compare him to the very best in the game. He is clearly, on paper at least, not as good as Clayton Kershaw of the Dodgers. During his career, Bumgarner has had a very good 104–76 record and a 123 ERA+. He has averaged almost one strikeout per inning and four strikeouts to every one walk. However, MadBum has never finished better than fourth place in Cy Young voting; never led the league in wins, ERA, or strikeouts; and never won 20 games in a season. In 2012, Bum improved his reputation for World Series pitching with seven shutout innings against the Tigers in Game Two, but he had pitched poorly in the previous rounds of the 2012 postseason.

Although Bumgarner's numbers during the regular season have not been comparable to those of Kershaw, Chris Sale, Max Scherzer, or Felix Hernandez, if you needed one pitcher of his era to win a World Series game, or a World Series, Bum would be your best option. Bum proved this in 2014. The Giants team that made it into the postseason that year, with the second wild card spot, was a strange one. They had some real strengths. Posey was the best catcher in the game. The Brandon brothers—Belt at first and Crawford at short—both were excellent defenders and better hitters than most casual fans realized. Joe Panik had provided top defense and useful hitting at second base after a midseason callup. Pablo Sandoval, the paunchy fan favorite known as the Kung Fu Panda, was an asset at third. However, two-thirds of the outfield was, due to injuries, made up of journeymen Travis Ishikawa and Gregor Blanco. Injuries had also decimated the pitching staff, making the team heavily dependent on their 27-year-old left-handed ace.

The notion of carrying a team is an overused cliché that is rarely applicable in baseball anymore, but MadBum came pretty close to doing that in the 2014 postseason. On their way to the championship, the Giants won 12 postseason games; MadBum won four of them. Twice he pitched complete-game shutouts. Over the course of 52.2 innings, he struck out 45, while walking six with an ERA of 1.03. MadBum's first game of that postseason was a one-game play-in against the Pirates in Pittsburgh. The Giants scored eight runs in that game, but Bumgarner didn't need all of them. He pitched a complete-game shutout, allowing only five Pirates to reach base, while striking out ten. The Giants advanced to the next round and were on their way.

After beating the Nationals in the divisional series in four games and the Cardinals in five in the NLCS, the Giants met a very tough Royals team in the World Series. Bumgarner was given the ball for Game One in Kansas City and pitched his worst World Series game ever, only lasting seven innings and giving up a run. However, the Giants won easily by a score of 7–1. His Game Five start in San Francisco was more like what Giants fans expected, as the lefty threw a shutout, striking out eight, walking none, and holding the Royals to three singles and a double.

Bumgarner had a nice World Series up to that point. He might have even won the World Series MVP for that performance. The Giants, however, still needed to coax one more win out of a shaky pitching staff. They lost Game Six 10–0, when the late Yordano Ventura shut them out. The Royals knocked Giants starter Jake Peavy out with five runs before the second inning was over. The Game Seven starting pitcher for the Giants also got knocked out before the end of the second inning. Lefty Jeremy Affeldt relieved Tim Hudson and, with the help from some fine defense by Panik and Crawford, held the Royals in check and left the game after four innings with the Giants holding on to a 3–2 lead.

In the twenty-first century, starting pitchers very rarely pitch in relief only three days after pitching a complete game, but the Giants needed 15 outs and Bumgarner was the best bet to get those outs. None of the more than 40,000 fans at Kaufmann Stadium were surprised to see Bumgarner making the long walk from the bullpen to the pitcher's mound in the bottom of fifth. The Royals immediately rallied as a single by Omar Infante and a sacrifice bunt by Alcides Escobar put the tying run in scoring position with only one out—this counted as a big rally when Madison Bumgarner was on the mound in October 2014. The next batter, Nori Aoki, hit a line drive to left, but Juan Perez made a nice running catch. Lorenzo Cain struck out, and that was the end of the rally,

Bumgarner was in control from there, allowing nobody on base until, with two outs in the bottom of the ninth, a very strange play occurred. With the Giants one out away from winning the game and the World Series, Alex Gordon, the Royals star left fielder, hit a soft line drive to left-center. It might have been catchable, or perhaps it should have been allowed to drop for a single. Instead, Juan Perez and Gregor Blanco, two players who were in the game primarily for their defense, misplayed the ball into a triple. The tying run was on third with the dangerous Salvador Perez at-bat. The Royals catcher quickly hit a high foul ball near third base, Pablo Sandoval pounded his chest, caught the ball, and collapsed onto the field—and the Giants were champions for the third time in five years.

One of the most important figures in the Giants three World Series championships was their manager, Bruce Bochy. Bochy has now managed, and won, more games than any manager in Giants history, other than John McGraw, who led the New York team for 31 years. Like Bochy, McGraw also won three World Series. Bochy has quietly become the best manager of his generation. He has earned this reputation largely through his work in the postseason. His career wining percentage is below .500, but in the postseason he has a record of 44–33, including 36–17 with the Giants.

Before coming to the Giants in 2007, Bochy managed the Padres for 12 years. He won one pennant there, but that 1998 Padre team could not compete with the Yankees in the World Series. Nonetheless, only 22 other men have managed their team to four different pennants, and only nine other managers have won three or more World Series. Bochy's accomplishment is even more impressive because none of his pennant-winning teams were preseason favorites; most were not expected to go far in the playoffs.

Bochy's postseason success stems from his strategic understanding that, in the postseason, every game is a must win. This has led him never to hesitate to pull a struggling starting pitcher, as he did with Tim Hudson in Game Seven of 2014. In perhaps Bochy's best managed game of the Giants run, Game Six of the 2010 NLCS, he took a struggling Jonathan Sanchez out of the game after only two innings. Bochy then coaxed seven innings of shutout baseball out of five pitchers, including two starters, Lincecum and Bumgarner. Bochy managed very aggressively in a nonelimination game as the Giants were ahead in the series 3–2 when the game began. Bochy, however, did not want to take his chances with a Game Seven, even though he had a rested Matt Cain ready to start that game. The strategy worked, as an eighth-inning home run by Juan Uribe put the Giants ahead for good by a score of 3–2. The Giants manager has also become a beloved figure among Giants fans. His gruff demeanor, calm temperament, plain-spoken style, and media savvy have all contributed to this. Bochy has also published a book of reflections on walking around various National League cities, including San Francisco.[13]

In recent years, the Giants have also begun to understand the unusual challenges and advantages of being located in San Francisco. The most glaring of these is that San Francisco is considerably more socially and politically progressive than any other big league city. This is particularly true when the entire Bay Area is compared to other big league metropolitan areas. This meant that the conservative, often devoutly Christian culture that characterizes many teams was not going to work for the Giants. Public pronouncements of Christian faith, conservative tweets, and the like are not the kind of thing that endears athletes to San Franciscans. The Giants have had many white players from the South on their championship teams who may hold conservative views. Bumgarner, Posey, Belt, and Peavy are among them. The political views of these players are not clear, but they have likely been offered guidance from the team on how to interact with the unique local fan base.

It also meant that players who might not have been quite so welcome on other teams were beloved in the Bay Area. This has included Hunter Pence, a star right fielder with a goofy and quirky public persona and reliever Sergio Romo, a proud Mexican American with deep roots in California. It has also meant that for some players like Barry Zito, an inconsistent lefty with a love of music, or Jake Peavy, a fan of the seminal Bay Area band the Grateful Dead, the Giants have been a perfect fit.

No player has been a better fit for the Giants than two-time Cy Young Award–winner Tim Lincecum. Lincecum won the award for being the best pitcher in the National League in 2008 and 2009. In 2010 he led the team to the World Series championship; however, beginning in 2012, he became increasingly inconsistent and ineffective, finishing his career with a few starts with the Angels in 2016.

Lincecum was physically unlike any other pitcher in baseball. The native of Washington State stands 5'11" and weighs 170 pounds. For most of his career, he wore his hair long and always, even when he grew a mustache, had a baby face. Lincecum also had been busted for possession of marijuana; after the Giants won their division in 2010, he famously screamed, "Fuck yeah!" into a live microphone belonging to a San Francisco television station.

For other teams, this kind of behavior would have been a problem, but it only increased Lincecum's and the Giants' popularity in San Francisco. Lincecum's long hair became a symbol for many Giants fans of how San Francisco baseball culture is different from that of other cities. At a time when marijuana laws are rapidly changing, Lincecum's pot smoking became a point of pride for many fans. The Giants, for their part, looked the other way as vendors sold T-shirts with "Let Timmy Smoke" emblazoned over a marijuana leaf.

THE DODGERS RETURN TO CONTENTION

The extraordinary success of the Giants from 2010 to 2014 has overshadowed a very strong ten-year period for the Dodgers. Beginning in 2008, the Dodgers have been one of baseball's most successful franchises, on and off the field. During the ten years from 2008 to 2017, the Dodgers won the NL West seven times, including four consecutive division crowns from 2013 to 2017. The Dodgers made it as far as the NLCS in 2008, 2009, 2013, and 2016, but lost each time, before finally winning the National League flag in 2017. They then lost a seven-game World Series to the Houston Astros. Thus, while the Giants were winning three World Series, the Dodgers were playing well, but coming up short in the postseason. The Dodgers also drew over 3.7 million fans in each of these years, except for 2011 and 2012, when their attendance dipped to 2.9 and 3.3 million fans.

On May 25, 2008, the Dodgers were in second place, 3½ games behind the Arizona Diamondbacks. Their record stood at 25–23. As the game began that day, the Dodgers were hosting the St. Louis Cardinals and hoping to avoid being swept at home. That day, they gave the ball to a rookie who had been the team's first-round pick in 2006. Dodgers fans were probably looking forward to seeing the pitcher, as he had been ranked the top prospect in the Dodgers organization in 2007.

Clayton Kershaw did not disappoint. The 20-year-old southpaw held the Cardinals to two runs on five hits and a walk, while striking out seven. Kershaw only lasted six innings and did not get a decision, but the Dodgers won that game in ten innings. Kershaw stayed in the Dodgers rotation for the rest of the season, finishing at 5–5 with a 4.26 ERA. Those numbers were relatively ordinary, but for a 20-year-old pitcher, they were impressive. The next year, 2009, Kershaw's record was 8–8, but his 2.79 ERA and 185 strikeouts in 171 innings indicated that he was better than his won–lost record.

Since then, Kershaw has been the best pitcher in baseball. He won the Cy Young Award in 2011, 2013, and 2014, while finishing in the top five for Cy Young voting in 2012, 2015, 2016, and 2017. He was also the league's MVP in 2014. Kershaw's defining skill is his ability to strike out batters while walking very few. As of 2017, he has struck out 4.19 batters for every one walk, while averaging 9.9 strikeouts per nine innings. Despite his extraordinary success in the regular season, Kershaw has not been successful in the postseason. His overall record of 7–7 with a 4.35 ERA over the course of 24 postseason games is very pedestrian and demonstrates why MadBum, not Kershaw, has earned the reputation of the best big-game pitcher of his generation.

Many people who watched baseball in the 1960s will resist this idea, but Kershaw is at least as good a pitcher as Koufax was and will soon eclipse him. It is difficult to compare players across eras, but Koufax and Kershaw were, or are, both dominant Dodgers lefties, so the comparison almost makes itself. Koufax's raw numbers are better. He won 25 games three times, while striking out more than 300 batters three times. Kershaw has never won more than 23 games in a season and only reached the 300-strikeout mark once. Koufax had 21 more wins in almost 400 more innings than Kershaw had at the end of 2017.

These numbers should be examined in the context of time and place that Koufax pitched—an extreme pitcher's era, when the mound was higher, when many teams played in pitcher's parks, and when few teams hit from top to bottom of the lineup. Therefore fewer runs were scored. When this is taken into consideration, the numbers tell a different story. Kershaw's ERA+ through 2017 was 161, a full 30 points higher than Koufax's career ERA+. This is an enormous difference. Thirty points of ERA+ separate a solid middle-of-the-rotation starter from a player who would be sent to the minors or, if the difference is in the other direction, a solid starter from a Cy Young candidate. The two pitchers have comparable WAR. Koufax accumulated 53.2 WAR, only 4.3 fewer than Kershaw's cumulative WAR through 2017.

Although the Dodgers have been resurgent in this period, they have no championships to show for it. From 2010 to 2014, the Giants won three World Championships and ten consecutive postseason series, counting the one-game play-in against the Pirates in 2014 as a series. However, during that five-year period, the Dodgers actually won more regular-season games than the Giants by a slight margin of 434–427. They made it to the postseason twice in those years. In 2013, they won the first round, but got eliminated in the second round of the playoffs. In 2014, they got knocked out in the first round.

Some of the dramatic difference between what these two teams achieved in this period can be attributed to luck. The Giants got some good breaks in the postseason and seemed to use 2011 and 2013 for retooling, but many Giants fans would probably argue that a big part of the difference is that while the Giants had the gruff genius of Bruce Bochy to get them through the playoffs, the Dodgers were led by Don Mattingly from 2011 to 2015.

In a postmortem of the Dodgers' defeat in the 2015 divisional series, Mattingly's last games in Dodgers blue, Matt Snyder of CBS summarized Mattingly's ability as a manager: "Manager Don Mattingly is an old-school manager who many new-school baseball minds believe makes questionable decisions when it comes to bunting, late-game personnel moves, dealing with the bullpen and starting lineups."[14] Mattingly was fired a few weeks after the postseason loss. Mattingly was replaced by Dave Roberts for the 2016 season, who got the team to the NLCS in his first year and is one of the game's best young managers. The Dodgers' lost that series to the Cubs. In 2017, Roberts guided the Dodgers to their first pennant in 29 in only his second year managing the team.

THE RIVALRY IN THE TWENTY-FIRST CENTURY

In recent years, particularly since the Giants started winning again, the rivalry has changed. It is no longer one-sided the way it was in the late 1970s and early 1980s. It is also still deeply felt by many fans. Ironically, given the initial tension between the Dodgers and the large Mexican American community in Los Angeles, much of the rivalry today occurs in Spanish, as both the Bay Area and Los Angeles have very large baseball-loving Latino populations.

The player who best represents this aspect of the rivalry is Sergio Romo. Romo grew up in Brawley, California, deep in Dodgers country, and was raised in a family of intense Dodgers fans. However, it was the Giants who selected him in the twenty-eighth round in 2005, and it was in San Francisco where he developed into a star. Relying on a filthy slider and mediocre fastball, Romo alternated between being a setup man and closer during the Giants World Series victories. In the final game of the 2012 World Series, he struck out the side. The game ended when Romo froze Tigers slugger Miguel Cabrera, who was expecting a slider, with a less-than-blazing fastball right down the middle. Romo, who is bearded, heavily tattooed, and Mexican American, then wore a long-sleeved T-shirt to the Giants' victory parade emblazoned with the words, "I only look illegal." This made him even more of a hero in progressive and heavily Latino San Francisco. Following the 2016 season, Romo signed a free-agent deal with the Dodgers. Romo pitched poorly for the Dodgers in 2017, posting an ERA of 6.12 in 25 innings before a midseason trade to the Rays.

Between 2012 and 2017, the Giants and Dodgers occupied the top two spots in the NL West four times. However, none of those pennant races were particularly close. Moreover, since MLB moved to a three-tier playoff system, consisting of divisions and a wild card, the nature of pennant races and rivalries themselves have changed. In 1951 and 1962, when the Giants and Dodgers met in a playoff to decide the National League champion, it was a rare end to a dramatic pennant race, but now every season ends in a league championship series. Additionally, until 1993, the structures made it impossible for division rivals to meet in the NLCS. That too has changed.

Thus, while the Giants finished second to the Dodgers in both 2014 and 2016, they went on to the playoffs anyway. This is one of the reasons the multi-tiered playoff system, in which fully one-third of all teams participate, has taken much of the excitement out of pennant races. Today, because the rules make it possible for historic rivals to play each other in the league champion-ship series, that is now the national stage for these rivalries. The Giants and

Dodgers have yet to occupy that stage together. Between 2008 and 2017, either the Giants or the Dodgers were in the NLCS a total of eight times, but they never played each other in that series.

This is a sharp contrast with baseball's other great rivalry. Since the multi-tier playoff system began, the Yankees and Red Sox have played each other three times in the American League Championship Series (ALCS). The 1999 ALCS was the first time these two teams had met in the postseason. Despite the historic nature of the series, only a true Yankees fan would describe that ALCS as a great one. The Yankees won easily in five games on their way to their second of three consecutive World Series victories.

The two teams met again in the 2003 and 2004 ALCS. Those two series were among the most exciting in playoff history. Both went the full seven games. The Yankees won the 2003 ALCS on a walk-off home run by Aaron Boone in the bottom of the twelfth inning of Game Seven. A year later, the Yankees won the first three games and looked like a lock to beat Boston yet again, but the Red Sox won the next four games. That was the first and only time a team has come back after trailing in a postseason series three games to none.

In recent years, the on-the-field intensity of the rivalry between the Dodgers and the Giants has not quite reached the level that it did in 1951 or 1962. Nor has it led to an NLCS between the two teams. However, in recent years the rivalry between the Yankees and the Red Sox has also lost some of its energy, as the two have not met in the postseason or fought each other for a division title since 2009. In that year, the Red Sox finished eight games behind a Yankees team that won 103 regular games, so even then the rivalry generated little excitement. This began to change again in 2017, when the Red Sox and Yankees finished first and second in a very close AL East race, but Boston had been in control for the last month or so of the season. The two teams did not meet in the postseason in 2017.

The Giants–Dodgers rivalry has always been as much about the fans as about the players on the field. One of the ugliest moments of the rivalry between the fans occurred on Opening Day 2011 in the parking lot of Dodger Stadium. The Giants were, for the first time ever since moving to the West Coast, seeking to defend their World Series title. The pitching matchup pitted Tim Lincecum, two-time Cy Young Award winner and hero of the 2010 postseason run, against Clayton Kershaw, the great Dodgers lefty, who would go on to win the first of his three Cy Young awards in 2011. Both pitchers were sharp that day as 56,000 fans saw the two aces go seven innings without giving up any earned runs. Kershaw was a little better, striking out nine and walking one, while scattering four hits.

Lincecum gave up five hits, while walking three. He only struck out five Dodgers, but in the bottom of the sixth, a walk, an error, and an errant pickoff throw by Posey gave the Dodgers a 1–0 lead. The Dodgers bullpen outpitched the Giants bullpen over the final two innings, as the Dodgers held on to win 2–1.

One of those 56,000 fans was Bryan Stow, a 42-year-old Giants fan from the Bay Area, who had driven down with two friends, Jeff Bradford and Corey Maciel, to watch the Giants play the Dodgers. Maciel described what happened after the game, as the three friends were trying to get to a taxi stand to get a ride back to their hotel.

> It turned from uncomfortable in the stadium to almost a hostile feeling in the parking lot. . . . Bryan and I were side by side and talking amongst ourselves. We're walking past this car. And I noticed there's a group of people. And, next thing, one of them comes from behind the car yelling, and pushes Bryan into me. . . . I turned around, and at that point, I see Jeff get punched in the face and get knocked to his back. And I just remember feeling stunned, completely stunned, almost paralyzed with the feeling of what is going on right now?[15]

When Maciel looked to see where Stow was in the melee that followed, he saw his friend on the ground being kicked in the head by one of the attackers. Stow was badly hurt. He spent nine months in a coma, suffered severe brain damage, and had to relearn basic tasks, like brushing his teeth. Stow was unable to resume his career as a paramedic and will struggle with the impact of this beating for the rest of his life.

Bryan Stow's beating was an ugly and, fortunately, isolated incident in the long bicoastal rivalry between the two teams. However, it is a reminder of the intensity of the specific Giants–Dodgers rivalry and also of how irrational sports-fan culture can be. The two men who assaulted Stow, Louie Sanchez and Marvin Norwood, pled guilty in a 2014 trial. A year later they were both sentenced to prison terms of fewer than ten years.

THE GIANTS AND DODGERS TODAY

Today the Giants and Dodgers have played in their West Coast homes for almost as long as they were in New York. They have both succeeded in building a brand and an image that fit well with their hometown. It took the Giants a bit longer, but by the new century, with a new ballpark, smart management, and a winning team, they were finally able to do this. Many visitors to San Francisco are eager to visit AT&T Park, while Dodger Stadium is now one of the game's great old ballparks, as only the Red Sox and Cubs have played longer in their current homes.

It is possible that no baseball teams will ever again be part of the fabric of a great city the way the Dodgers, Giants, and Yankees were in the 1950s in New York; however, given our current era, the Giants and Dodgers come close. Both teams are strongly identified with their cities, are regularly among the league leaders in attendance, and are by far the most popular baseball teams in their regions. Both ballparks have also crept into popular entertainment in quirky and funny ways. In 2015 the HBO show *Silicon Valley* set their season premier partially in AT&T Park. The main characters in the show, tech wizards with a valuable new startup, attended a party in their honor at the ballpark. In a 2004 episode of *Curb Your Enthusiasm,* one of the best of the many television programs set in Los Angeles, Larry David, the star actor and lead character, solicits a prostitute so that he can use the carpool lane to get to a Dodgers game. That episode, which included crowd scenes at the game, later led to the acquittal of Juan Catalan. Catalan had been arrested for a murder he claimed not to have committed. His alibi, that he was at a Dodgers game at the time of the murder, was proven to be true because he was in one of the crowd scenes of that episode.[1] This was another chapter in the long relationship between Hollywood and the Dodgers, going back to before Wes Parker made a cameo appearance on *The Brady Bunch* in 1970.

The identities the Dodgers and Giants have created over the last several decades don't seem related at all to their earlier New York days, but for years the reminders were very present. The last Los Angeles Dodger to have played for Brooklyn was Don Drysdale, who retired in 1969. In May 1972, the Giants traded Willie Mays to the Mets, giving New York fans another chance to see one of their heroes play every day. Mays had been the last San Francisco Giant to have played for the New York version of the team.

The connections, however, were deeper than that. Horace Stoneham owned the Giants until 1976. The manager of the Giants that year was Bill Rigney, who had been a New York Giants infielder from 1946 to 1953 and managed the team from 1956 to 1960. The O'Malley family, first Walter and then his son Peter, ran the Dodgers until 1998. Tommy Lasorda, the colorful Dodgers manager who guided the team to four pennants and two World Championships from 1976 to 1996, pitched for the team in Brooklyn, albeit in a total of only eight games, in 1954 and 1955.

Although it is still possible to find elderly New Yorkers who remember when the Giants and Dodgers played in New York and who still view those days as baseball's golden era, no fan under 60 has any firsthand recollections of the Brooklyn Dodgers or New York Giants. The housing developments that stand where the Polo Grounds and Ebbets Field used to be have now been home to generations of families. The Mets have a huge and devoted, if somewhat star-crossed, fan base, many of whose parents, grandparents, and even great-grandparents had been Dodgers or Giants fans.

In San Francisco and Los Angeles, you will still occasionally find an elderly baseball fan who grew up watching the Seals or the Angels, the PCL version, but there are not many people from that generation remaining either. However, there are now grandparents in both of those cities who grew up watching the Giants and Dodgers and who tell their grandkids about Koufax, Drysdale, and Garvey, or Mays, McCovey, and Bonds, while taking them to see Kershaw and Corey Seager or Posey and Bumgarner. The San Francisco Giants and Los Angeles Dodgers are so deeply woven into the fabric of twenty-first-century baseball that, as difficult as it may be for fans over 60 to believe, there are now millions of baseball fans who are probably only vaguely aware of where these two teams used to play.

THE GIANTS AND DODGERS CHANGED BASEBALL

In 1957, the year the Dodgers and Giants ended their time in New York, baseball was the most important sport in American culture and society; it was also the tail-end of an 11-year period when New York was by far the most important baseball city in the world. At the same time, MLB—or, as it was better understood at the time, the American and National Leagues—was a minor industry, where most franchises played in front of mostly empty ballparks. Most players were not well compensated, while owners often finished the year in the red. Integration was going slowly. Nobody even thought of an Asian player making it to the big leagues, and the first Dominican player was just beginning his career. Television was starting to become the most important medium through which Americans got information and entertainment, but baseball had not quite figured out whether this was an opportunity or a problem.

In the 60 years since the move, MLB has become much wealthier and more global and tech savvy (a phrase that did not exist in 1957). Major League Baseball also became a more national organization that demonstrated its hegemony by weakening or destroying independent leagues, barnstorming, Negro Leagues, and other forms of baseball that were still part of the broader landscape of the game in the 1950s.

We know that these things occurred during the decades after the Giants and Dodgers moved west. This question of the extent to which there was any causality between these developments is critical to determining the impact that decisions made by Horace Stoneham and Walter O'Malley in the mid-1950s had on the development and growth of MLB. It is very difficult, probably impossible, to answer this question with any certainty, not least because it cannot be known what would have happened if these two teams had not moved when they did.

If the Giants and Dodgers had not moved west in the late 1950s, something else would have happened. Perhaps MLB would have put two expansion teams in those two cities. Perhaps two less-celebrated franchises would have been the first to California. It is possible that a revived PCL could have expanded and become a third major league. Maybe that league would have outpaced MLB in bringing in the top players from Asia and the Caribbean. None of these things happened, so we cannot know how those developments might have changed the trajectory of big league baseball. Maybe the economic boom of the 1960s would have revolutionized the major leagues even without two storied franchises anchoring the efforts to make the industry truly national.

Nonetheless, it should be apparent that nothing that happened in baseball over the last 60 years was inevitable, despite how it may look now. It is easy to imagine an alternate history in which, when the American League expanded in 1961, the Angels became the first major league team in Los Angeles, and the second expansion team went to San Francisco instead of Washington.[2] That may have been the most likely outcome if the Dodgers and Giants had not moved, but there is no concrete reason to think expansion teams would have succeeded in these new cities, which were steeped in self-confidence and a long history of PCL baseball.

In the big picture, these hypotheticals are not so relevant because we know what happened in Los Angeles and San Francisco in the last 60 years. We know that the Giants and Dodgers established significant beachheads for MLB outside of its traditional midwestern and northeastern base and that these western teams helped make MLB a truly national industry for the first time. We know that the success of the Dodgers and, after a fashion, the Giants, in their new homes made it much easier for MLB to continue to expand southward and westward until the industry eventually spanned the entire country.

We also know that the two most important stars of the 1960s played for the Giants and Dodgers and that their stardom was rooted in the New York Giants and Brooklyn Dodgers. One had been a star in New York because the Giants were among the first teams, second perhaps only to the Dodgers, to aggressively seek African American players. By the time Willie Mays played his first game in Seals Stadium in 1958, he already enjoyed a national reputation because of his body of work in the Polo Grounds.

The other star, Sandy Koufax, was a fringe player when he played for the Dodgers in Brooklyn, but his path to the Dodgers is significant. As a high school and college student, Koufax was a raw talent. There is never any certainty that talents of the kind displayed by Koufax on the sandlots and during his brief time at the University of Cincinnati will translate into the big leagues. The Dodgers decided to take a chance on Koufax. The Dodgers took chances on many young players, most of whom never made it, but Koufax was special. Koufax had two things going for him that made him particularly valuable to the Dodgers. First, he was from Brooklyn. In those days before the amateur draft, teams took a greater interest in local prospects, believing that these players were potentially good for business and could help bond the team with its home city—or, in the case of the Dodgers, home borough. Second, Koufax's Judaism also made him appealing, because the Dodgers understood the value of having a Jewish player on a team based in Brooklyn. Thus, while Koufax became a star in Los

Angeles, and became much more than just a big league pitcher who happened to be Jewish, he ended up with the Dodgers at least in part for reasons that were specific to that franchise while it was in Brooklyn.

We also know that MLB became a much bigger national industry in the 1960s, the decade when the Giants–Dodgers rivalry grew even more intense than it had been in the 1950s. This was also the first era in which MLB became more international, led by the Giants in particular. During these years, the Giants crafted some excellent, if ultimately hard-luck, teams by building on the early advantage they had dating back to their last years in New York, when they were one of the first teams to aggressively scout the Caribbean. Latino stars like Orlando Cepeda and Felipe Alou were part of the New York Giants farm system in the late 1950s. Alou was instrumental in bringing his younger brothers Matty and Jesus to the San Francisco Giants. Additionally, he had grown up with Juan Marichal. Alou's relationship with Marichal helped the Giants sign the first great Dominican pitcher.

In 1969, baseball again underwent some significant changes. The two leagues were split into divisions for the first time, meaning that the pennant would be decided not by regular season record, but by a best-of-five playoff between the winners of each division. Each league also added two teams; the American League continued its westward expansion, adding teams in Seattle and Kansas City, where the Royals replaced the recently departed Athletics. The Seattle Pilots only lasted one year before moving to Milwaukee and becoming the Brewers. The National League added two teams—another team on the West Coast, the San Diego Padres, and, for the first time ever, a team outside the United States, the Montreal Expos. Beginning in 1969, there were five teams in California, meaning that the Golden State had become absolutely central to MLB.

THE POST POST-MOVE YEARS

From 1969 on the Giants and Dodgers were never again quite as much at the heart of MLB's changing story and evolution as they had been in the decade and a half or so between Bobby Thomson's shot heard 'round the world in 1951 and the Marichal–Roseboro fight in 1965. The designated hitter rule happened in the other league. Although the Dodgers were, in an important sense, present at the creation of free agency, the labor strife and complex player–owner relationships that were so important to baseball from the early 1970s through mid-1990s touched every team. Indeed, if one had to choose a team through which to tell the free-agent story, that team would probably be the Yankees. Barry Bonds was the best and most visible player caught in the scandals around performance-enhancing drugs, but the PED controversy played out across MLB as a whole, not just on the Giants. There were still, however, important episodes during this period when events for the two teams, particularly Los Angeles, reflected important developments and evolution for MLB. Fernandomania in 1981 and Nomomania 14 years later are the best examples of this.

All of this needs to be considered when attempting to evaluate the impact on MLB of the Dodgers and Giants going to California in 1958. In the years preceding the move, Walter O'Malley and Horace Stoneham were no more seeking to save MLB than they were trying to destroy New York City. Nobody ever accused them of the former; however, generations of baseball fans believed the latter accusation to be the case—particularly New Yorkers, both in the five boroughs and spreading across the nation in the postwar years, who saw their beloved team taken away from them. The Giants and Dodgers moved, because it was increasingly apparent that if the right team or teams moved to California they could make a lot of money; the teams that got there first would have a big advantage. From this rather quotidian sentiment, O'Malley and Stoneham set in motion something that, if it didn't quite save MLB, certainly modernized, expanded, and improved the game.

NOTES

INTRODUCTION

1. Willie, Mickey, and the Duke have become almost synonymous with baseball in New York in the 1950s, but there were only four years (1954–57) when all three played center field full time in New York. Mantle was in right field in 1951, Mays missed most of 1952 and almost all of 1953 due to military service, and the Giants and Dodgers moved west following the 1957 season.

2. An example of a fictional treatment of the Dodgers' departure is David Ritz, *The Man Who Brought the Dodgers Back to Brooklyn* (New York: Simon and Schuster, 1981). Dan Bern's "If the Dodgers Had Stayed in Brooklyn" (n.d.), http://danbern.com/lyrics/if-the-dodgers-had-stayed-in-brooklyn/, is a musical example of this Dodgers nostalgia.

3. Sam Anderson, "Exorcising the Dodgers," *New York Magazine,* Sept. 16, 2007. This essay was written a few weeks short of 50 years after the Dodgers and Giants played their final home games in New York, but was still a reflection of how almost all New Yorkers still viewed these events.

4. John Rosengren, *The Fight of Their Lives: How Juan Marichal and John Roseboro Turned Baseball's Ugliest Brawl into a Story of Forgiveness and Redemption* (Guilford, Conn.: Lyons Press, 2014), 87.

5. Andrew Goldblatt, *The Giants and the Dodgers: Four Cities, Two Teams, One Rivalry* (Jefferson, N.C.: McFarland, 2003).

6. This data, as well as much of the data about specific games, statistics, seasons, and players, is drawn from https://www.baseball-reference.com, Sports Reference's invaluable and enormously fun online baseball encyclopedia.

7. Before moving to Baltimore, the Browns had made some noise about moving to Los Angeles, but the leadership of that city did not respond enthusiastically to those overtures.

8. Brett Smiley, "'Baseball Is Dying': A 100-Year History of Doomsday Proclamations," Fox Sports (Mar. 12, 2015), https://www.foxsports.com/buzzer/story/baseball-is-dying-proclamations-031215 (italics in original).

9. Bryan Curtis, "The Dead Ball Century," Grantland (Oct. 7, 2014), http://grantland.com/the-triangle/the-dead-ball-century-mlb-baseball-playoffs-john-thorn-mlb-historian-baseball-decline-articles/ (italics in original).

10. Bill James, *The New Bill James Historical Baseball Abstract* (New York: Free Press, 2001), 224, 252.

11. The Braves represented Boston in the 1948 World Series and Milwaukee in the 1957 World Series.

12. I looked at a span of 11 years, rather than merely a decade, because the 1947–57 period is bound clearly by Jackie Robinson's debut on one side and the move on the other. Similarly, 1958 was the first year after the move, and 1968 the last season before the leagues were broken into two divisions.

13. James R. Walker and Robert V. Bellamy Jr., *Center Field Shot: A History of Baseball on Television* (Lincoln: Univ. of Nebraska Press, 2008), 107.

14. Ibid., 122–23.

15. "MLB World Series Preview Historical U.S. TV Ratings," Nielson Newswire (Oct. 22, 2008), http://www.nielsen.com/us/en/insights/news/2008/mlb-world-series-preview-historical-us-tv-ratings.html; "Will 'Super Bowl XLVIII' TV Viewership Set a New Record? (Poll + Ratings History)," TV by the Numbers (Feb. 1, 2014), http://tvbythenumbers.zap2it.com/sports/will-super-bowl-xlviii-tv-viewership-set-a-new-record-poll-ratings-history/233590/.

16. Ralph Andreano, *No Joy in Mudville: The Dilemma of Major League Baseball* (Cambridge, Mass.: Schenkman Publishing, 1965), xiv.

17. These numbers, sometimes called a player's "slash lines," refer to his batting average, on-base percentage, and slugging percentage. In this case, those are Herman's aggregate numbers for the years in question. Throughout the book, slash lines will be presented to give a quick overview of a player's offensive value. Generally speaking, if the last two numbers in the slash line add up to .800 or more, that is a very good season or player; if they add up to over about .950, the player is an MVP candidate for a single season or a Hall of Fame candidate over the course of a career. However, these numbers are not adjusted for ballpark era. Herman played in an era when there was a lot of offense, so his numbers are not quite as good as they seem at first glance.

18. Roger Kahn, *The Boys of Summer* (New York: Signet, 1973), xi–xii (italics in original).

19. Brian Cronin, "Did Reese Really Embrace Robinson in '47?" *ESPN* (Apr. 15, 2014), http://espn.go.com/blog/playbook/fandom/post/_/id/20917/did-reese-really-embrace-robinson-in-47.

20. Jerald Podair, *City of Dreams: Dodger Stadium and the Birth of Modern Los Angeles* (Princeton, N.J.: Princeton Univ. Press, 2017), 216.

21. Pete Hamill, "Keith," in *The Greatest Baseball Stories Ever Told: Thirty Unforgettable Tales from the Diamond,* edited by Jeff Silverman (Guilford, Conn.: Lyons Press, 1981), 181. Carter ended up playing one year for the Los Angeles Dodgers, as a 37-year-old in 1991.

22. Eddie Frierson, "Christy Mathewson," in *Deadball Stars of the National League,* edited by Tom Simon (Washington, D.C.: Brassey's, 2004).

23. McGraw was less successful in the World Series. His Giants team won three World Series, lost six, and refused to play in the 1904 World Series.

24. Josh Wilker, *Cardboard Gods: An All-American Tale Told through Baseball Cards* (New York: Seven Footer Press, 2010). Lucas, unlike the other Garys, never even played for the Giants.

1. BASEBALL THEN AND NOW

1. For more on Alvin Dark's struggles with that Giants team, see, for example, Felipe Alou, with Arnold Hano, "Latin-American Ballplayers Need a Bill of Rights," *Sport Magazine,* Nov. 1963, 21.

2. Television Bureau of Advertising, "Total and TV Households," TVB (2016), https://www.tvb.org/Portals/0/media/file/TV_Households.pdf.

3. Jacques Barzun, "God's Country and Mine," in *The Second Fireside Book of Baseball,* edited by Charles Einstein (New York: Simon and Schuster, 1958).

4. Roger Angell, *The Summer Game* (1972; repr., Lincoln, Neb.: Bison Books, 2004).

5. This is an estimate based on the 154-game season, in which each team had 77 home games. However, since doubleheaders were common at the time, I assumed 72 home dates per season per team.

6. This figure is based on each team having 81 home dates a year. By the year 2000, doubleheaders were extremely rare, so I did not adjust for that.

7. See Ballparks of Baseball (2017), http://www.ballparksofbaseball.com/.

8. "Average TV Ratings of World Series Games in the United States from 2000 to 2017," Statista (2018), https://www.statista.com/statistics/235714/world-series-tv -ratings-in-the-us/.

9. "Average TV Viewership of World Series Games in the United States from 2000 to 2017 (in Millions)," Statista (2018), https://www.statista.com/statistics /235678/world-series-tv-viewership-in-the-united-states/.

10. Michael Haupert, "MLB's Annual Salary Leaders Since 1874," Society for American Baseball Research (2012), http://sabr.org/research/mlbs-annual-salary -leaders-1874-2012; Bureau of Labor Statistics, "CPI Inflation Calculator," https:// www.bls.gov/data/inflation_calculator.htm.

11. See Lincoln Mitchell, *Will Big League Baseball Survive? Globalization, the End of Television, Youth Sports, and the Future of Major League Baseball* (Philadelphia: Temple Univ. Press, 2016).

2. THE OLDEST RIVALRY IN BASEBALL

1. Until 1898, Brooklyn and New York were separate cities.

2. The latter has culture.

3. Lawrence Ritter and Donald Honig, *The Image of Their Greatness: An Illustrated History of Baseball from 1900 to the Present* (New York: Crown, 1979), 1.

4. Don Jensen, "John McGraw," Society for American Baseball Research, Baseball Biography Project, http://sabr.org/bioproj/person/fef5035f (accessed Jan. 12, 2018).

5. For more on Frisch's impact on the Hall of Fame, see Joe Posnanski, "Breaking Down the Hall," Joe Blogs (Dec. 7, 2012), http://joeposnanski.com/breaking -down-the-hall/.

6. Christy Mathewson, *Pitching in a Pinch, or Baseball from the Inside* (New York: Grosset and Dunlap, 1912), Kindle edition, chap. 3.

7. Lawrence Ritter and Donald Honig, *The 100 Greatest Baseball Players of All Time* (New York: Crown, 1981), 71.

8. Cait Murphy, *Crazy '08: How a Cast of Cranks, Rogues, Boneheads, and Magnates Created the Greatest Year in Baseball History* (Washington, D.C.: Smithsonian Books, 2007), 191–93.

9. Frank Graham, *The Brooklyn Dodgers: An Informal History* (1945; repr., Carbondale: Southern Illinois Univ. Press, 2002).

10. Jack Kavanaugh and Norman Macht, *Uncle Robbie* (Cleveland: Society for American Baseball Research, 1999), 185.

11. Arthur Daley, "Uncle Robbie and the Brooks" [1951], in *A Brooklyn Dodgers Reader*, edited by Andrew Paul Mele (Jefferson, N.C.: McFarland, 2004), 26.

12. Harold Parrott, "When Ebbets Field Was a Bad Joke" [1976], in *A Brooklyn Dodgers Reader*, edited by Andrew Paul Mele (Jefferson, N.C.: McFarland, 2004), 42.

13. Kavanaugh and Macht, *Uncle Robbie*, 21.

14. Ibid., 23.

15. Graham, *Brooklyn Dodgers*, 47–48.

16. Kavanaugh and Macht, *Uncle Robbie*, 51.

17. Damon Runyon, "1923: New York Giants 5, New York Yankees 4" [1923], in *The Fireside Book of Baseball, Volume I*, edited by Charles Einstein (New York: Simon and Schuster, 1956) (italics in original). Stengel was only 32 at the time of the home run.

18. Steven Goldman, *Forging Genius: The Making of Casey Stengel* (Washington, D.C.: Potomac Books, 2005), 153.

19. Scott Simon, "Brooklyn, 1947" [2002], in *A Brooklyn Dodgers Reader*, edited by Andrew Paul Mele (Jefferson, N.C.: McFarland, 2004), 107.

20. Robert E. Murphy, *After Many a Summer: The Passing of the Giants and Dodgers and a Golden Age in New York Baseball* (New York: Union Square Press, 2009), 20.

21. Wendell Cox Consultancy, "City of New York and Boroughs: Population and Population Density from 1790," Demographia (2001), http://www.demographia.com/dm-nyc.htm.

22. Michael Fallon, *Dodgerland: Decadent Los Angeles and the 1977–78 Dodgers* (Lincoln: Univ. of Nebraska Press, 2016), Kindle edition.

23. My grandfather, for example, left the Lower East Side of Manhattan, where he had been born in 1907, and moved to the Bronx when he was around 11 or 12. For the rest of his life, which lasted well into the 1990s, he described that move as going to the "country."

24. For more about Robinson's on-the-field contributions, see Lincoln Mitchell, "How Good a Player Was Jackie Robinson?" HuffPost (Apr. 17, 2013), https://www.huffingtonpost.com/lincoln-mitchell/how-good-a-player-was-jac_b_3099879.html.

25. Graham, *Brooklyn Dodgers*, 110.

26. "Terry Predicts Giants Will Finish among First Three," *New York Herald Tribune*, Jan. 25, 1934, 19.

3. NEW YORK IN THE 1950S

1. Martin Shefter, "New York's National and International Influence," in *Capital of the American Century: The National and International Influence of New York City*, edited by Martin Shefter (New York: Russell Sage Foundation, 1993), 1.

2. U.S. Census data as reported and analyzed by the New York Department of City Planning, "Current and Projected Populations: Current Estimates of New

York City's Population for July 2016," NYC Planning, http://www1.nyc.gov/site /planning/data-maps/nyc-population/current-future-populations.page (accessed Jan. 2, 2018).

3. U.S. Census Bureau, "Table 33. New York—Race and Hispanic Origin for Selected Large Cities and Other Places: Earliest Census to 1990" (July 13, 2005), http://www.census.gov/population/www/documentation/twps0076/NYtab.pdf.

4. Campbell Gibson and Kay Jung, "Historical Census Statistics on the Foreign-Born Population of the United States: 1850–2000," Working Paper No. 81 (Washington, D.C.: U.S. Census Bureau, Population Division, 2006), 74, table 23, https://www.census.gov/population/www/documentation/twps0081/twps0081.pdf (accessed Jan. 2, 2017).

5. José L. Vázquez Calzada, *La población de Puerto Rico y su trayectoria histórica* (Río Piedras, P.R.: Escuela Graduada de Salud Pública, Recinto de Ciencias Médicas, Universidad de Puerto Rico, 1988), 286; for 1970–90 data, see Francisco L. Rivera Batiz and Carlos Santiago, *Island Paradox: Puerto Rico in the 1990s* (New York: Russell Sage Foundation, 1996), 45.

6. New York City Department of Planning, *Puerto Rican Migration to New York City* (Feb. 1957), 1.

7. U.S. Census Bureau, "Table 33. New York."

8. OPS (On-Base Plus Slugging) is a statistic that seeks to measure a player's offensive value by aggregating his on-base and slugging percentages. OPS+ normalizes that statistic across contexts to make it easier to compare players from different eras. An OPS+ of 100 is league average for that time and place. An OPS+ of 120 is an All-Star candidate; over 140, an MVP and potentially, if sustained over a career, a Hall of Famer. Williams's 190 is second only to that of Babe Ruth.

9. WAR (Wins Above Replacement) is a statistic that seeks to measure the value of a player with one number. It is created through a complex formula, but is very useful and easy to understand. A season of six or more WAR is excellent. Eight or more WAR in a season usually makes a player an MVP candidate. However, in bad years, players can accumulate negative WAR.

10. Dom Forker, *The Men of Autumn* (New York: Signet, 1990). With reference to the Brooklyn Dodgers, see Kahn, *The Boys of Summer*.

11. Kahn, *The Boys of Summer*, xii.

12. Andrew Paul Mele, ed., *A Brooklyn Dodgers Reader* (Jefferson, N.C.: McFarland, 2004), xii.

13. See "The Glory Days: New York Baseball, 1947–1957," Museum of the City of New York (June 27–Dec. 31, 2007), http://www.mcny.org/exhibition/glory-days. This exhibit featured a section on Bobby Thomson's famous 1951 home run. While I was looking at that part of the exhibit, an older man who looked to be in his late 60s or early 70s stood next to me and groaned audibly. When I asked him if he remembered that home run, he responded that he had been in the military in Korea during that series and had bet his entire month's pay on the Dodgers. More than 50 years later, he was still upset about the Giants' dramatic come-from-behind victory.

14. George Will, "Fifties Baseball," *The Story of the Game, the Story of America*, PBS (1994), http://www.pbs.org/kenburns/baseball/capital/georgewill.html.

15. Harvey Frommer, *New York City Baseball: The Last Golden Age* (Madison: Univ. of Wisconsin Press, 2004), 32.

16. Ibid., 33.

17. "The Glory Days: New York Baseball, 1947–1957."

18. Harold Rosenthal, *The Ten Best Years of Baseball: An Informal History of the 1950s* (New York: Van Nostrand Reinhold, 1979).

19. Frommer, *New York City Baseball.*

20. Carl Prince, *Brooklyn's Dodgers: The Bums, the Borough, and the Best of Baseball, 1947–1957* (Oxford: Oxford Univ. Press, 1996).

21. Ibid., 42. Other notable Yankees fans who were born or raised in Brooklyn in the 1930s and 1940s include Rudolph Giuliani, who made a television commercial based on that peculiarity during his successful 1993 mayoral campaign, and noted New York haberdasher and raconteur Joseph D'Anna.

22. Woody Allen, *Manhattan* (United Artists, 1979).

23. Don DeLillo, *Underworld* (New York, Scribner, 1997), 14–15.

24. Ibid., 60.

25. See, for example, Robert Weintraub, *The Victory Season: The End of World War II and the Birth of Baseball's Golden Age* (New York: Little, Brown and Company, 2013); Bill Gutman, *The Golden Age of Baseball, 1941–1964* (Charlotte, N.C.: Baker and Taylor, 1992); and Dave Heller and Bob Wolff, *Facing Ted Williams: Players from the Golden Age of Baseball Recall the Greatest Hitter Who Ever Lived* (New York: Sports Publishing, 2013).

26. Murphy, *After Many a Summer,* 73.

27. Roberto Gonzalez Echeverria, *The Pride of Havana: A History of Cuban Baseball,* (Oxford: Oxford Univ. Press, 1999), 9.

28. Adrian Burgos Jr., *Playing America's Game: Baseball, Latinos, and the Color Line* (Berkeley: Univ. of California Press, 2007), 194.

29. Ibid., 224–25.

30. Rosengren, *Fight of Their Lives,* 42.

31. James, *New Bill James Historical Baseball Abstract.*

32. Rick Swaine, "Jackie Robinson," Society for American Baseball Research, Baseball Biography Project, http://sabr.org/bioproj/person/bb9e2490 (accessed Jan. 12, 2018).

33. Maria Aspan, "Andy Rooney Regrets a Racist Comment in Recent Column," *New York Times,* Aug. 27, 2007, http://www.nytimes.com/2007/08/27/business/media/27rooney.html.

34. John Updike, "Hub Fans Bid Kid Adieu," *New Yorker,* Oct. 22, 1960.

35. Musial had grown up in Donora, Pennsylvania, where African Americans and whites played ball together even in the 1930s. Musial was a star basketball player as well as baseball player as a youth and had played on an integrated basketball team. In a strange quirk of baseball history, one of the African American players on that team was Buddy Griffey. Griffey's son Ken was a standout outfielder for the Reds, Yankees, Braves, and Mariners during the 1970s, 1980s, and early 1990s. Buddy Griffey's grandson, Ken Griffey Jr., became an even better player than his father and was elected to the Baseball Hall of Fame in 2016. Griffey received 99.3 percent of the vote on the first ballot, even more than Musial. Contemporary fans probably don't want to hear it, but, due to his durability and sustained excellence, Musial was the better player.

36. Frommer, *New York City Baseball,* 95.

37. Ibid., 96.

38. "1940–1949 Ballpark Attendance," Ballparks of Baseball (2017), http://www
.ballparksofbaseball.com/1940-1949-mlb-attendance/.

39. Art Smith, "And Joy Reigned—Unrefined," *New York Daily News,* Oct. 5, 1955.

4. BASEBALL ON THE WEST COAST

1. The Angels became the California Angels in 1965, the Anaheim Angels in 1997, and have gone by the awkward moniker the Los Angeles Angels of Anaheim since 2005.

2. Another famous athlete who graduated from Galileo High School was O. J. Simpson.

3. Dennis Snelling, *The Greatest Minor League: A History of the Pacific Coast League, 1903–1957* (Jefferson, N.C.: McFarland, 2012), Kindle edition, preface.

4. Michael Lomax, "A Reshuffling Market: The Pacific Coast League's Efforts to Become a Third Major League and How The Braves Made Milwaukee Famous," paper presented at the North American Society for Sport History annual conference, Springfield, Mass., May 2001, available through Fisher Digital Publications (Feb. 22, 2013), https://fisherpub.sjfc.edu/nepca/conference/2012/55/.

5. Snelling, *Greatest Minor League,* 11

6. Ibid., 37.

7. Quoted in Brent Kelly, *The San Francisco Seals, 1946–1956* (Jefferson, N.C.: McFarland, 2002), 269.

8. Charles Einstein, *A Flag for San Francisco* (New York: Simon and Schuster, 1963), 4.

9. U.S. Census Bureau, "Census of Population and Housing, 1920," vol. 3, "Composition and Characteristics of the Population by States" (Washington, D.C.: Government Printing Office, 1921), https://www2.census.gov/prod2/decennial
/documents/41084484v3_TOC.pdf; U.S. Census Bureau, "Census of Population and Housing, 1930: Population," vol. 3, part 1, "Reports by States: Alabama–Missouri" (Washington, D.C.: Government Printing Office, 1931), https://www2.census.gov
/prod2/decennial/documents/10612963v3p1_TOC.pdf .

10. Richard Walker, "Another Round of Globalization in San Francisco," *Urban Geography* 17.1 (1996): 60–94.

11. Kevin Starr, *Inventing the Dream: California through the Progressive Era* (Oxford: Oxford Univ. Press, 1985), 193–94.

12. John Hibner, "Last Hurrah for the Seals," SABR Research Journal Archives, http://research.sabr.org/journals/last-hurrah-for-the-seals (accessed Jan. 13, 2018). Also see Ballparks of Baseball (2017), http://www.ballparksofbaseball.com/.

13. Kelly, *San Francisco Seals,* 11.

14. Bill Weiss and Marshall Wright, "Top 100 Teams: 44. 1922 San Francisco Seals," *MiLB.com,* http://www.milb.com/milb/history/top100.jsp?idx=44 (accessed Jan. 13, 2018). Also see Ballparks of Baseball (2017), http://www.ballparksofbaseball
.com/.

15. Jerry Cohen, email exchange with author, Sept. 12–13, 2016.

16. Bill Weiss and Marshall Wright, "Top 100 Teams: 1. 1934 Los Angeles Angels," MiLB, http://www.milb.com/milb/history/top100.jsp?idx=1 (accessed Jan. 6, 2018).

17. Theodore H. White, *The Making of the President, 1960* (New York: Pocket Books, 1961), 335–36 (italics in original).

18. Walker and Bellamy, *Center Field Shot,* 98.

19. Mitchell, *Will Big League Baseball Survive?* 24–26, discussed how the decline of the Negro Leagues had begun before Jackie Robinson's debut.

20. Williams's mother was Mexican American.

21. Campbell Gibson and Kay Jung, "Historical Census Statistics on Population Totals By Race, 1790 to 1990, and By Hispanic Origin, 1970 to 1990," Working Paper No. 56 (Washington, D.C.: U.S. Census Bureau, Population Division, 2002), https://www.census.gov/content/dam/Census/library/working-papers/2002/demo/POP-twps0056.pdf.

22. Jay Bergman, "Short Stay: Black Baseball Briefly Had West Coast Home," *Orange County Register,* Aug. 21, 2013, http://www.ocregister.com/articles/league-378201-baseball-oakland.html.

23. Francisco E. Balderrama and Richard A. Santillan, *Mexican American Baseball in Los Angeles* (Charleston, S.C.: Arcadia, 2011).

24. Campbell Gibson, "Population of the 100 Largest Cities and Other Urban Places in the United States: 1790 to 1990," Working Paper No. POP-WP027 (Washington, D.C.: U.S. Census Bureau, Population Division, 1998), http://www.census.gov/library/working-papers/1998/demo/POP-twps0027.html.

25. U.S. Census Bureau, "Statistical Abstract of the United States," 81st edition, (Washington, D.C.: Government Printing Office, 1960), 2:18–21, table 14, https://www2.census.gov/library/publications/1960/compendia/statab/81ed/1960-02.pdf.

5. THE MOVE

1. See, for example, Neil Sullivan, *The Dodgers Move West* (New York: Oxford Univ. Press, 1987); Murphy, *After Many a Summer;* Prince, *Brooklyn's Dodgers;* and Kahn, *The Boys of Summer.* Goldblatt, *Giants and the Dodgers,* also analyzes the move, but with less of an emphasis on its impact on New York.

2. Few people have had as much influence on New York City as Robert Moses. To a great extent, we live in Robert Moses's New York. Thoroughfares like the Cross Bronx Expressway or the Triborough Bridge, which are still essential for the daily functioning of New York, were, for better and worse, envisioned and built by Moses. Weekend getaways like Jones Beach and the roads that take people there, as well as the paucity of parks in lower-income communities, are also largely Moses's doing. Robert Caro's *The Power Broker: Robert Moses and the Fall of New York* (New York: Vintage Books, 1974) remains by far the best and most comprehensive work on Moses as well as one of the best biographies of anybody.

3. Paul Hirsch, "Walter O'Malley Was Right," in *Endless Seasons: Baseball in Southern California,* edited by Jean Hastings Ardell and Andy McCue, *The National Pastime,* no. 41 (Phoenix: Society for American Baseball Research, 2011), 81.

4. Caro, *Power Broker,* 1018.

5. Murphy, *After Many a Summer,* 103.

6. In 1948, the Yankees were second in overall attendance to the Indians. From 1953 to 1957, the Yankees were second in attendance to the Milwaukee Braves.

7. Art Rosenbaum, "DiMaggio and Heath Discuss Majors in S.F.," *San Francisco Chronicle,* Nov. 13, 1954.

8. Doris Kearns Goodwin, *Wait Till Next Year—A Memoir* (New York: Simon and Schuster, 1998).

9. New York City Department of Planning, *The Newest New Yorkers: Characteristics of the City's Foreign-Born Population,* NYC DCP #13–10 (New York, 2013), https://www1.nyc.gov/assets/planning/download/pdf/data-maps/nyc-population /nny2013/nny_2013.pdf.

10. Gary S. Henderson, "Los Angeles and the Dodger War, 1957–1962," *Southern California Quarterly* 62.3 (Fall 1980): 261–89.

11. Bill Leiser, "Giants Will Move Before Yankees Do," *San Francisco Chronicle,* Mar. 4, 1954. This story was more or less a spring-training filler, but it demonstrates that talk of the Yankees moving was sufficiently widespread that a counter-argument needed to be made, and that the talk of the Giants moving was strong even as they began a spring training when their star center fielder was back from the military and, as Leiser could not then have known, were on their way to winning the World Series.

12. Robert Garratt, *Home Team: The Turbulent History of the San Francisco Giants* (Lincoln: Univ. of Nebraska Press, 2017), 24.

13. Ibid., 16.

14. Bill Leiser, "'Save the Seals' Club Launches Campaign," *San Francisco Chronicle,* June 9, 1957.

15. Wrigley Field was the home of the American League Los Angeles Angels during their inaugural 1961 season.

16. Don Zminda, "A Home Like No Other: The Dodgers in L.A. Memorial Coliseum," in *Endless Seasons: Baseball in Southern California,* edited by Jean Hastings Ardell and Andy McCue, *The National Pastime,* no. 41 (Phoenix: Society for American Baseball Research, 2011), 84.

17. U.S. Census Bureau, "Census of Population, 1960," 3 vols. (Washington, D.C.: Government Printing Office, 1961).

18. Alex Bevk, "Looking Back on the Past Lives of Candlestick Point before It Becomes a Mall," Curbed San Francisco (Nov. 18, 2014), https://sf.curbed.com /2014/11/18/10020580/looking-back-on-the-past-lives-of-candlestick-point-before -it-becomes.

19. Wade Avery, "Candlestick before and after Stadium Built," FoundSF (Nov. 8, 2013), http://www.foundsf.org/index.php?title=Candlestick_Before_and_After _Stadium_Built.

20. Garratt, *Home Team,* 51.

21. Peter Hartlaub, "Our SF: Transportation Thrives after a Muddy History," *San Francisco Chronicle,* July 11, 2015.

22. Greg Proops, "Buzzers," *The Smartest Man in the World Podcast* (Jan. 13, 2014), https://itunes.apple.com/us/podcast/the-smartest-man-in-the-world/id401055309.

23. Podair, *City of Dreams,* xii.

24. Ibid., xiii.

25. Sullivan, *The Dodgers Move West,* 100.

26. Bob Timmerman, "Vote No on B? Why? Looking Back 50 Years," The Griddle (Mar. 10, 2008), https://griddle.baseballtoaster.com/archives/920926.html.

27. Ibid. (capitals in original).

28. Ibid. (capitals in original).

29. John H. M. Laslett, *Shameful Victory: The Los Angeles Dodgers, the Red Scare, and the Hidden History of Chavez Ravine* (Tucson: Univ. of Arizona Press, 2015), Kindle edition, chap. 3.

30. Ibid., chap. 4.

31. "Prop. B Won in 9 of 15 Districts," *Los Angeles Times* (June 2, 1958), quoted in OAC: Online Archive of California (2009), http://www.oac.cdlib.org/view?docId=hb7n39p500&brand=oac4&doc.view=entire_text.

32. Podair, *City of Dreams*, 197.

33. Ibid., 74

34. Ibid., 15

6. FIRST SEASONS IN CALIFORNIA

1. Frank Finch, "Drysdale and Gomez to Start Big League Opener in Bay Area," *Los Angeles Times,* Apr. 15, 1958.

2. Jeremy Lehrman, *Baseball's Most Baffling MVP Ballots* (Jefferson, N.C.: McFarland, 2016), 107, describes that vote as "dreadful but understandable," due to Wills setting the stolen base record that year.

3. Michael Leahy, *The Last Innocents: The Collision of the Turbulent Sixties and the Los Angeles Dodgers* (New York: Harper Collins, 2016), 5.

4. Zimmer appeared in 17 games for the Dodgers in 1956, but did not play in the World Series that year. However, he played in the 1955 World Series.

5. Steve Delsohn, *True Blue: The Dramatic History of the Los Angeles Dodgers, Told by the Men Who Lived It* (New York: Harper Collins, 2002), 63.

6. Einstein, *A Flag for San Francisco,* 185–86.

7. Murray Chass, "Baseball: A Final Out That Continued for Forty Years," *New York Times,* June 7, 2002.

8. Einstein, *A Flag for San Francisco,* 10.

9. Mays missed most of 1952 and 1953 due to military service.

10. Mays would go on to win the award every year until 1968.

11. *Minneapolis Tribune,* Apr. 10, 1951, p. 7. See also John Saccoman, Willie Mays, Society for American Baseball Research, Baseball Biography Project (Jan. 2014), http://sabr.org/bioproj/person/64f5dfa2.

12. James S. Hirsch, *Willie Mays: The Life, the Legend* (New York: Scribner, 2010), 96.

13. My wife is not a big baseball fan, but she is married to one, and both our sons are avid baseball players. Years ago when I supported my son's desire to play a Little League game on Rosh Hashanah, she responded like many Jewish mothers before her, "Sandy Koufax didn't pitch on Yom Kippur." My unhelpful response was "and when Asher pitches like Sandy Koufax, he can take that day off."

14. Jane Leavy, *Sandy Koufax: A Lefty's Legacy* (New York: Harper Collins, 2002), 169.

15. Most fans today remember the aging Reggie Jackson in the late 1970s and 1980s, who was best suited for the designated hitter role, but earlier in his career he had the speed and arm to play center field occasionally.

16. Hirsch, *Willie Mays*, 469, 473.

17. Carol E. Lee, "Say, Hey! Mays Gives Obama Tips," Politico (July 14, 2009), https://www.politico.com/story/2009/07/say-hey-mays-gives-obama-tips-024939.

18. John Fogerty, "Centerfield," *Centerfield* (Geffen, 1985).

19. Einstein, *A Flag for San Francisco*, 100.

20. Roger Guenveur Smith's "Juan and John," was a 2009 one-man play about the incident. The most comprehensive book on the incident is Rosengren, *Fight of Their Lives*.

21. Leonard Koppett, "Marichal Clubs Roseboro with a Bat," *New York Times*, Aug. 22, 1965.

22. Sid Ziff, "Dodgers on Marichal: Kick Him Out," *Los Angeles Times*, Aug. 23, 1965, C4.

23. Juan Marichal, with Lew Freedman, *Juan Marichal: My Journey from the Dominican Republic to Cooperstown* (Minneapolis: MVP Books, 2011), 125–28.

24. Leahy, *Last Innocents*, 275.

25. Rosengren, *Fight of Their Lives*, 112.

26. Hirsch, *Willie Mays*, 438–39.

27. Leahy, *Last Innocents*, 292.

28. Rosengren, *Fight of Their Lives*, 116.

29. WHIP (Walks and Hits per Inning Pitched) is a statistic that, essentially, seeks to measure the number of baserunners a pitcher allows per inning—hence the lower the number, the better.

30. Robert Fitts, *Mashi: The Unfulfilled Baseball Dreams of Masanori Murakami, the First Japanese Major Leaguer* (Lincoln: Univ. of Nebraska, 2014), iBook edition, 461.

31. Richard Goldstein, "Alvin Dark, 92, Dies; Led Giants to Pennants as Captain and Manager," *New York Times*, Nov. 13, 2014, https://www.nytimes.com/2014/11/14/sports/baseball/alvin-dark-giants-shortstop-and-manager-dies-at-92.html.

32. Ibid.

33. Hirsch, *Willie Mays*, 327. "Rig's" refers to Bill Rigney, who managed the first 58 games; "Sheehan's" refers to Tom Sheehan, who managed the remaining 96.

34. Dick Young, "Young Ideas," *New York Daily News*, Aug. 26, 1965.

35. Alou, "Latin-American Ballplayers Need a Bill of Rights."

36. Leavy, *Sandy Koufax*, 202.

37. Salary data in this section from www.baseballreference.com.

38. Buzzie Bavasi, "The Great Holdout," *Sports Illustrated*, May 15, 1967.

39. Leavy, *Sandy Koufax*, 202 (capitals in original).

40. Delsohn, *True Blue*, 25.

41. Leahy, *Last Innocents*, 91.

42. Robert F. Garratt, *Home Team: The Turbulent History of the San Francisco Giants* (Lincoln: Univ. of Nebraska Press, 2017), 75.

7. AFTER MAYS AND KOUFAX

1. Mantle is said to have not taken care of himself, causing him to age quickly and forcing him to retire in 1968, a few years after he stopped being an effective player. While it is true that Mays lasted longer than Mantle and was still a star

as late as 1971, this conventional wisdom is not entirely accurate. Mantle was as much a victim of the pitcher-friendly era of the middle and late 1960s and the absence of sophisticated quantitative analysis as he was of age and drink. Although Mantle had slowed down a bit by 1964 or so, he was still an effective player. Much of his value in these years came through his combination of walking and hitting home runs—patience and power in the parlance of twenty-first-century baseball analysis. From 1965 to 1968, the supposed decline years for the great Mantle, he hit .254/.386/.450, good for an OPS+ of 149. Most players who sustain an OPS+ that high over the course of their careers are easily elected to the Hall of Fame. Mantle's .237 batting average in 1968 overshadowed his very respectable on-base percentage of .385 and his decent slugging percentage of .398. In that great year of the pitcher, those numbers were good enough for ninth in OPS in the American League.

2. The Pilots moved to Milwaukee and became the Brewers for the 1970 season. Although they existed for only one year, the Pilots will always be remembered as Jim Bouton's team in his seminal baseball diary, *Ball Four* (1970; repr., New York: Macmillan, 1990).

3. For more on those great A's teams, see Bruce Markusen, *Baseball's Last Dynasty: Charlie Finley's Oakland A's* (Dallas: Master's Press, 1998), and Tom Clark, *Champagne and Baloney: The Rise and Fall of Finley's A's* (New York: Harper and Row, 1976).

4. The Yankees actually added two star relievers between the 1977 and 1978 seasons. The other, another former Red, Rawly Eastwick, never produced as a Yankee and was swapped to the Phillies. Signing two top relievers would have been overkill in a normal situations, but was even stranger given that the American League Cy Young Award winner in 1977 had been a third Yankee reliever, Sparky Lyle.

5. Righetti pitched well, if unspectacularly, as a starter in 1982 and 1983, but was switched to the closer role for the 1984 season. This move was not a wise one for the Yankees, but was viewed by many as an attempt by Yankees owner George Steinbrenner to save face after the great Yankees closer Goose Gossage went to the San Diego Padres as a free agent.

6. Beginning in 1976, the designated hitter was used in every other World Series. In 1986 the rule was changed so that the designated hitter would be used in games in the American League park, but not in the National League park.

7. Garvey missed the last 62 games of the 1983 season after dislocating a thumb on July 29, thus ending his consecutive game streak. A lesser-known story about that streak is that in the same season, on June 25, after getting a double and helping the visiting Padres beat the Giants at Candlestick Park, Garvey, who was particularly hated in San Francisco, had dinner at Prego, a popular Italian restaurant on Union Street in San Francisco. During the meal, several rowdy teenage Giants fans spotted him in the restaurant and waited for him to come outside. Following the meal, Garvey engaged in some friendly, but tense banter with the youths. As he walked away, one of them, who was wearing a Yankees cap, yelled, "You'll never break Lou Gehrig's record." For years, my friends believed that my comment had put some kind of a curse on Garvey.

8. Fallon, *Dodgerland*, 297–99.

9. Steve Wulf, "Too Good to Be True," *Sports Illustrated*, Apr. 25, 1983.

10. "At Last, Acceptance for Garvey," *New York Times*, May 17, 1981.

11. Delsohn, *True Blue*, 112–13.

12. Pat Jordan, "Trouble in Paradise with Steve and Cindy Garvey," *Inside Sports,* Aug. 31, 1980.

13. Rick Reilly, "America's Sweetheart," *Sports Illustrated,* Nov. 27, 1989.

14. Greg Proops, *The Smartest Book in the World* (New York: Touchstone, 2015), 137.

15. Glenn Burke and Erik Sherman, *Out at Home: The True Story of Glenn Burke* (New York: Berkley Books, 1995), 8.

16. Sarah Kaplan, "The Trials of Baseball's First Openly Gay Player, Glenn Burke, Four Decades Ago," *Washington Post,* Aug. 17, 2015.

17. Michael Smith, "The Double Life of a Gay Dodger," *Inside Sports,* Oct. 1982.

18. See, for example, Mark Whicker, "Former L.A. Dodger Glenn Burke Was a Trailblazer for Gay Athletes," *Los Angeles Daily News,* July 18, 2015; John Branch, "Posthumous Recognition: MLB to Recognize Glenn Burke as Baseball's Gay Pioneer," *New York Times,* July 14, 2014; and "The Price Glenn Burke Paid for Coming Out," NPR (May 5, 2013), https://www.npr.org/2013/05/05/181410089/the-price -glenn-burke-paid-for-coming-out.

19. Smith, "Double Life of a Gay Dodger."

20. He was traded for Billy North, the last member of the championship teams still on the A's. This somewhat belies the notion that bigotry was the only reason Burke was traded. North, a speedy centerfielder, played very well with the Dodgers in 1978. He had a .371 on-base percentage and stole 27 bases, sharing center field with Rick Monday and batting second when he was in the lineup.

21. Burke and Sherman, *Out at Home,* 17.

22. ERA+ is a measure of ERA (Earned Run Average) that normalizes that statistic over era and home field, making it easier to make comparisons across generations. An ERA+ of 100 is league average; an ERA+ of 120 is what might be expected from a good starting pitcher. An ERA+ of 140 or better would make somebody a Cy Young candidate in most seasons. Generally speaking, ERA+ is more useful for evaluating starting pitchers.

23. Jeff Katz, *Split Season: 1981* (New York: Thomas Dunne Books, 2015), iBook edition, 240. The Phillies were the defending World Series winners, making that series particularly important. The notion of Pete Rose asking for a photo with an opposing player, which Rose claimed was for his son, shows how big Fernando was. Rose was known as one of the most intense competitors of his era and rarely made gestures like that.

24. Delsohn, *True Blue,* 149–50.

25. George Vecsey, "Sports of the Times: Adios, Freddie, Adios," Mar. 29, 1991, *New York Times.*

26. Burgos, *Playing America's Game,* 235.

27. From 1977 to 1981, Garvey had 16.3 WAR, and Smith 16.7. Baker and Davey Lopes both had 15.8. This difference is essentially a margin of error. Ron Cey had 22.4 WAR, more than any of his teammates. However, from 1977 to 1978, Smith had an OPS+ of 165 compared to Garvey's 130. This is a very big difference.

28. Willie Weinbaum, "The Legacy of Al Campanis," *ESPN* (Apr. 1, 2012), http:// www.espn.com/espn/otl/story/_/id/7751398/how-al-campanis-controversial-racial -remarks-cost-career-highlighted-mlb-hiring-practices.

29. "1980 Presidential General Election Data Graphs—California," Dave Leip's Atlas of U.S. Presidential Elections (2012), http://uselectionatlas.org/RESULTS/ datagraph.php?year=1984&fips=6&f=0&off=0&elect=0.

30. "Giants Approve Sale—Would Go to Toronto," *San Francisco Chronicle*, Jan. 10, 1976.

31. Harry Jupiter, "Moscone Says He'll Fight to Keep Giants," *San Francisco Chronicle*, Jan. 10, 1976.

8. GLOBALIZATION, PEDS, AND THE RIVALRY SINCE 1990

1. Bob Nightingale, "Nomomania Grips L.A. and Japan," *Los Angeles Times*, July 4, 1995. Bo Jackson was a tremendous athlete who was a star in both the NFL and MLB, with the Kansas City Royals, before injuries derailed his career.

2. Acey Kohrogi, "Nomo Attendance Boost," interviewed by Mark Langill, Watase Media Arts Center, Japanese American National Museum (Mar. 21, 2014), https://www.youtube.com/watch?v=IRw0JfcV0Gg.

3. Joan Ryan, "Dodger Nomo One of a Kind: Japanese Rookie Pitcher Takes 'Nomomania' to Texas," *San Francisco Chronicle*, July 11, 1995.

4. Murray Chass, "Baseball: Baseball's Giants Reach Agreement to Move to Florida," *New York Times*, Aug. 8, 1992.

5. Howard Bryant, *Juicing the Game: Drugs, Power, and the Fight for the Soul of Major League Baseball* (New York: Viking, 2005), 76, 342.

6. Joe Sheehan, "A-Rod, Legend: The Case for Appreciating Alex Rodriguez's Greatness, *Sports Illustrated*, Aug. 8, 2016.

7. Joe Sheehan, "The Big Lie," *Joe Sheehan Newsletter* 75 (Aug. 4, 2013).

8. Bryant, *Juicing the Game*, 194–95.

9. From 1989 to 1998, Griffey was an outstanding player, hitting .300/.379/.568, winning nine Gold Gloves, and stealing 149 bases while being caught only 53 times—good for 65.6 WAR. Bonds's .299/.429/.581 slash line was better than Griffey's. Bonds won one fewer Gold Glove, but stole 360 bases while being caught 102 times over these years. Not surprisingly his 84.1 WAR from 1989 to 1998 is significantly higher than Griffey's over the same years.

10. See "Bud Selig Hints Hank Aaron Is Still Baseball's Home Run King," *Associated Press*, Apr. 8, 2014.

11. The previous three were 1974 and 1988 (A's–Dodgers) and 1989 (A's–Giants).

12. Henry Schulman, "Collapse: Monkey Perches on Giants' Backs," *San Francisco Chronicle*, Oct. 27, 2002.

13. Bruce Bochy, *A Book of Walks* (Soquel, Calif.: Wellstone, 2015).

14. Matt Snyder, "Dodgers NLDS Exit a Good Excuse for Dodgers to Fire Don Mattingly?" CBS Sports (Oct. 16, 2015), https://www.cbssports.com/mlb/news/dodgers-nlds-exit-a-good-excuse-for-dodgers-to-fire-don-mattingly/.

15. "Bryan Stow's Friends Describe Brutal Attack outside Dodger Stadium," *Rock Center with Brian Williams*, NBC News (Dec. 19, 2011).

9. THE GIANTS AND DODGERS TODAY

1. Patrick McTeevy, "L.A. to Pay Man Cleared of Murder," *Los Angeles Times*, Mar. 8, 2007.

2. The Washington Senators were an expansion team in 1961 because the original Washington Senators had moved to Minnesota and become the Twins after the 1960 season.

INDEX